Richard R. Bowker

Copyright, its law and its literature

Being a summary of the principles and law of copyright, with especial reference to

books

Richard R. Bowker

Copyright, its law and its literature
Being a summary of the principles and law of copyright, with especial reference to books

ISBN/EAN: 9783742833235

Manufactured in Europe, USA, Canada, Australia, Japa

Cover: Foto ©Lupo / pixelio.de

Manufactured and distributed by brebook publishing software
(www.brebook.com)

Richard R. Bowker

Copyright, its law and its literature

ITS LAW AND ITS LITERATURE

*BEING A SUMMARY OF THE PRINCIPLES AND LAW OF COPY-
RIGHT, WITH ESPECIAL REFERENCE TO BOOKS*

BY

R. R. BOWKER

WITH A BIBLIOGRAPHY OF LITERARY PROPERTY

BY

THORVALD SOLBERG.

NEW YORK
Office of THE PUBLISHERS' WEEKLY
LONDON: SAMPSON LOW, MARSTON, SEARLE & RIVINGTON
1886

PREFATORY NOTE.

THE present work is an attempt to give in brief and simple shape a comprehensive view—such as did not exist, despite an evident need—of the principles, history, and present law of copyright, domestic and international. It was first published, in chapters, as editorial articles in the PUBLISHERS' WEEKLY, July to October, 1885 ; it has since been revised and extended to the spring of 1886. Its preparation has involved careful study, not only of the leading copyright authorities, such as Copinger on the Law of Copyright (2d edition, London, 1881), and Drone on Copyright (Boston, 1879), respectively the foremost English and American legal treatises on the subject, but of numerous other sources of information, such as the early Parliamentary law reports ; the Morrill report to Congress in 1873, and the valuable Report, with digest and Evidence, of the British Royal Copyright Commission to Parliament in 1878 ; the papers of Mr. H. D. Macleod and Mr. G. H. Putnam in Lalor's " Cyclopædia of Political Science ;" Griswold's Synopsis of Copyright Decisions (Bangor, 1883), and Spalding's handy alphabetical abridgment of the Law of Copyright (Philadelphia, 1878) ; besides many volumes, reports, magazine articles, and newspaper clippings, contained in the copyright collection of the PUBLISHERS' WEEKLY office or reprinted in its columns. Mr. A. R. Spofford, Librarian of Congress, has kindly gone over the proofs critically and made valuable corrections, and I am indebted also to Mr. S. E. Dawson, of Montreal, for revision of the portion relating to Canadian law and practice. It has been impracticable, within the compass of the work, to give references to authorities ; but these can largely be supplied from the tables of cases and indexes of Copinger and Drone ; and most of the bills, reports, etc., of recent years will be found in full in the volumes of the PUBLISHERS' WEEKLY. I have tried, however, to present a summary which will be found trustworthy as well as readable, which carefully discriminates between settled principles of law, judicial constructions, and mooted points, and which, except in the preliminary chapter, where the theory of copyright is discussed, and in the last, on copyright reform, avoids for the most part the interpolation of the writer's personal opinions. The frequent use of the word " probably" or its equivalent suggests how unsettled is the condition of copyright law.

I trust this summary may be of service as well in the reform of domestic copyright as in the promotion of international copyright. The completeness and efficiency of the protection of property by a State is a chief test of its civilization, and it is to be hoped that the United States will not long remain almost the only exception among civilized nations in rejecting international copyright. This national disgrace should be blotted out.

Only those who know by hard experience the difficulties of bibliographical work can appreciate fully the invaluable bibliography of literary property, compiled by Mr. Thorvald Solberg, which complements this little treatise.

R. R. BOWKER.

NEW YORK, February, 1886.

CONTENTS.

PART I.

PART II.

A SUMMARY OF

THE PRINCIPLES AND LAW OF COPYRIGHT,

WITH ESPECIAL REFERENCE TO BOOKS.

BY

R. R. BOWKER.

.

COPYRIGHT.

I.

THE NATURE AND ORIGIN OF COPYRIGHT.

COPYRIGHT (from the Latin *copia*, plenty) means, in general, the right to copy, to make plenty. In its specific application it means the right to multiply copies of those products of the human brain known as literature and art.

There is another legal sense of the word "copyright" much emphasized by several English justices. Through the low Latin use of the word *copia*, our word "copy" has a secondary and reversed meaning, as the pattern to be copied or made plenty, in which sense the schoolboy copies from the "copy" set in his copy-book, and the modern printer calls for the author's "copy." Copyright, accordingly, may also mean the right in copy made (whether the original work or a duplication of it), as well as the right to make copies, which by no means goes with the work or any duplicate of it. Said Lord St. Leonards : " When we are talking of the right of an author we must distinguish between the mere right to his manuscript, and to any copy which he may choose to make of it, as his property, just like any other personal chattel, and the right to multiply copies to the exclusion of every other person. Nothing can be more distinct than these two things. The common law does give a man who has composed a work a right to it at composition, just as he has a right to any other part of his personal property ; but the question of the right of excluding all the world from copying, and of himself claiming the exclusive right of forever copying his own composition after he has published it to the world, is a totally different thing." Baron Parks, in the same case,

pointed out expressly these two different legal senses of the word copyright, the right *in* copy, a right of possession, always fully protected by the common law, and the right *to* copy, a right of multiplication, which alone has been the subject of special statutory protection.

There is nothing which may more properly be called property than the creation of the individual brain. For property means a man's very *own*, and there is nothing more his own than the thought, created, made out of no material thing (unless the nerve-food which the brain consumes in the act of thinking be so counted), which uses material things only for its record or manifestation. The best proof of *own*-ership is that, if this individual man or woman had not thought this individual thought, realized in writing or in music or in marble, it would not exist. Or if the individual, thinking it, had put it aside without such record, it would not, in any practical sense, exist. We cannot know what " might have beens" of untold value have been lost to the world where thinkers, such as inventors, have had no inducement or opportunity to so materialize their thoughts.

It is sometimes said, as a bar to this idea of property, that no thought is new—that every thinker is dependent upon the gifts of nature and the thoughts of other thinkers before him, as every tiller of the soil is dependent upon the land as given by nature and improved by the men who have toiled and tilled before him, a view of which Henry C. Carey has been the chief exponent in this country. But there is no real analogy—aside from the question whether the denial of individual property in land would not be setting back the hands of progress. If Farmer Jones does not raise potatoes from a piece of land Farmer Smith can ; but Shakespeare cannot write " Paradise Lost" nor Milton " Much Ado," though before both Dante dreamed and Boccaccio told his tales. It was because of Milton and Shakespeare writing, not because of Dante and Boccaccio who had written, that these immortal works are treasures of the English tongue. It was the very self of each, *in propria persona*, that gave these form and worth, though they used words that had come down from generations as the common heritage of English-speaking men. Property in a stream of water, as has been pointed out, is not in the atoms of the water but in the flow of the stream.

Property right in unpublished works has never been effectively questioned—a fact which in itself confirms the view that intellectual property is a natural inherent right. The author has "supreme control" over an unpublished work, and his manuscript cannot be utilized by creditors as assets without his consent. " If he lends a copy to another," says Baron Parks, " his right is not gone ; if he sends it to another under an implied undertaking that he is not to part with it or publish it he has a right to enforce that undertaking." The receiver of a letter, to whom the paper containing the writing has undoubtedly been given, has no right to publish or otherwise use the letter without the writer's consent. The theory that by permitting copies to be made, an author dedicates his writing to the public, as an owner of land dedicates a road to the public by permitting public use of it for twenty-one years, overlooks the fact that in so doing the author only conveys to each holder of his book the right to individual use, and not the right to multiply copies, as though the landowner should not give but sell permission to individuals to pass over his road, without any permission to them to sell tickets for the same privilege to other people. The owner of a right does not forfeit a right by selling a privilege.

It is at the moment of publication that the undisputed possessory right passes over into the much-disputed right to multiply copies, and that the vexed question of the true theory of copyright property arises. The broad view of literary property holds that the one kind of copyright is involved in the other. The right to have is the

right to use. An author cannot use—that is, get beneficial results from his work, without offering copies for sale. He would be otherwise like the owner of a loaf of bread who was told that the bread was his until he wanted to eat it. That sale would seem to contain " an implied undertaking " that the buyer has liberty to use his copy but not to multiply it. Peculiarly in this kind of property the right of ownership consists in the right to prevent use of one's property by others without the owner's consent. The right of exclusion seems to be indeed a part of ownership. In the case of land the owner is entitled to prevent trespass to the extent of a shot-gun, and in the same way the law recognizes the right to use violence, even to the extreme, in preventing others from possession of one's own property of any kind. The owner of a literary property has, however, no physical means of defence or redress ; the very act of publication by which he gets a market for his productions opens him to the danger of wider multiplication and publication without his consent. There is, therefore, no kind of property which is so dependent on the help of the law for the protection of the real owner.

The inherent right of authors is a right at what is called common law—that is, natural or customary law. So far as concerns the undisputed rights before publication, the copyright laws are auxiliary merely to common law. Rights exist before remedies ; remedies are merely invented to enforce rights. " The seeking for the law of the right of property in the law of procedure relating to the remedies," says Copinger, " is a mistake similar to supposing that the mark on the ear of an animal is the cause, instead of the consequence, of property therein." After the invention of printing it became evident that new methods of procedure must be devised to enforce common law rights. Copyright became therefore the subject of statute law, by the passage of laws imposing penalties for a theft which, without such laws, could not be punished.

These laws, covering naturally enough only the country of the author, and specifying a time during which the penalties could be enforced, and providing means of registration by which authors could register their property rights, as the title to a house is registered when it is sold, had an unexpected result. The statute of Anne, which is the foundation of present English copyright law, intended to protect authors' rights by providing penalties against their violation, had the effect of limiting those rights. It was doubtless the intention of those who framed the statute of Anne to establish, for the benefit of authors, specific means of redress. Overlooking, apparently, the fact that law and equity, as their principles were then established, enabled authors to use the same means of redress, so far as they held good, which persons suffering wrongs as to other property had, the law was so drawn that in 1774 the English House of Lords (against, however, the weight of one half of English judicial opinion) decided that, instead of giving additional sanction to a formerly existing right, the statute of Anne had substituted a new and lesser right to the exclusion of what the majority of English judges held to have been an old and greater right. Literary and like property to this extent lost the character of copy*right*, and became the subject of copy-*privilege*, depending on legal enactment for the security of the private owner. American courts, wont to follow English precedent, have rather taken for granted this view of the law of literary property, and our Constitution, in authorizing Congress to secure " for limited terms to authors and inventors the exclusive right to their respective writings and discoveries," was evidently drawn from the same point of view, though it does not in itself deny or withdraw the natural rights of the author at common law.

II.

THE EARLY HISTORY OF COPYRIGHT.

Our traditions of the blind Homer, singing his Iliad in the multitudinous places of his protean nativity, do not vouchsafe us any information as to the *status* of authors in his day. But there is mention in Roman literature of the sale of " playright" by the dramatic authors, as Terence, and Rome had booksellers who sold copies of poems written out by slaves, and who seem to have been protected by some kind of " courtesy of the trade," since Martial names certain booksellers who had specific poems of his for sale. Horace complains that the Sosius brothers, his publishers, got gold while he got only fame ; but this may have been a pre-historic " author's grumble," and it is probable that some kind of payment was made to authors.

There is, nevertheless, no valid evidence of the protection of book-property until the invention of printing. This raised, of course, many new questions, wherever the guardians of the law were set to their chronic task of applying old ideas of right to new conditions. At first the " privileges " were granted chiefly to printers, but possibly as the representatives of the writers. The first recorded instance is in 1491, when Venice gave to the publicist Peter of Ravenna and the publisher of his choice the exclusive right to print and sell his " Phœnix." The Italian States encouraged printing by granting to different printers exclusive rights for fourteen years, more or less, of printing specified classics, a practice certainly not founded on authors' rights, but rather on a theory of eminent domain and State monopoly of such property. Similar privileges were issued in Germany, the first at Nuremberg, 1501, for the works of a nun-poet who had been dead for six hundred years, and some of these

provided penalties against reprinters. General acts providing both protection and penalties were passed in Germany as early as 1660. In France, from the times of Louis XII., " letters of the king" forbid booksellers, printers, and other persons to " introduce foreign impressions" (meaning, it is supposed, unauthorized reprints) of the books to which such letters were appended. They were usually issued to printers. In 1556 a general ordinance of Henry II. defined literary property.

In England a Royal Printer was appointed in 1504, and to his successor, Richard Pynson, in 1518, the first printing " privilege" was issued, in the form of a prohibition for two years of the printing by any other person of a certain speech to which this first English copyright notice was appended. Henry VIII. granted many such privileges, and in 1533 appeared the first complaint of piracy, that of Wynken de Worde, who obtained the king's privilege for his second edition of Witinton's Grammar, because Peter Trevers had pirated it from the edition of 1523. In 1530 the first English copyright to an author was granted to John Palsgrave, who, having published a French grammar at his own expense, received a privilege for seven years. Up to the middle of the sixteenth century " copyrights" were in form printers' licenses, and even in this case Palsgrave seems to have been recognized rather because he published his own book than because he wrote it.

The " Stationers' Company," chartered in 1556, was in part a device to prevent seditious printing, by prohibiting any printing in England except by those registered in its membership. In 1558, under a second charter, its by-laws provided that every one who printed a book should register it and pay a fee, and those who failed to do this, or who printed another member's book, were to be fined. In 1559 fines of this last sort, and in 1573 sales of " copy," are entered. The practice now grew up of granting patents or monopolies to persons for a whole class of books, and the Stationers' Company itself held that for almanacs up to a very late period. These monopolies were defied, and the Star Chamber decree of 1566, disabling offending printers from exercising their trade and prescribing three months' imprisonment, did not avail. In 1640 the Star Chamber and all the regulations of the press were abolished, but the abuse of unlicensed printing led to a new licensing act in 1643, which prohibited printing or importing without consent of the *owner*, on pain of forfeiture of copies to the owner, and which renewed the order that all books should be entered in the register of the Stationers' Company. The early registers still exist in Stationer's Hall, near Paternoster Row, London, in quaint and almost undecipherable chirography, and some of them have been reissued in *fac-simile*. It was against the licensing act of this date that Milton, in 1644, printed his " Areopagitica," but he particularly excepts from his criticism of the act the part providing for " the just retaining of each man his several copy, which God forbid should be gainsaid."

In 1649 Parliament provided a penalty of 6s. 8d. and forfeiture for the piracy of registered books, and prohibited presses except at London, Finsbury, York, and the universities, and in 1662 it added the requirement of deposit of a copy at the king's library and at each of the universities. To prevent fraudulent changes in a book after licensing, it was further required that a copy be deposited with the licenser at the time of application—apparently the origin of our record-deposit. With the expiration of these acts in 1679 legislative penalties lapsed, and piracy became common. Charles II. in 1684 renewed the charter of the Stationers' Company, approved its register, and confirmed to proprietors of books " the sale, right, power, and privilege and authority of printing, as has been usual heretofore." The licensing act of 1649-'62 was revived in 1685, and renewed up to 1694, although the booksellers now petitioned against it, and eleven peers protested against subjecting learning to a mercenary and perhaps ignorant licenser, and destroying the property of authors in their copies. The law lapsed because of the indignation of the Commons against the arbitrary power of the license, but the result was the abolition of statutory penalties, leaving the punishment of piracy a matter of damages at common law, requiring a separate action for each copy sold, usually against irresponsible people. Piracy again flourished. The right at common law seems, however, to have been unquestioned, and the Court of Common Pleas held that a plaintiff who had purchased from the executors of an author was owner of the property at common law. Owners of literary property petitioned Parliament, 1703 to 1709, for security and redress, declaring that the property of English authors had always been held as sacred among the traders, that conveyance gave just and legal title, that the property was the same with houses and other estates, and that existing "copies" had cost at least £50,000, and had been used in marriage settlements and were the subsistence of many widows and orphans. This led to the famous statute of Anne, passed March, 1710, " for the encouragement of learning," which remains the practical foundation of copyright in England and America to-day.

DEVELOPMENT OF STATUTORY COPYRIGHT IN ENGLAND.

THE statute of Anne, the foundation of the present copyright system, which took effect April 10, 1710, gave the author of works then existing, or his assigns, the sole right of printing for twenty-one years from that date and no longer ; of works not printed, for fourteen years and no longer, except in case he were alive at the expiration of that term, when he could have the privilege prolonged for another fourteen years. Penalties were provided, which could not be exacted unless the books were registered with the Stationers' Company, and which must be sued for within three months after the offence. If too high prices were charged, the Queen's officers might order them lowered. A book could not be imported without written consent of the owner of the copyright. The number of deposit copies was increased to nine. The act was not to prejudice any previous rights of the universities and others.

This act did not touch the question of rights at common law, and soon after its statutory term of protection on previously printed books expired, in 1731, lawsuits began. The first was that of Eyre *vs.* Walker, in which Sir Joseph Jekyll granted, in 1735, an injunction as to " The Whole Duty of Man," which had been first published in 1657, or seventy-eight years before. In this and several other cases the Court of Chancery issued injunctions on the theory that the legal right was unquestioned. But in 1769 the famous case of Millar *vs.* Taylor, as to the copyright of Thomson's " Seasons," brought directly before the Court of King's Bench the question whether rights at common law still existed, aside from the statute and its period of protection. In this case Lord Mansfield and two

other judges held that an author had, at common law, a perpetual copyright, independent of statute, one dissenting justice holding that there was no such property at common law. In 1774, in the case of Donaldsons *vs.* Beckett, this decision was appealed from, and the issue was carried to the highest tribunal, the House of Lords.

The House of Lords propounded five questions to the judges. These, with the replies,* were as follows :

I. Whether at common law, an author of any book or literary composition had the sole right of first printing and publishing the same for sale ; and might bring an action against any person who printed, published, and sold the same without his consent ? Yes, 10 to 1 that he had the sole right, etc., and 8 to 3 that he might bring the action.

II. If the author had such right originally, did the law take it away, upon his printing and publishing such book or literary composition ; and might any person afterward reprint and sell, for his own benefit, such book or literary composition against the will of the author ? No, 7 to 4.

III. If such action would have lain at common law, is it taken away by the Statute of 8th Anne ? And is an author, by the said statute, precluded from every remedy, except on the foundation of the said statute and on the terms and conditions prescribed thereby ? Yes, 6 to 5.

IV. Whether the author of any literary composition and his assigns, had the sole right of printing and publishing the same in perpetuity, by the common law ? Yes, 7 to 4.

* The votes on these decisions are given differently in the several copyright authorities. These figures are corrected from 4 Burrow's Reports, 2408, the leading English parliamentary reports, and are probably right.

V. Whether this right is any way impeached, restrained, or taken away by the Statute 8th Anne? Yes, 6 to 5.

These decisions, that there was perpetual copyright at common law, which was not lost by publication, but that the statute of Anne took away that right and confined remedies to the statutory provisions, were directly contrary to the previous decrees of the courts, and on a motion seconded by the Lord Chancellor, the House of Lords, 22 to 11, reversed the decree in the case at issue. This construction by the Lords, in the case of Donaldsons *vs.* Beckett, of the statute of Anne, has practically " laid down the law" for England and America ever since.

Two protests against this action deserve note. The first, that of the universities, was met by an act of 1775, which granted to the English and Scotch universities and to the colleges of Eton, Westminster, and Winchester (Dublin was added in 1801) perpetual copyright in works bequeathed to and printed by them. The other, that of the booksellers, presented to the Commons February 28, 1774, set forth that the petitioners had invested large sums in the belief of perpetuity of copyright, but a bill for their relief was rejected. In 1801 an act was passed authorizing suits for damages [at common law, as well as penalties under statute] during the period of protection of the statute, the need for such a law having been shown in the case of Beckford *vs.* Hood, wherein the court had to " stretch a point" to protect the plaintiff's rights in an anonymous book, which he had not entered in the Stationers' Register. An act of 1814 extended copyright to twenty-eight years and for the remainder of the life of a surviving author, and relieved the author of the necessity of delivering the eleven library copies, except on demand. These deposit copies were reduced to five by the act of 1836.

In 1841, under the leadership of Sergeant Talfourd, a great debate on copyright, in which Macaulay took a leading part in favor of restricted copyright, was started in the Commons, which resulted in the act of 1842 (5 and 6 Victoria), repealing the previous acts, and presenting a new code of copyright. It practically preserved, however, the restrictions of the Statute of Anne.

The copyright term was made the author's lifetime and seven years beyond, but in any event at least forty-two years. The Judicial Committee of the Privy Council may authorize publication of a posthumous work in case the proprietor of the copyright refuse to publish. Articles in periodicals, etc. have the same copyright term, but they revert to the author after twenty-eight years. Subsequent acts extend copyright to prints and like art works, designs for manufactures, sculptures, dramas, musical compositions, lectures, for various terms and under differing conditions.

The present law of England as to copyright, says the Report of the Royal Copyright Commission, in a Blue Book of 1878, " consists partly of the provisions of fourteen Acts of Parliament, which relate in whole or in part to different branches of the subject, and partly of common law principles, nowhere stated in any definite or authoritative way, but implied in a considerable number of reported cases scattered over the law reports." The Digest, by Sir James Stephen, appended to this Report, is presented by the Commission as " a correct statement of the law as it stands." This Digest is, perhaps, the most valuable single contribution yet made to the literature of copyright, but the frequency with which such phrases occur as " it is probable, but not certain," " it is uncertain," " probably," " it seems," show the state of the law, " wholly destitute of any sort of arrangement, incomplete, often obscure," as says the Report itself. The Digest is accompanied, in parallel columns, with alterations suggested by the Commission, and it is much to be regretted that their work failed to reach the expected result of an Act of Parliament. The evidence taken by the commissioners forms a second Blue Book, also of great value. A new copyright law is now under consideration in England.

It seems possible that, under the precedent of the acts of 1775 and 1801, the common law rights practically taken away by the statute of Anne could be restored by legislation. Its restrictions have not only ruled the practice of England ever since, but they were embodied in the Constitution of the United States, and have influenced alike our legislators and our courts.

THE HISTORY OF COPYRIGHT IN THE UNITED STATES.

THE Constitution of the United States authorized Congress " to promote the progress of science and useful arts by securing for limited times, to authors and inventors, the exclusive right to their respective writings and discoveries." Previous to its adoption, in 1787, the nation had no power to act, but on Madison's motion, Congress, in May, 1783, recommended the States to pass acts securing copyright for fourteen years. Connecticut in January, 1783, and Massachusetts in March, 1783, had already provided copyright for twenty-one years. Virginia in 1785, New York and New Jersey in 1786, also passed copyright acts, and other States were considering them,—thanks to the vigorous copyright crusade of Noah Webster, who travelled from capital to capital,—when the United States statute of 1790 made them unnecessary. This act followed the precedent of the English act of 1710, and gave to authors who were citizens or residents, their heirs and assigns, copyrights in books, maps, and charts for fourteen years, with renewal for fourteen years more, if the author were living at expiration of the first term. A printed title must be deposited before publication in the clerk's office of the local United States District Court ; notice must be printed four times in a newspaper within two months after publication ; a copy must be deposited with the United States Secretary of State within six months after publication ; the penalties were forfeiture and a fine of fifty cents for each sheet found, half to go to the copyright owner, half to the United States ; a remedy was provided against unauthorized publication of manuscripts.

This original and fundamental act was followed by others :—in 1802, requiring copyright record to be printed on or next the title-page, and including designs, engravings, and etchings ; in 1819, giving United States Circuit Courts original jurisdiction in copyright cases ; in 1831 (a consolidation of previous acts), including musical compositions, extending the term to twenty-eight years, with renewal for fourteen years to author, widow, or children, doing away with the newspaper notice except for renewals, and providing for the deposit of a copy with the district clerk (for transmission to the Secretary of State) within three months after publication ; in 1834, requiring record of assignment in the court of original entry ; in 1846 (the act establishing the Smithsonian Institution), requiring one copy to be delivered to that, and one to the Library of Congress ; in 1856, securing to dramatists the right of performance ; in 1859, repealing the provision of 1846 for the deposit of copies, and making the Interior Department instead of the State Department the copyright custodian ; in 1861, providing for appeal in all copyright cases to the Supreme Court ; in 1865, one act again requiring deposit with the Library of Congress, within one month from publication, another including photographs and negatives ; in 1867, providing $25 penalty for failure to deposit. This makes twelve acts bearing on copyright up to 1870, when a general act took the place of all, including " paintings, drawings, chromos, statues, statuary, and models or designs intended to be perfected as works of the fine arts." This did away with the local District Court system of registry, and made the Librarian of Congress the copyright officer, with whom printed title must be filed before, and two copies deposited within ten days after, publication. In 1873-74 the copyright act was included in the Revised Statutes as Sections 4948 to 4971 (also see Secs. 629 and 699), and in 1874 an amendatory act made legal a short form of record, " Copyright, 18—, by A. B.," and relegated labels to the Patent Office.

The act of 1790 received an interpretation, in 1834, in the case of Wheaton *vs.* Peters (rival law reports), at the bar of the United States Supreme Court, which placed copyright in the United States exactly in the *status* it held in England after the decision of the House of Lords in 1774. The court referred directly to that decision as the ruling precedent, and declared that by the statute of 1790 Congress did not affirm an existing right, but created a right. It stated also that there was no common law of the United States, and that (English) common law as to copyright had not been adopted in Pennsylvania, where the case arose. So late as 1880, in Putnam *vs.* Pollard, claim was made that this ruling decision did not apply in New York, which, in its statute of 1786, expressly "*provided*, that nothing in this act shall extend to, affect, prejudice, or confirm the rights which any person may have to the printing or publishing of any books or pamphlets at common law, in cases not mentioned in this act." But the N. Y. Supreme Court decided that the precedent of Wheaton *vs.* Peters nevertheless held.

As in the English case of Donaldsons *vs.* Beckett, the decision in the American ruling case came from a divided court. The opinion was handed down by Justice McLean, three other judges agreeing, Justices Thompson and Baldwin dissenting, a seventh judge being absent. The opinions of the dissenting judges (see Drone,

p. 43 *et seq.*) constitute one of the strongest statements ever made of natural rights in literary property, in opposition to the ruling that the right is solely the creature of the statute. " An author's right," says Justice Thompson, " ought to be esteemed an inviolable right established in sound reason and abstract morality."

. The application of copyright law, unlike that regarding patents, is solely a question of the courts. The Librarian of Congress is simply an officer of record, and makes no decisions, as is well stated in his general circular in reply to queries :

" I have to advise you that no question concerning the validity of a copyright can be determined under our laws by any other authority than a United States Court. This office has no discretion or authority to refuse any application for a copyright coming within the provisions of the law, and all questions as to priority or infringement are purely judicial questions, with which the undersigned has nothing to do.

" A certificate of copyright is *prima facie* evidence of an exclusive title, and is highly valuable as the foundation of a legal claim to the property involved in the publication. As no claim to exclusive property in the contents of a printed book or other article can be enforced under the common law, Congress has very properly provided the guarantees of such property which are embodied in the " Act to revise, consolidate, and amend the statutes relating to patents and copyrights," approved, July 8, 1870. If you obtain a copyright under the provisions of this act, you can claim damages from any person infringing your rights by printing or selling the same article ; but upon all questions as to what constitutes an infringement, or what measure of damages can be recovered, all parties are left to their proper remedy in the Courts of the United States."

The many perplexities that arise under our complicated and unsatisfactory law, as it stands at present, suggest the need here, as in England, of a thorough re-modelling of our copyright system.

WHAT CAN BE COPYRIGHTED.

THE United States law (Revised Statutes, Secs. 4948-71, being the act of July 8, 1870; also amendatory act of June 18, 1874) mentions as subjects of copyright "any book, map, chart, dramatic or musical composition, engraving, cut, print, photograph or negative thereof . . . painting, drawing, chromo, statue, statuary . . . models or designs intended to be perfected as works of the fine arts," and excludes (amendment of 1874), as subject only to registry in the Patent Office, prints or labels not "connected with the fine arts" but "designed to be used for any other articles of manufacture." The English laws now cover much the same ground. The United States statute expressly provides, however, that "nothing in this chapter shall be construed to prohibit the printing, publishing, importation or sale of any book, map, chart, dramatic or musical composition, print, cut, engraving, or photograph, written, composed or made by any person not a citizen of the United States nor resident therein."

The word "book" covers the great body of copyright property, and has been many times the subject of judicial construction giving the most comprehensive meaning to the term. The English judges early held that protection "could not depend upon the form of the publication ;" "that a composition on a single sheet might well be a book within the meaning of the Legislature ;" and that "any composition, whether large or small, is a book within the meaning of this Act." The law of 5 and 6 Vict. (1842) afterward specifically construed the word "book" "to mean and include every volume, part or division of a volume, pamphlet, sheet of letterpress, sheet of music, map, chart or plan, sep-

arately published." The law of the United States makes no definition of the term, but our judges have followed the English precedent, Judge Thompson holding, in Clayton vs. Stone, that a "book" "may be printed only on one sheet," and that "the literary property intended to be protected by the Act is not to be determined by the size, form or shape . . . but by the subject - matter," and Judge Leavitt, in Drury vs. Ewing, that a diagram for cutting dresses, with directions, printed on a single sheet, being "the product of thought and mental toil," was a "book" within the benefit of the law.

In fact, though all English and American statutes have been avowedly for "the encouragement of learning" and "the progress of science and useful arts," the courts have construed the laws to cover in the widest sense any "useful book." They have denied copyright protection only to works having absolutely no literary quality, such as advertisements (unless they contain original literary matter) and advertising cuts, labels, blank-books, or a cricket score-card ; and even booksellers' and other trade catalogues, having descriptive notes or distinctive arrangement and combination, can be copyrighted. Compilations of existing materials, from common sources, arranged and combined in an original and useful form, receive the same protection as wholly original matter, and Mr. Drone schedules English or American judicial constructions extending this principle to : (1) general miscellaneous compilations ; (2) annotations consisting of common materials ; (3) dictionaries ; (4) books of chronology ; (5) gazetteers ; (6) itineraries, road and guide-books ; (7) directories ; (8) maps and charts ; (9) calendars ; (10) catalogues ; (11) mathematical tables ; (12) a list of hounds ; (13) abstracts of titles to lands ; and collections of (14) statistics, (15) statutory forms, (16) recipes and (17) designs.

The copyright in such cases may be in the combination and arrangement only, or it may be also in any original material included with other material. Quantity is not an essential element in copyright so much as "substantial importance ;" an English court protected a passage of only sixty words, and a Scotch justice contended that Walter Scott's change of a single word in "Glenallan's Earl" authorized a copyright for the new edition, though another law lord differed, and the case was decided on other grounds. In the case of new editions, a few colorable alterations or unimportant notes will not justify a new copyright, but, as in the case of Lockhart's notes to Scott, the courts will protect notes of substantial worth, though the copyright on the text or on other notes printed with them has expired. In any case, the copyright on a new edition, whether made by re-writing, extending, condensing, annotating, or otherwise altering, runs independently of the term of the original or any other edition, covers only the new parts, and cannot prevent the issue by others of the original or any other edition on which copyright has expired.

"A book must include every part of the book ; it must include every print, design or engraving which forms part of the book, as well as the letter-press therein, which is another part of it," according to the ruling decision of Vice-Chancellor Parker, in the English case of Bogue *vs.* Houlston. This precedent would doubtless be accepted by American courts, following Drone, who says : "The copyright protects the whole and all the parts and contents of a book : when the book comprises a number of independent compositions, each of the latter is as fully protected as the whole." The practice of some publishers in copyrighting a magazine and also specific articles or engravings, seems, therefore, a work of supererogation. On the other hand, copyright cannot extend to any part of a book not subject in itself to copyright, as a part written by a foreigner. The general copyright is not, however, vitiated as to copyrightable portions by its seeming to cover non-copyrightable portions, as was held by Lord Kenyon in Cary *vs.* Longman. But when copyright is claimed on a work partly composed of uncopyrightable matter the courts may require the claimant on interrogatories to designate which parts are and which are not original. "If the parts cannot be separated," says Drone, "it would seem that copyright will not vest in any of it."

A copyright owner cannot prevent another person from publishing the matter contained in his book, if invented or collected independently, or from making "fair use" of its contents. Two map-makers or cataloguers, collecting accurately and completely at first hand the same *data*, would naturally make the same map or catalogue, and each would equally be entitled to copyright. It has even been held that the collected material might be used by a second compiler as a guide in a second compilation, if subjected to original verification, as in the case of a street directory. In this respect, copyright law differs from patent law, where a first use bars others from the same field. But under the general rule as to "fair use," the great proportion of copyright perplexities are to be found—relating to compilation, abridgment, translation, quotation, and dramatization. Such cases are usually decided on the individual matters of fact in each case.

In respect to *abridgments* and translations, the courts have held to precedents which the best writers, such as Curtis, Drone and Copinger, declare to be contradictory to the true principles of copyright law. In 1740 Lord Hardwicke, deciding against a mere reprint, "colorably shortened only," of Sir Matthew Hale's "Pleas of the Crown," declared that he would not restrain "a real and fair abridgment," and in 1774 Lord-Chancellor Apsley, after consultation with Blackstone, held that an abridgment of Hawkesworth's "Voyages," involving understanding and skill, was not plagiarism or a copyright wrong, but "an allowable and meritorious work." In the leading American case of Story's "Commentaries," Justice McLean, while expressing his own opinion that "an abridgment, if fairly made, contains the principle of the original work, and this constitutes its value," added, "But a contrary doctrine has long been established in England . . . and in this country the same doctrine has prevailed. I am, therefore, bound by precedent, and I yield to it, in this instance, more as a principle of law than a rule of reason or justice." Similarly, in Lawrence *vs.* Dana, in 1869, Justice

Clifford declared that "an abridgment ought to be regarded as an infringement . . . but the opposite doctrine has been too long established to be considered open to controversy."

In regard to *translations*, the only direct precedent is the American case of "Uncle Tom's Cabin," in 1853, in which Mrs. Stowe had copyrighted not only the original work, but a German translation which she had caused to be made ; Justice Grier held that she could not recover against another person who was issuing another German translation, since it was not "*copies* of her *book*." This case was previous to the stat ute permitting authors to reserve the right of translation.

In regard to *dramatization*, the leading cases are English : it has been held that the mere copyrighting of a book cannot prevent dramatization, but that copyright of a work in dramatic form before its literary publication does prevent other dramatization of the literary work.

It is not improbable that the prevailing sentiment of the best authorities will ultimately overthrow the above precedents, but the law as to abridgments should be definitely amended, as proposed by the English commission, so that no abridgment of a copyright work can be published without the owner's consent. The precedents cited apply, of course, only to books copyrighted without reservation of rights ; in England the right of translation may be reserved under the international copyright provisions, notice being given on title page, and in America the Revised Statutes (Sec. 4952) enact that "authors may reserve the right to dramatize or to translate their own works," which is done, under the Official Regulations, by notifying the Librarian of Congress of such reservation, for record, and by printing the words "Right of translation reserved" or "All rights reserved" below the copyright notice. There is no provision against any translation, abridgment, etc., of a book not copyrighted ; nor can any person do more, in any case, than copyright his own translation, abridgment, etc. He cannot prevent any other person making independent use of the original which he has used unless he is himself the owner of the original.

The question of how much *quotation* is within the limits of "fair use" is almost entirely a question of fact to be decided by the court in the individual case : the leading case hereafter will probably be that of the publishers of "Gordon's memoirs" against the *Pall Mall Gazette* for undue quotation, now pending in England.

The state of the law regarding *titles* is also somewhat confusing. There seems to be no copyright protection for the title of a book *per se*, but it may be considered an essential part of the book. Judge Shepley held (1872) that "the right secured is the property in the literary composition—the product of the mind and genius of the author—and not in the name or title given to it. The title does not necessarily involve any literary composition ; it may not be, and certainly the statute does not require that it should be, the product of the author's mind . . . It is a mere appendage, which only identifies, and frequently does not in any way describe, the literary composition itself . . . If there were no piracy of the copyrighted book there would be no remedy . . . for the use of a title which could not be copyrighted independently of the book." The English rulings are to the effect that a title has no copyright protection except as part of a book, but that the use of a title to attract purchasers on the supposition that they are getting another book previously known by that title is a fraud punishable at common law. General titles cannot in any way be protected : the publishers of the "Post-Office Directory," England, and of "Irving's Works," America, were both defeated in attempts to prevent the use of those titles. Judge Curtis, in the N. Y. Superior Court, decided in 1874, in the case of a play, that "the use of the word 'Charity' as a designation for any work of art or literature cannot ordinarily be monopolized by any one person." The specific title "The Two Orphans" was, however, protected at common law in another case. In the case, also, of the specific title "Trial and Triumph," 1876, Vice-Chancellor Malins enjoined quite another book under the same title, though the title was chosen in ignorance of the first book and in entire good faith. So, also, in the title "Splendid Misery," used by Miss Braddon in 1879, the English judge was inclined to support the copyright claim of Mr. Hazlewood, who had used it in 1874, until it was shown that a third novelist had used it in 1801, so that it had become, in a measure, common property.

Titles are rather to be considered as trademarks, which may be registered in the United States under Secs. 4937-4947 of the Revised Statutes and protected by the statutory penalties, or may be protected on general principles of equity. In the "Chatterbox" cases, 1884-85,

Judge Wheeler's injunction restraining the use of this " name or word, or any name or word substantially identical therewith," in or upon any juveniles of the general character of the English book of that name, rests on principles of trade-mark and not of copyright, but thus a measure of international copyright is indirectly secured. In the English case of " Belgravia" Lord Cairns also seemed to think that there could not be copyright in a single word, but this question is avoided by considering a title as a trade-mark.

It was laid down, in the case of " Belgravia," that there can be no claim to protection for the title of an unpublished book, no matter what expenditure has been made or advertising done, and this holds in trade-mark as well as in copyright law. " There is no such thing as property in a trade-mark as an abstract name," ruled Judge Shepley, 1872, for a trade-mark simply shows that certain goods " were manufactured by a certain person." Nor can an abandoned title, in the case of a periodical, be held against a person starting a new periodical of that name, providing it does not purport to be a continuation of the old, according to a French case quoted by English authorities.

There can be no copyright in an immoral book, and Lord Eldon, in Southey vs. Sherwood, carried this doctrine so far as to deny the common law right of an author in a non-innocent manuscript, because there could be no right to hold what there was no right to sell. His opinion, resulting in the wide sale of a book which the author desired to suppress, has been severely criticised by later authorities. There can be no copyright in blasphemous, seditious, or libellous books ; but though this rule was very strictly enforced by English judges a century ago, the later courts hesitate to rule strictly on this point, lest the rule be perverted to sectarianism or despotism. There can be no copyright in books involving fraud, as those which spuriously obtain salable value by being represented to be the work of writers who did not write them, or to contain matter which they do not contain ; but this rule does not extend to books under assumed names or innocently pretending to be what they are not, as when Horace Walpole's " Castle of Otranto " was put forward as a translation from the Italian. There can be no statutory copyright in books not yet published, but simply projected, just as there can be no copyright in a title not representing any book.

There is nothing in copyright law corresponding to the *caveat* in patent law.

In regard to *periodicals* and books published in *parts*, as also in regard to encyclopædias and other composite books, there are no specific statutory provisions in the United States, but they come under the general designation of books. Each issue of a magazine or other periodical must therefore be separately entered as though a separate book, although the title may be registered as a trade-mark once for all. All copyrightable matter contained in the issue would then be copyrighted, as before noted. It seems probable that even a daily newspaper could thus be copyrighted day by day at a cost of $365 per year, so as to protect all its original material of substantial literary value. A daily Price-List of the New York Cotton Exchange was so entered day by day for some time, but the question of maintaining such a copyright seems never to have been tested in court. The New York *Sun* copyrights its Sunday cable letter separately. A specific act to protect news for twenty-four hours has been proposed in Congress, but never passed. A book, published in more than one volume or part, the portions not complete in themselves, is probably protected by copyright entry of the first part ; but, of course, all parts must be deposited in the Library of Congress. The statutes of Great Britain provide specifically that a work published in parts or a periodical may be fully protected by copyright entry of the first part, but the word " newspaper " does not occur in the definitions of the Act. When the London *Times's* memoir of Beaconsfield was reprinted as a penny pamphlet, the *Times* brought suit as a matter of common-law right, but the judge held that a newspaper was copyrightable under the statute, and therefore that a common-law suit could not hold. It was held by Mr. Justice Molesworth, in Melbourne, Australia, that a newspaper proprietor had copyright in special news telegrams, and another paper was enjoined from using them.

Lectures are protected in England by statutory provision, provided the lecturer gives notice to two justices at the place of reading that he reserves his rights. There is no statutory provision in this country, but the courts seem disposed to protect a lecturer on the common law ground that the lecture read is not published by reading, and can be controlled as a manuscript. Newspapers have, however, in practice freely republished lectures. Probably, when this is done with consent of the author, he loses copyright, on the ground that non-copyrighted articles in a non copyrighted periodical cannot have protection ; but if done without his consent, the publication by another party cannot deprive him of his rights. It is suggested that the law should permit free report without vitiating book copyright, unless the lecturer forbids such report preceding his lecture.

The general rules as to books govern the other articles of publication mentioned in the Revised Statutes, but it should be noted that in the case of dramatic and musical compositions, in addition to copyright covering publication in print, there is " playright," covering performance. This rests partly upon principles of common law and partly upon the statute ; it opens a wide field, into which this summary will not enter.

VI.

THE OWNERSHIP AND DURATION OF COPYRIGHT.

THE English law secures copyright to an author or his assigns ; the United States Constitution mentions "authors and inventors," and the Revised Statutes name "any citizen of the United States or resident therein, who shall be the author, inventor, designer, or proprietor of any kind, and the executors, administrators, or assigns of any such person" as the persons in whom copyright may lodge. The Librarian of Congress accordingly issues copyright certificates for books as to an "author" or "proprietor" only, assuming usually that an editor is the "author" and a publisher the "proprietor," and never going behind the claim set forth in the application.

The author of a book is the person primarily entitled to copyright. He may sell or otherwise transfer his production before it is copyrighted, in which case the new proprietor obtains all the common-law rights of property, both in the manuscript and its publication, including the right to copyright. This common-law right, including the right to copyright, may extend, Mr. Drone argues, to the finder of an unpublished manuscript, provided no one successfully disputes his ownership of his find, if the manuscript be copyrightable ; but there are no decisions on this point. Or a copyright may be taken out by another person (as the publisher of the book), impliedly in trust for the author, as is a usual custom among American publishers. The proprietor is defined to mean "the representative of an artist or author who might himself obtain copyright."

The copyright officer makes no inquiry into the right of the claimant, and that question, in any of its bearings, must be settled by the courts. When one person is employed by another to prepare a book, or an article which is part of a book, the authorship may inhere in the employer, if the design of the work is so far his as to make him the virtual creator and the actual writer a deputy merely ; but the courts have held that he is not an author who "merely suggests the subject, and has no share in the design or execution of the work." In any case, however, the proprietary right, including the right to secure copyright, depends upon the contract, implied or express, between employer and employed, and the courts will decide this according to the common law of contracts. In the case of a book "with illustrations by John Leech," where Leech retained the copyright of the designs, though the publishers owned the wood on which he had drawn them, an English court held to a distinction between the copyright and the right to the material, and directed the publishers to waive their lesser right and surrender the cuts, in view of the circumstances of the contract. Most of the cases arising as to ownership are in fact issues at common property law and not at copyright law, (as the American case in which Mr. Clemens vainly sought to restrain the use of his name, "Mark Twain," in a collection of his uncopyrighted papers, the court holding that whoever has a right to publish has a right to state authorship, though an author can restrain from the publication over his name of things he did not write,) and this summary does not undertake to present the laws of contract between author and publisher. The copyright is in the author, unless he has consented to part with it ; but this consent may be implied in the circumstances of employment. The particular application of this general principle must be determined by the facts in each case.

When a salaried law reporter had been employed by the State of New York under a law that the copyright of the Reports should vest in the State, Judge Nelson held as valid an entry by the Secretary of State, " in trust for the State of New York," though no formal assignment had been made. When, as in the case of a cyclopædia, many persons are employed at the offices of an employer, using his materials and facilities, and especially if on salary, the courts would undoubtedly uphold his full proprietorship in their work. Where outside persons contributed special articles, the presumption would probably be that the ownership of the copyright, for that special publication, vested in the employer, but that neither he, without the author's consent, nor the author, without his consent, could publish the article in other competing shape. There may be joint authorship in a work of common design, in which case the joint authors will become owners in common of the undivided property ; but mere alterations or work on specific parts could not justify claim to more than such alterations or parts. No person, though a citizen, can obtain copyright in work of which any but a citizen or resident is the author, though the latter be in his employ. But it seems that a foreigner may enter copyright in the work of a citizen or resident author—it being foreign authorship, not ownership, which the law refuses to protect, though this point has not been judicially determined.

' A *resident*, under the American decisions, is a person who intends to reside permanently in this country. It is decided by the *intention* of the resident. A person who is residing here without intention of permanence cannot maintain copyright. For English copyright, on the contrary, a person temporarily residing in Her Majesty's dominions is considered a resident.

The *assignment* of copyright opens vexed questions. The Revised Statutes provide for penalties against any one who shall print, publish, or import a copyrighted book," without the consent of the proprietor of the copyright first obtained in writing, signed in presence of two or more witnesses," as also against any one who shall sell or expose for sale such issue. They also provide that " copyrights shall be assignable in law, by any instrument of writing, and such assignment shall be recorded in the office of the Librarian of Congress within sixty days after its execution ; in default of which it shall be void against any subsequent purchaser or mortgagee for a valuable consideration, without

notice." The section first cited follows the phraseology of the early English statute, under which the English courts have held that assignments must be in writing, attested by two witnesses ; the later statute of Victoria modifies this language, and the later English decisions, as to whether an assignment must be in writing, are confusing, if not contradictory. The section providing for the record of assignment somewhat patterns the method of registration of assignment provided by the English statute, but there left optional. The American law on this point has not been judicially construed ; it seems probable that a written transfer would be required, but possibly not its attestation by two witnesses. The safe method of transfer, both in England and this country, is by writing, under attest of two witnesses, duly recorded in the copyright office. But assignment of common-law rights (as in an unpublished manuscript) may doubtless be by word of mouth. A proprietor can probably assign part of his copyright, as the right to dramatize ; he can probably assign his rights for a portion of the term of copyright, or for another country, but probably not for a limited portion (as a particular State) of this country. But none of these points are judicially determined. Only an author, his widow, or children can obtain a renewal, but this renewal right can probably be assigned. It is possible that an author who assigns in specific words his entire rights bars himself as well as his assignee from the benefit of renewal.

The *duration* of all copyrights in this country is uniformly twenty-eight years, dating from the time of recording the title, with a renewal of fourteen years, securable only by the author, or, if he be dead at the expiration of the term, by his widow or children. No other heirs or persons can renew. In England the term of book copyright is the life-time of the author and seven years after his death, or forty-two years from first publication, whichever is the longer. The copyright in other articles varies according to the specific law. The Copyright Commission propose, for all copyright articles as well as books, a term of life and thirty years after the author's death, according to the German fashion, or in case of anonymous and posthumous books and encyclopædias, thirty years from the date of deposit in the British Museum, an anonymous author to have the right during the thirty years to obtain the full term by publishing an edition with his name.

The English law contains a specific provision that in the case of articles in periodicals (but not in an encyclopædia) the right to publish in separate form shall revert to an author after twenty-eight years ; the Commission purposes a term of three years, during which time also the author as well as the general owner may bring suit against piracy. No specific provision on this point exists in this country.

VII.

THE ENTRY AND PROTECTION OF COPYRIGHTS.

IN the United States the Revised Statutes and the official "Directions for securing copyright" promulgated thereunder by the Librarian of Congress, prescribe exactly the method of entering copyright, and unless the statute is precisely complied with, the copyright is not valid. Said Mr. Justice Sawyer, in Parkinson *vs.* Laselle : " There is no possible room for construction here. The statute says no right shall attach until these acts have been performed ; and the court cannot say, in the face of this express negative provision, that a right shall attach unless they are performed. Until the performance as prescribed, there is no right acquired under the statute that can be violated." And in the case of the play "Shaughraun," Boucicault *vs.* Hart, in 1875, Mr. Justice Hunt held, as regards copyrights in general : ' The work must be published within a reasonable time after the filing of the title-page, and two copies are by the statute made necessary to be performed, and we can no more take it upon ourselves to say that the latter is not an indispensable requisite to a copyright than we can say it of the former." The Supreme Court laid down this general doctrine in Wheaton *vs.* Peters, in reference to the statutes of 1790 and 1802, and the later statutes are most explicit on this point. In the same case of Wheaton *vs.* Peters, Mr. Justice McLean, in delivering the judgment of the Supreme Court, held that while the right " accrues," so that it may be protected in chancery, on the recording of the title of a book, it must be perfected by complying with the other requisites before a suit at law for violation of copyright can be maintained.

Under the present laws, the statutory requisites are :

1. The delivery at the office of the Librarian of Congress, or deposit in the mails to his address, *before publication*, of a printed copy of title, or, in the case of a painting, etc., of a description of the same. Any postmaster is required, if requested, to receipt for such title or description. No affidavit or form of application is prescribed ; but the applicant should give his full name and address, and state whether he claims copyright as author, designer, or proprietor. With each application should be sent one dollar, of which fifty cents is for recording the entry and fifty cents for the certificate of entry which the Librarian returns by mail. If the certificate is not desired at this time, only fifty cents need be sent.

"The *printed title* required may be a copy of the title-page of such publications as have title-pages. In other cases, the title must be printed expressly for copyright entry, with name of claimant of copyright. The style of type is immaterial, and the print of a type-writer will be accepted. But a separate title is required for each entry, and *each* title must be printed on paper as large as commercial note. The title of a *periodical* must include the date and number."

2. The insertion, in every copy published, on the title-page or page following, in the case of a book, or the inscription on the face or mounting of other articles, of the notice, " Entered according to Act of Congress, in the year . . . . by . . . . in the office of the Librarian of Congress at Washington," or of the short form, " Copyright, 18 . . , by . . ." This exact phraseology and order of words must be followed, and it has been held that any inaccuracy in the name of the copyright proprietor (as in the English case of Sampson Low, Son & Co.,

vs. Routledge, by Vice-Chancellor Kindersley) or in the date of the entry (as in the American case of Baker *vs.* Taylor, when 1847 was put for 1846) makes the copyright invalid. A later decision of an American court held, however, that where a copyright notice gave the year 1866, while the true date was 1867, there was no harm done to the public, because a year of the copyright (which really ended in 1895 instead of 1894) was given to the public, whereas in the previous case an additional year was claimed. This decision, however, is not a safe precedent. A microscopic objection that N. Sarony (instead of Napoleon Sarony) was not a *name* was promptly quashed.

The original copyright entry must appear in every reprint of the first edition ; and it would seem that this entry should also appear in every new edition newly copyrighted, as well as the new notice, so long as it is desired to protect the matter contained in the old edition. But the decision of Justice Clifford, in Lawrence *vs.* Dana, rules this to be superfluous. The statute does not expressly prescribe that the notice shall appear in successive volumes after a first, and in Dwight *vs.* Appleton, 1840, it was held that this was not necessary ; but it is safer to print in all, especially if issued at different dates. The official "Directions" indeed prescribe that a separate copyright is to be taken out for each volume ; but this seems to be unsettled in the law, although it has been the general practice from the beginning. The law imposes a penalty of $100 upon any person who shall use the copyright notice without obtaining copyright.

3. The deposit, *within ten days after publication,* of two copies of the best edition of each book or other article, or, in the case of a painting, etc., within ten days after completion, of a photograph of the same (at least of cabinet size), with the Librarian of Congress or in the mails to his address. It is safer to address "To the Librarian of Congress" than to that officer by his personal name. The Librarian furnishes "free penalty labels" for mailing deposit copies, on application, and any postmaster is required, if requested, to receipt for such copies. The Librarian furnishes blank receipts for publications, if desired. The Librarian of Congress may recover a penalty of $25, by an action of debt, for omission to make such deposit. Under the laws existing in 1843, the Attorney-General held that if a book were deposited after the statutory time, opyright would avail nevertheless from the date

of such deposit ; but the judicial interpretations of the existing law hold that a copyright is not valid if deposit is not made *within the ten days.* The nature of this requirement is apt to be overlooked. The Librarian of Congress has been in the habit of sending out a reminder *after* the expiration of the ten days ; but response to this would not help the copyright owner. The volume may be sent before publication, for instance, with the title-page at the time of entry. The law also requires the deposit of "a copy of every subsequent edition wherein any substantial changes shall be made," but there is no decision as to whether omission to do this would in any way invalidate the original copyright.

Publication consists in publicly offering for sale, or gratuitously circulating, from which act the ten days would count. A consignment of an edition, in which sale before a certain time is prohibited, is not publication, but a consignment which is practically a sale is, for "a sale naturally imports publication." It is not certain whether first publication abroad defeats copyright here. The official "Directions" declare that "the time within which any work copyrighted may be issued from the press is not limited by any law or regulation, but depends upon the discretion of the proprietor ;" but Justice Hunt held, as before quoted, that it must be "within a reasonable time." The official "Directions," say that "a copyright may be secured for a projected work as well as for a completed one,"—but this refers, of course, to entering the title of books about to be published, and is not meant to contravene the legal decisions that there can be no copyright in works not in being.

The Copyright Office is required by law to give copyright certificates for fifty cents each, and for the same fee it furnishes information as to a given copyright to any person. The original application and printed title are filed away together, after the title has been copied into one of the prepared blank books known as the "Copyright Record," in which there is a continuous numbering for the year, and which becomes the main record. From this index-cards are made, and kept in an alphabetic card-catalogue, giving the name of the book, the author, and the publisher, so that information can be obtained at once. This card-catalogue is not accessible to the public, but its information is furnished on request. In each certificate of copyright the title and claimant of copyright are entered upon a prepared blank, and the entries in the Record book are fac similes of the certificates given. The date of deposit of volumes is given in the Record book, and also in the certificate *when the title and volume are sent at one time.*

To procure the fourteen years' *renewal* beyond the original twenty-eight years, " the author, inventor, or designer, if he be still living and a citizen of the United States or resident therein, or his widow or children, if he be dead," must, "*within six months before* the expiration of the first term," record the title or description a second time, and comply " with all other regulations in regard to original copyrights." The fees are the same as for original copyrights "Applications for renewal," according to the official "Directions," "must be accompanied by explicit statement of ownership, in the case of the author, or of relationship, in the case of his heirs, and must state definitely the date and place of entry of the original copyright. Within two months from the date of said renewal the renewer must publish a copy of the record " in one or more newspapers printed in the United States, for the space of four weeks." An assignee cannot obtain a renewal, although an author may contract with the assignee to take out and to convey to him the benefit of a renewal ; he may also contract not to renew, and so bar his own right.

An *assignment,* made by any instrument of writing, " shall be recorded in the office of the Librarian of Congress within sixty days after its execution ; in default of which," says the statute, " it shall be void as against any subsequent purchaser or mortgagee for a valuable consideration, without notice." The fee for this record and certificate is $1, and for a certified copy of any record of assignment $1.

The *penalties* and *procedure* in cases under the copyright law are specifically determined by statute. The penalty for false use of the copyright notice is $100, recoverable one half for the person who shall sue for such penalty, and one half to the use of the United States. The penalty for printing, publishing or importing, or knowingly selling or exposing for sale unlawful copies of any book whose title is duly recorded, without consent of the proprietor " first obtained in writing, signed in presence of two or more witnesses," is forfeiture of all copies to the proprietor, and such damages as may be recovered in a civil action by such proprietor in any court of competent jurisdiction. An English decision holds that an importer is not innocent because he does not know that an importation includes copyright matter ; and the wording of our law implies the same, though an American decision held that a partner or employer is not chargeable with statute penalties for acts done without his knowledge by a partner or agent. The penalty against an infringer in the case of all other copyright articles, except books and dramatic compositions, is forfeiture to the proprietor of all plates on which the article shall be copied, and every sheet thereof, and $1 for every sheet thereof ; or, in the case of a painting, statue or statuary, $10 for every copy thereof found in his possession—one half to go to the proprietor and the other half to the use of the United States. The penalty for infringement of " play-right" is damages to be assessed by the court. at not less than $100 for the first and $50 each for subsequent performances. A person who unlawfully prints a manuscript is liable to the proprietor " for all damages." Any action must be commenced within two years after the cause has arisen. The general issue may be pleaded, and special matter given in evidence. The Circuit and District Courts having circuit jurisdiction may grant injunctions for copyright wrongs upon bill in equity. The Circuit Courts have jurisdiction " of all suits at law or in equity arising under the patent or copyright laws of the United States," with writ of error or appeal to the Supreme Court of the United States.

VIII.

STATUTORY COPYRIGHT IN OTHER COUNTRIES.

COPYRIGHT in America has been so much modelled on English statutes, decisions, and precedents, that previous papers have presented many of the points of copyright law in the United Kingdom. There are two essential points of difference, however, between the British and American copyright systems. Copyright there depends essentially upon first publication, not upon citizenship ; and registration and deposit, which are here a *sine quâ non*, are there only necessary previous to, and as a basis for, an infringement suit. A book first published in the United Kingdom (England, Scotland, Wales, and Ireland) is *ipso facto* copyright throughout Her Majesty's Dominions, whether it be from a natural born or naturalized subject of the Queen, wherever resident ; or from a person who is at the time of publication on British soil, colonies included, and so "temporarily a subject of the crown—bound by, subject to, and entitled to the benefit of the laws," even if he made a journey for this express purpose ; or, probably but not certainly, by an alien friend not resident in the United Kingdom nor in a country with which there is a copyright treaty. Under the statute of Anne, it was decided by the Law Lords, in the case of Boosey *vs.* Jefferys (overruling Jefferys *vs.* Boosey), that a person not a British subject or resident was not entitled to copyright because of first publication in England, but the statute of 5 and 6 Victoria was construed to alter this. In the ruling case under the last-named statute, Routledge *vs.* Low (on appeal from Low *vs.* Routledge), Lords Cairns and Westbury laid down explicitly that first publication was the single necessity, and that copyright was not strengthened by residence ; but Lord Cranworth

objected and Lord Chelmsford doubted whether this was good law. It is because of this doubt that American authors have been accustomed to make a day's stay in Montreal on the date of English publication of their books—possibly a wise precaution, though probably unnecessary. It was unanimously held, in the case last cited, that to acquire copyright throughout the British Dominions the work must be published within the *United Kingdom* ; it is probable, but uncertain, that first publication in one of the colonies, for instance, confines copyright to that colony under its local law alone. Simultaneous publication elsewhere does not, however, vitiate British copyright. If a portion of a work only be first published in the United Kingdom, that portion is protected and only the other parts of the book can be reprinted without permission. The practical effect of all this is to give an international copyright under provisions of the domestic law.

Registration in England is made at Stationers' Hall, London ; the requirement should certify that the applicant is the proprietor of the copyright of the book, should give *accurately* the title, name of publisher, and place of publication, name and place of abode of the proprietor of the copyright, and date of first publication ; and should be dated, signed, and witnessed. The fee is five shillings ($1.25) for registration, and five shillings for certificate of entry. Assignments are also to be recorded—the fee being also five shillings. Blank forms are furnished by the Stationers' Company. No suit can be brought for the piracy of a book until this registration is made, but after registration the copyright proprietor may obtain penalties for piracy committed before registration — an anomaly which the Copyright Commission propose to correct by confining penalties to acts committed after registration. The law also requires the deposit of one copy of the best edition with the British Museum, within one month if published in London, three months if elsewhere in the Kingdom, twelve months if elsewhere in the British Dominions ; and the delivery to the Stationers' Company, if demanded in writing within twelve months from publication, of one copy of the edition of which the largest number is printed, for each of four designated libraries, at Oxford, Cambridge, Edinburgh, and Dublin. Neglect to deposit does not vitiate the copyright, but involves a penalty of five pounds. The British statute, unlike the American, does not require any notice of copyright registration to appear in the work, proceeding, apparently, upon the presumption that all publications are registered, without notice.

There is also a registry for paintings, drawings, and photographs kept at Stationers' Hall, and on these no suits can be brought for acts committed prior to registration. In other articles, as drama, no registry is required. The terms and conditions for the various articles other than books subject to copyright vary greatly under the several acts protecting them.

The universities have perpetual copyright in works given to them outright, so long as these are printed by their own presses for their sole benefit and advantage. The Crown seems to have the right to grant patents to the Crown printers for the exclusive printing of the authorized version of the Bible, of the Book of Common Prayer, and probably of Acts of Parliament. To prevent suppression of books, the Judicial Committee of the Privy Council, on complaint that a copyright proprietor, after the death of an author, withholds a work from republication, are empowered to authorize the complainant to issue it, under conditions within their discretion.

Copyright in Canada is a perplexity of perplexities, because it is regulated by two sets of statutes—the Imperial, applicable to the whole British Empire, and the Canadian, applicable to the Dominion of Canada alone. A work copyrighted in the United Kingdom is copyright in Canada, but a Canadian copyright holds only for Canada. The " Foreign Reprints act," passed by the British Parliament in 1847, authorized the suspension of that portion of the Imperial statute which forbade the importation of foreign reprints of English books into Canada.

As a condition of the permission so granted, the Canadian Legislature passed a law subjecting reprints so admitted to a customs duty of twelve and one half per cent, to be finally paid over to the British author. The returns were ridiculously small—only £1084 in the ten years ending in 1876. In 1875, the Dominion Legislature passed a Copyright act, limited in its application, of course, to Canada, which after some delay was approved by the Queen. The English lawyers, however, thought it necessary to pass another Imperial act, by which it was provided that when English authors authorized the reprinting of their books for the Canadian market, such reprints (although not piracies) could not be imported into Great Britain. This law makes it possible to issue in Canada cheap reprints of English works without interfering with the more costly English editions.

These laws, apparently so complex, do not conflict. Each is good *pro tanto.* The net result of the whole mass of combined legislation may be summarized as follows :

1. The works of a British author cannot be reprinted in Canada without his permission, but, if he does not comply with the Canadian law, reprints may be imported into Canada from foreign countries.

2. The works of a British author who complies with the Canadian law can neither be reprinted in, nor imported into, Canada without his permission.

The circuitous way in which American authors are able to avail themselves of both these laws results from judicial interpretations of the Imperial statute.

Canada grants copyright for twenty-eight years to such as are *bona fide* residents of Canada, or who are citizens of any country which has an international copyright with the United Kingdom. The condition essential is printing and publication in Canada. The plates may be made elsewhere, but the impressions must be printed in Canada. Prior, or even simultaneous, publication is not necessary. The copyright will not commence until publication and registration. The cases of serial publications are provided for, and under certain conditions a temporary protection of a month is afforded to books passing through the press.

As an instance of the operation of these laws, the case of " Prince and Pauper," by Mark

Twain, may be cited. This book is copyrighted in England—therefore it cannot be *printed* in Canada. But an edition can be and has been quietly printed out of Canada and imported and sold freely in Canada.

The French copyright system is the most liberal in existence. All copyrights, whether for literary, dramatic, musical, or artistic works, now extend fifty years beyond an author's death (law of 1866) ; the State has copyright in perpetuity over works published by its order or by its agents, but in a private copyright lapsing to the State for lack of heirs, the exclusive right is extinguished. To obtain a right of action in cases of piracy, the law requires the deposit of two copies of a book at the Ministry of the Interior at Paris (or at the Prefecture, if in the departments), for which a receipt is given. The decree of March, 1852, still in force, protects works of foreigners published abroad from piracy on French territory, on the sole condition of deposit as above, and any foreigner who publishes in France is on the same footing as a French author.

Copyright throughout the German Empire extends thirty years beyond an author's death—a period which the British Copyright Commission propose to adopt. Works of academies, etc., and anonymous works are protected for thirty years from date of publication ; but an author by disclosing and registering his name can obtain copyright on an anonymous book for the full term. On a joint work the thirty years counts from the death of the last survivor. An author may reserve rights of translation by so announcing on his title-page, provided an authorized translation be commenced within one and finished within three years. Translations are protected as though original books. Piracy is punished by forfeiture, damages, and fine or imprisonment. The law provides for expert associations in each German State, nominated by the government, to advise the judges. Proceedings must be begun within three years from the act of piracy and within three months of its coming to the knowledge of the aggrieved party. A general registry book is kept at Leipzig, open to public inspection, for every entry in or extract from which fifteen sgr. (about thirty-six cents) is charged, and the entry is printed in the *Börsenblatt*, at the expense of the copyright proprietor. The law protects all works of native authors, whether published in or out of the German Empire, *and* works by a foreigner published by a firm having its place of business or a branch office within the German Empire.

In both Holland and Belgium copyright in books has been for the author's life and twenty years after, but only on works printed and published within the country, and of which three copies, signed by printer and publisher, have been deposited with the communal authorities. New and more liberal systems are under consideration in both countries. Previous to the French Revolution Holland acknowledged the author's right as a perpetual one.

Norway grants copyright for life and fifty years, and formerly required no registration. But by a new law of June 20, 1882, a literary register was established at the University in Christiania, in which register must be entered all claims of copyright—literary and artistic—a fee of one crown (about twenty-seven cents) being charged for each entry. And of each new work and new edition so entered, one copy of the work must be deposited in the University Library at the time of publication ; and *in addition* the law demands that of each book, print, lithograph, wood-cut, and musical composition, published during the year, a complete and perfect copy must be sent, not later than the end of January of the year next following, to the University Library. The printer is responsible for this last deposit, and a failure to deposit is subject to fine of from two to fifty crowns for each work. But for such deposits a claim for payment may be made when a work costs over ten crowns ($2.68).

Spain grants copyright for life and eighty years thereafter,—publishers of anonymous and pseudonymous works having the same rights as authors until proof of the real author is made,— providing entry is made in the Register of Intellectual Property within one year and two copies deposited. In default of registry a work becomes public property. Portugal grants copyright for life and thirty years ; six copies must be deposited at the Lisbon Library.

Italy grants full copyright for life or forty years, whichever is longer. After forty years from first publication, or, if the author live beyond that date, after his death, a second term of forty years begins, in which any person, on duly declaring his intention, may republish a work, on condition of paying five per cent royalty to the copyright proprietor. The State may expropriate any work after the death of an author on paying to the proprietor a compensation named by three experts. Government and society publications are copyrighted only for twenty years. An author may reserve rights of translation for ten years. Three copies must be deposited, and a declaration made of reservation of rights ; these declarations are published for each six months in the Official Gazette.

Hayti, within a year, has adopted a copyright law with some unusual features. An author holds exclusive right during life ; the widow through her life ; the children for twenty years further, or other heirs, if there are no children surviving, for ten years. Unauthorized reprints are confiscated on the complaint of the proprietor of the copyright ; and the author recovers from the reprinter the price of a thousand, or from a bookseller of two hundred copies, reckoned at the retail price of the author's edition.

Copyright also exists in Austria-Hungary—for life and thirty years after, no registry or deposit being required ; Sweden, formerly perpetual, now for life and fifty years, no registration ; Denmark, for life and thirty years, no registration or deposit ; Switzerland, for life or thirty years ; Russia, for life and fifty years, registration but not deposit being required, with complicated provisions as to new editions ; Turkey, for forty years, or twenty for translations ; Greece, for fifteen years, subject to royal extension ; Mexico, which has perpetual literary copyright, registration and deposit being obligatory ; Venezuela, for life and fourteen years, or deposit and registration ; Chili, for life and five years ; Brazil, for life and ten years ; Japan, for thirty years, with extension to forty-five.

IX

INTERNATIONAL COPYRIGHT IN EUROPE.

WITH the growth of civilization, the practice of protecting in all countries the property of the citizen of any one has also grown, until it is now a generally recognized principle. This principle, applied to literary property, has resulted in international copyright among most civilized nations. The United States remains a not honorable exception.

The first provision for international copyright was made by Prussia in 1836, by a law which provided that any country might secure copyright for its authors in Prussia on granting reciprocal privileges. A copyright convention was concluded between the members of the German Confederation in 1837. England followed, in 1838, with the Act 1 and 2 Victoria, an "Act for securing to authors, in certain cases, the benefit of international copyright," which empowered the Queen, by an Order in Council, to direct that the author of a book first published in a foreign country should have copyright in the United Kingdom, on certain conditions, providing that country conferred similar privileges on English authors. The act of 1844 (7 and 8 Victoria) extended this privilege to prints, sculpture, and other works of art, and provided for international playright. It expressly denied the privilege, however, to translations of foreign works, and it was not until 1852 (act of 15 and 16 Victoria) that provision was fully made for translations and dramatic compositions, the latter with the proviso that "fair imitations or adaptations" of foreign plays or music might be made. The latest act on international copyright, that of 1875 (38 Victoria), repealed this proviso, and authorized the Queen, by Orders in Council, to protect foreign plays against this kind of piracy. The domestic copyright acts, however, provide, on the condition of first publication in the United Kingdom, a practical measure of international copyright. Great Britain has copyright treaties with Germany (1846-55, those with Prussia and the minor States extended to the Empire, but apparently not including Würtemberg and Bavaria), France (1851), Belgium (1854), Spain (1857), and Italy (1860, that with Sardinia extended to the Kingdom).

Copyright by treaty, under approval of Orders in Council, for works first published in other countries, is restricted to the terms provided by British domestic law for the several copyright articles, but may vary within these terms according to the treaty with each country. As a condition of copyright, each work *must* be registered, and a copy of the first edition and of every subsequent edition containing additions or alterations deposited, at Stationers' Hall, for transmission within a month to the British Museum. The time and place of first publication abroad must be included in the registry; the fee for registration is one shilling only. Translations are protected for five years, on the additional conditions that the original shall have been registered and deposited in the one country within three months after first publication in the other; that the author notify his reservation on the title-page of the original, and that the authorized translation shall begin to appear within one year, and be completed within three years, from the registration and deposit. The several treaties of Her Majesty with the powers above-named are in almost identical language, and grant the full terms provided by the British domestic laws. The treaties generally include a proviso that duties on books, etc., imported into the treaty country shall not be above a stated sum. In the case of France there is to be no duty either way.

The British Copyright Commission have proposed that registration and deposit in London shall not be necessary, but that a copy of entry in any foreign register, attested by a British consular agent, shall be *prima facie* evidence of title ; and that the right to translate shall in any case abide with the author for three years, and if within that time an authorized translation be published, it shall be copyright for ten years.

France, by the decree of 1852, protects works published abroad without regard to reciprocity, providing the formalities of deposit are complied with previous to a suit for infringement ; but it also has treaties with several nations. In none of them, except those with England and Spain, is *deposit* required in the foreign country, and four of the countries which require *registration* permit that it shall be performed at their legations in Paris.

A curious outcome results from the wording of the Anglo-French treaty taken in connection with French law. Any foreign work being entitled by the latter to copyright on publication and deposit in France, and British protection being assured by treaty to all works copyrighted in France and properly registered and deposited in England, it seems to follow that an American, for instance, by obtaining French copyright under French law can obtain English copyright under the Anglo-French treaty. This might hold in the case of books already published in America and not first published in England.

Germany extends copyright privileges to foreign works issued by publishers having a place of business or branch office in Germany, without regard to reciprocity. Otherwise the rights of foreign authors are regulated by the several treaties in force with other nations.

In Belgium and Holland the law protecting works *published* and *printed* in the country, on deposit of certified copies, seems to cover books by foreign authors. Belgium has definite treaties with Great Britain, France, Germany, Holland, Spain, Portugal, Italy, Switzerland, and Russia, guaranteeing to their citizens the rights of Belgian subjects, with reciprocal provisions. The law proposed extends its privileges alike to native and foreign authors, but to the latter for no longer than the term of copyright in their country.

In Norway and Sweden the domestic law provides for its extension to citizens of other countries, on condition of reciprocity. In Sweden every anonymous or pseudonymous book is considered as of Swedish authorship in default of proof to the contrary.

Spain bases international copyright on "complete reciprocity between the two contracting powers," each of which shall treat the other as "the most favored nation," and does not require the fulfilling of any formality. It thus extends the protection of its domestic law to subjects of any foreign State whose law recognizes the right of intellectual property, and it has treaties with Great Britain, France, Belgium, Holland, Portugal, and Italy. Under Spanish law, it is stated, the foreign proprietor can exercise his right of property in Spain in accordance with the laws of *his own* country.

Portugal gives protection to foreigners on condition of reciprocity. Italy, Austria, and Russia have copyright treaties with other countries. Greece protects foreigners for fifteen years, on condition of reciprocity. Switzerland offers treaty protection to citizens of "foreign States who exercise reciprocity, and who by moderate duties on the production of Swiss literature and art facilitate their sale ;" but such treaties are binding only in the cantons which agree to them.

At the time of the Universal Exposition in Paris in 1878, the French *Société des Gens de Lettres* issued invitations for an International Literary Congress, which was held in Paris, under the presidency of Victor Hugo, commencing June 4, 1878. From this came the International Literary Association, which held subsequent Congresses at London in 1879, at Lisbon in 1880, at Vienna in 1881, at Rome in 1882, at Amsterdam in 1883, at Brussels in 1884, and at Antwerp in 1885, at which the extension of international copyright was discussed and advocated.

The Congress at Antwerp, in 1885, ratified the following proposition : "The author's right in his work constitutes an inherent right of property. The law does not create, but merely regulates it."

Partly at the initiation of this Association, and at the invitation of the Swiss Government, semi-official conferences of representatives of the several nations were held at Berne in September, 1883, and September, 1884. At the first of these, the following draft, submitted by the International Literary Association, was substantially adopted as the basis for a general convention of civilized nations :

1. The authors of literary or artistic works published, represented, or executed in one of the contracting States, shall enjoy, upon the sole condition of accomplishing the formalities required by the laws of that State, the same rights for the protection of their works in the other States of the Union, whatever the nationality of the authors may be, as are enjoyed by natives of the States.

2. The term literary or artistic works comprises books, pamphlets, and all other writings ; dramatic and dramatico-musical works ; musical compositions, with or without words, and arrangements of music ; drawings, paintings, sculptures, engravings, lithographs, maps, plans, scientific sketches, and generally all other literary, artistic, and scientific works whatsoever, which may be published by any system of impression or reproduction whatsoever.

3. The rights of authors extend to manuscript or unpublished works.

4. The legal representatives and assignees of authors shall enjoy in all respects the same rights as are awarded by this convention to authors themselves.

5. The subjects of one of the contracting States shall enjoy in all the other States of the Union during the subsistence of their rights in their original works the exclusive right of translation. This right comprises the right of publication, representation, or execution.

6. Authorized translations are protected in the same manner as original works. When the translation is of a work which has become public property, the translator cannot prevent the work from being translated by others.

7. In the case of the infringement of the above provisions, the courts having jurisdiction will apply the laws enacted by their respective legislatures, just as if the infringement had been committed to the prejudice of a native. Adaptation shall be considered piracy, and treated in the same manner.

8. This convention applies to all works that have not yet become public property in the country in which they were first published at the time of coming into force of the convention.

9. The States of the Union reserve to themselves the right of entering into separate agreements among themselves for the protection of literary or artistic works, provided that such agreements are not contrary to any of the provisions of the present convention.

10. A Central International Office shall be established, at which shall be deposited by the Governments of the States of the Union the laws, decrees, and regulations affecting the rights of authors which have already been or shall hereafter be promulgated in any of the said Governments. This office shall collect the laws, etc., and publish a periodical print in the French language, in which shall be contained all the documents and information necessary to be made known to the parties interested.

At the 1884 Conference the draft was modified to the following :

1. Authors placing themselves within the jurisdiction of the contracting countries will be afforded protection for their works, whether in print or manuscript, and will have all the advantages of the laws of the different nations embraced in the Union.

2. These privileges will be dependent upon the carrying out of the conditions and formalities prescribed by the legislation of the author's native country, or of the country in which he chooses to first publish his work, such country being, of course, one of those included in the convention.

3. These stipulations apply alike to editors and authors of literary works, as well as to works of art published or created in any country of the Union.

4. Authors within the jurisdiction of the Union will enjoy in all the countries the exclusive rights of translation of their works during a period of ten years after publication in any one country of the Union of an authorized translation.

5. It is proposed that it shall be made legal to publish extracts from works which have appeared in any country of the Union, provided that such publications are adapted for teaching or have a scientific character. The reciprocal publication of books composed of fragments of various authors will also be permitted. It will be an indispensable condition, however, that the source of such extracts shall at all times be acknowledged.

6. On the other hand, it will be unlawful to publish, without special permission of the holder of the copyright, any piece of music, in any collection of music used in musical academies.

7. The rights of protection accorded to musical works will prohibit arrangements of music containing fragments from other composers, unless the consent of such composer be first obtained.

This is to form the basis of a proposed International Copyright Union, similar to the Postal Union, and steps have already been taken in Great Britain to amend the English law to permit association with it.

X.

THE INTERNATIONAL COPYRIGHT MOVEMENT IN AMERICA.

SIMULTANEOUSLY with the earliest legislation for international copyright among European states, there was a movement in the same direction in the United States. In February, 1837, Henry Clay presented to the Senate a petition of British authors asking for copyright privileges in this country. It was referred to a select committee, whose members were Clay, Webster, Buchanan, Preston, and Ewing, which reported favorably a bill for international copyright. The report took high ground in favor of the rights of authors :

" That authors and inventors have, according to the practice among civilized nations, a property in the respective productions of their genius, is incontestable ; and that this property should be protected as effectually as any other property is, by law, follows as a legitimate consequence. Authors and inventors are among the greatest benefactors of mankind. . . . It being established that literary property is entitled to legal protection, it results that this protection ought to be afforded wherever the property is situated. . . . We should be all shocked if the law tolerated the least invasion of the rights of property, in the case of merchandise, whilst those that justly belong to the works of authors are exposed to daily violation, without the possibility of their invoking the aid of the laws."

No action was taken on this report, nor on an invitation extended by Lord Palmerston the succeeding year, 1838, for the co-operation of the American Government in an international copyright arrangement.

Mr. George P. Putnam, himself a publisher, revived the question in 1840, in a pamphlet prepared by him and by Dr. Francis Lieber, " An Argument in behalf of International Copyright," said to be the first publication on this subject in this country. In 1843 he procured the signatures of ninety-seven publishers, printers, and binders to a petition which was presented to Congress, setting forth that the absence of international copyright was " alike injurious to the business of publishing and to the best interests of the people." A counter-memorial from Philadelphia objected that international copyright " would prevent the adaptation of English books to American wants." Mr. Dickens's tour in 18.. stimulated interest in this subject, and there were high hopes of some result.

In 1853 Edward Everett, then Secretary of State, negotiated through the American Minister in London, John F. Crampton, a treaty providing simply that authors, etc. entitled to copyright in one country should be entitled to it in the other, on the same conditions and for the same term. The Committee on Foreign Relations of the Senate reported the Everett treaty favorably, but it was tabled in Committee of the Whole. Five New York publishers addressed a letter to Mr. Everett, supporting a convention, providing the work should be registered in the United States before publication abroad, issued here within thirty days after publication abroad, and wholly manufactured in this country. It was in this year that Henry C. Carey published his famous " Letters on International Copyright," in which he held that ideas are the common property of society, and that copyright is therefore indefensible. In 1858 Mr. Morris, of Pennsylvania, introduced into the House a bill on the basis of remanufacture by an American publisher within thirty days of publication abroad, but it does not seem to have been considered.

The matter slumbered until 1868—after Mr. Dickens's second visit in 1867—when a committee consisting of George P. Putnam, S. Irenæus Prime, Henry Ivison, James Parton, and Egbert Hazard, issued an appeal for "Justice to Authors and Artists," calling a meeting, which was held under the presidency of W. C. Bryant, April 9th, 1868. A "Copyright Association" was then organized, with Mr. Bryant as President and E. C. Stedman as Secretary, whose primary object was "to promote the enactment of a just and suitable international copyright law for the benefit of authors and artists in all parts of the world." A memorial to Congress, asking early attention for a bill "to secure in all parts of the world the right of authors," but making no recommendations in detail, was signed by one hundred and fifty-three persons, including one hundred and one authors and nineteen publishers. A bill was introduced in the House this same year by J. D. Baldwin, of Massachusetts, which provided for copyright on foreign books wholly manufactured here and published by an American citizen. This was reported favorably by the Library Committee, which said : "We are fully persuaded that it is not only expedient, but in a high degree important, to the United States to establish such international copyright laws as will protect the rights of American authors in foreign countries and give similar protection to foreign authors in this country. It would be an act of national honor and justice in which we should find that justice is the wisest policy for nations and brings the richest reward." The bill was, however, recommitted and never more heard of.

In 1870 what has since been known as the Clarendon treaty was proposed to the American Government by Lord Clarendon on behalf of the British Government, through Sir Edward Thornton, then British Minister at Washington. This was modelled on the treaties existing between Great Britain and other European nations, and provided that an author of either country should have full protection in the other country to the extent of its domestic law, on the sole condition of registration and deposit in the other country within three months after its first publication in the country in which it first appeared, the convention to continue in force for five years, and thence from year to year, unless twelve months' notice of termination were given. This was criticised (in Messrs. Harper's letter of November 25th, 1878) as a scheme "more in the interest of British publishers than either of British or American authors," on the ground that British

publishers would secure American with British copyright, and give no opportunity to American houses to issue works of English authors.

The next year the following resolution, offered by Mr. S. S. Cox, was passed by the House, December 18th, 1871 :

"*Resolved*, That the Committee on the Library be directed to consider the question of an international copyright, and to report to this House what, in their judgment, would be the wisest plan, by treaty or law, to secure the property of authors in their works, without injury to other rights and interests ; and if in their opinion Congressional legislation is the best, that they report a bill for that purpose."

Mr. Cox had himself presented, December 6th, 1871, a bill for international copyright on a basis of reciprocity, providing foreign works should be wholly manufactured in the United States and published by American citizens, and be registered, deposited, and arrangements for such publication made within three months of first publication in the foreign country. This bill was supported in Committee of the Whole by speeches from Mr. Archer, of Maryland, and Mr. Storm, of Pennsylvania, but opposed by Mr. Kelley, of Pennsylvania, who presented the following resolution :

"*Whereas*, It is expedient to facilitate the reproduction here of foreign works of a higher character than that of those now generally reprinted in this country ; and *whereas* it is in like manner desirable to facilitate the reproduction abroad of the works of our own authors ; and *whereas* the grant of monopoly privileges, in case of reproduction here or elsewhere must tend greatly to increase the cost of books, to limit their circulation, and to increase the already existing obstacles to the dissemination of knowledge : Therefore,
"*Resolved*, That the joint Committee on the Library be and it hereby is instructed to inquire into the practicability of arrangements by means of which such reproduction, both here and abroad, may be facilitated, freed from the great disadvantages that must inevitably result from the grant of monopoly privileges such as are now claimed in behalf of foreign authors and domestic publishers."

Mr. Cox's resolution was acted upon in 1872 by the new Library Committee, which invited the co-operation of authors, publishers, and others interested in framing a bill. At meetings of New York publishers, January 23d and February 6th, 1872, a bill prepared by Mr. W. H. Appleton and accepted by Mr. A. D. F. Randolph, Mr. Isaac E. Sheldon, and Mr. D. Van Nostrand, of a committee, was approved by a majority vote. It provided for copyright on foreign books issued under contract with an American publisher, "wholly the product of the mechanical industry of the United States," and registered within one month and published within three months from the foreign issue, stipulating that if a work were out of print for three months the copyright should lapse. This was in line with a letter printed by Mr. W. H. Appleton in the London *Times*, October, 1871, denying that there was any disposition in the United States to withhold justice from English authors, but objecting to any "kind of legal saddle for the English publisher to ride his author into the American book-market;" in response to which Herbert Spencer, John Stuart Mill, Froude, Carlyle, and others had signed a memorial to Lord Granville expressing a willingness to accept a copyright on the condition of confining American copyright to American assigns of English authors, and excluding English publishers. Mr. Appleton's bill was opposed in a minority report by Mr. Edward Seymour, of the Scribner house, on the ground that it was "in no sense an international copyright law, but simply an act to protect American publishers"; that the desired "protection" could be evaded by English houses through an American partner; and that the act was objectionable in prohibiting stereos, in failing to provide for cyclopædias, and in enabling an American publisher to exclude revised editions. A meeting of Philadelphia publishers, January 27th, 1872, opposed international copyright altogether, in a memorial declaring that "thought, when given to the world, is, as light, free to all;" that copyright is a matter of municipal (domestic) law; that any foreigner could get American copyright by becoming an American citizen; and that "the good of the whole people and the safety of republican institutions" would be contravened by putting into the hands of foreign authors and "the great capitalists on the Atlantic seaboard" the power to make books high. The Executive Committee of the Copyright Association met in New York, February 2d, 1872, and put forward Mr. Charles Astor Bristed's bill securing copyright, after two years from date of passage, to citizens of other countries granting reciprocity all the rights of American citizens.

The Library Committee gave several hearings on the subject, February 12th and later, and among other contributions to the discussion received a letter from Messrs. Harper taking ground that "any measure of international copyright was objectionable because it would add to the price of books, and thus interfere with the education of the people;" and a suggestion from John P. Morton, of Louisville, to permit general republication on payment of a ten per cent royalty to the foreign author. The same suggestion, providing for five per cent royalty, as brought forward by Mr. John Elderkin, was introduced, in a bill, February 21st, 1872, by Mr. Beck in the House, and Mr. Sherman in the Senate.

The Committee, in despair over these conflicting opinions, presented the celebrated Morrill report of February 7th, 1873, Senator Lot M. Morrill being the chairman, including a tabular comparison of the prices of American and English books. It said that "there was no unanimity of opinion among those interested in the measure," and concluded:

In view of the whole case, your committee are satisfied that no form of international copyright can fairly be urged upon Congress upon reasons of general equity, or of constitutional law; that the adoption of any plan for the purpose which has been laid before us would be of very doubtful advantage to American authors as a class, and would be not only an unquestionable and permanent injury to the manufacturing interests concerned in producing books, but a hindrance to the diffusion of knowledge among the people, and to the cause of universal education; that no plan for the protection of foreign authors has yet been devised which can unite the support of all or nearly all who profess to be favorable to the general object in view; and that, in the opinion of your committee, any project for an international copyright will be found upon mature deliberation to be inexpedient.

This was decidedly a damper to the cause, and the movement lapsed for some years.

The question rested until 1878, when, under date of November 25th, Messrs. Harper addressed a letter to Mr. Evarts, Secretary of State, suggesting that previous failures were due "to the fact that all such propositions have originated from one side only, and without prior joint consultation and intelligent discussion," reiterating "that there was no disinclination on the part of American publishers to pay British authors the same as they do American authors," and that "American publishers simply wished to be assured that they should have the privilege of printing and publishing the books of British authors;" indicating "the likelihood of the acceptance by the United States of a treaty which should recognize the interests of all parties;"

and proposing a Conference or Commission of eighteen Americans and Englishmen—three authors, three publishers, and three publicists to be appointed on each side, by the American Secretary of State and the British Secretary for Foreign Affairs—which should consider and present the details of a treaty.

They also presented, as a suggested basis of action, what came to be known as the "Harper draft," a modification of the Clarendon treaty, providing that there should be registration in both countries *before* publication in the country of origin ; that international registration should be in the name of the author—if a *citizen* of the United States, at Stationers' Hall, London ; if a *subject* of Her Majesty, at the Library of Congress, Washington ; and that "the author of any work of literature manufactured and published in the one country shall not be entitled to copyright in the other country unless such work shall be also manufactured and published therein, by a subject or citizen thereof, within three months after its original publication in the country of the author or proprietor ; but this proviso shall not apply to paintings, engravings, sculptures, or other works of art ; and the word 'manufacture' shall not be held to prohibit printing in one country from stereotype plates prepared in the other and imported for this purpose."

This draft was approved by fifty-two leading American authors, including Longfellow, Holmes, Emerson, and Whittier, in a memorial dated August, 1880. The American members of the International Copyright Committee, appointed by the Association for the Reform and Codification of the Law of Nations, Messrs. John Jay, James Grant Wilson, and Nathan Appleton, also memorialized the Secretary of State, under date of February 11th, 1880, in favor of this general plan, specifying "within from one to three months" as the manufacturing limit. It was also approved by the great body of American publishers, although Messrs. Putnam, Scribner, Holt, and Roberts in signing took exception to certain of the restrictions, especially to the time limit of three months. Mr. George Haven Putnam set forth the views of his house in a paper before the New York Free Trade Club, January 29th, 1879, afterward printed as *Economic Monograph* No. XV., "International Copyright considered in some of its relations to ethics and political economy." In this he suggested simultaneous registration in both countries, republication within six months, and

restriction of copyright protection here for the first ten years of the term to books printed and bound in the United States and published by an American citizen.

An interesting series of replies from American authors, publishers, etc., as to methods for international copyright, to queries from the PUB-LISHERS' WEEKLY will be found in v. 15, commencing with No. 7, Feb. 15, 1879

The "Harper draft" was submitted in September, 1880, by Mr. Lowell to Earl Granville, who replied, March, 1881, that the British Government favored such a treaty, but considered an extension of the republication term to six months essential, and to twelve months much more equitable. In the same month the International Literary Association adopted a report favoring an agreement, but protesting against the manufacturing clause and time limit. This position was also taken at several meetings of London publishers, and Mr. F. R. Daldy was sent to America to further the English view. Sir Edward Thornton, British Minister at Washington, was instructed to proceed to the consideration of the treaty, provided the term for reprint could be extended, and both President Garfield and Secretary Blaine were understood to favor the completion of a treaty. With the death of Garfield the matter ended for the time.

It was revived once more in 1884. A new copyright association, the American Copyright League, had been organized in 1883, chiefly through the efforts of George P. Lathrop, Edward Eggleston, and R. W. Gilder, and there was a general revival of interest in the question. On January 9, 1884, Mr. Dorsheimer, of New York, introduced into the House his bill for international copyright, which provided for the extension of copyright to citizens of countries granting reciprocal privileges, so soon as the President should issue his proclamation accepting such reciprocity, for the life of the author, or for twenty-five years, providing he should live longer than that time. This bill was the occasion of a general discussion. The Copyright League addressed a letter to Mr. Dorsheimer urging the modification of the above limitations, and it was particularly pointed out that the confining of copyright to an author's life-time would render literary property most insecure. The League also addressed a letter to the Secretary of State, urging the completion of a treaty with Great Britain, to which Mr. Frelinghuysen replied, January 25, 1884, that while the negotiation as to the Harper draft had not been interrupted, he thought the object might be attained by a simple amendment to our present copyright law, based on reciprocity, after which a simple convention would suffice to put the amendment in force. Mr. Dorsheimer's bill was referred to the House Committee on the Judiciary, and reported favorably, with amendments extending the copyright term to twenty-eight years, without regard to the decease of the author, with renewal for fourteen years. The amended bill also provided that such copyright should cease in case reciprocity was withdrawn by another country ; that there should be no copyright in works already published, and that the provisions of the domestic copyright law should as far as applicable extend also to foreign copyrights. On the 19th of February Mr. Dorsheimer moved to make his bill the special order for February 27, but his motion failed of the necessary two-thirds vote, 155 voting aye, 98 nay and 55 not voting. There was considerable opposition on the part of those who insisted upon the re-manufacture of foreign books in this country, and Mr. Dorsheimer privately expressed himself as willing to accept, although not willing to favor, amendments in that direction if they were necessary to insure the passage of the bill. A circular letter of inquiry sent out by the PUBLISHERS' WEEKLY in March, 1884, showed a general desire on the part of American publishers in favor of international copyright. Of fifty-five leading publishers who answered, fifty-two favored and only three opposed international copyright. Out of these, twenty-eight advocated International Copyright pure and simple ; fourteen favored a " manufacturing clause ;" the others did not reply on this point. Congress adjourned, however, without taking definite action.

President Arthur, in his message of December, 1884, put himself on record as favoring copyright on the basis of reciprocity. The Dorsheimer

bill was re-introduced by Mr. English, January 5, 1885, and on January 6 Senator Hawley introduced " the Hawley bill " into the Senate. This latter, which covered all copyright articles, while Mr. Dorsheimer's had been confined to books, was understood to be favored by the Copyright League ; it extended copyright to citizens of foreign States, on a basis of reciprocity, for books or other works published after the passage of the bill, by repealing those parts of the Revised Statutes confining copyright to " citizens of the United States or resident therein." No action was taken, however, on either the Dorsheimer or the Hawley bill. A bill brought forward in the PUBLISHERS' WEEKLY of December 6, 1884, was intended, by a form admitting of easy amendment, to facilitate the passage of some kind of bill extending the principle of copyright to citizens of foreign countries under limitations set forth in subsequent sections of the bill.

In his first annual message, 1885, President Cleveland referred favorably to the negotiations at Berne, and with the opening of the Forty-ninth Congress two bills were introduced into the Senate, that of Senator Hawley (December 7, 1885), being essentially his bill of the previous year, and that of Senator Chace (January 21, 1886), a new bill, based on a plan put forward some years previously by Mr. Henry C. Lea and now supported by the Typographical Union and other labor organizations. The Hawley bill is on a simple basis of reciprocity ; the Chace bill requires registry within fifteen days and deposit of the best *American* edition within six months from publication abroad, at a fee of $1, to be used in printing a list of copyright books for customs use ; the prohibition of importations ; and the voiding of copyright when the American manufacturer abandons publication. They are both before the Senate Committee on Patents, which has given several hearings to those interested in the subject.

XI.

COPYRIGHT PROGRESS—AUTHORS AND PUBLISHERS.

THE unsettled and confused state of copyright law, as shown in the previous chapters, makes desirable a thorough revision of our domestic copyright code, and the pending organization of an International Copyright Union, similar to the existing International Postal Union, with the proposed revision and assimilation to a general system of the domestic law of England and other countries, makes the time opportune.

The copyright term adopted by Germany, of the author's life and thirty years thereafter, promises to become the standard statutory term, giving the control and returns of all his works directly to the author and his heirs or assigns into the period of a third generation and avoiding all questions as to the date of commencement of copyright or the lapse at different times of copyright on different works. With an adequate term, extending the benefit of an author's works into the days of his children and grandchildren, the question of perpetuity of copyright, except as an acknowledgment of an author's inherent right in his own product, is comparatively unimportant. There are, indeed, two considerations which go far to reconcile the upholders of authors' rights to a statutory term, waiving rights at common law. An indeterminate copyright would bring, if sold by the author, little if any more "outright" price than one for the term designated ; and if the author retains copyright for his own proper heirs, his duties to his own posterity are fairly limited (as in the precedent of the law of entail) to his grandchildren. Beyond the term designated, the publisher or other beneficiary holding the exclusive right would have little natural relation to the original producer, and the reversion may very

fairly be to the public. Moreover, in the case of material property, where a material exists, it is difficult enough to keep a title clear from generation to generation ; it might be still more difficult in the case of immaterial property.

The adoption of an adequate term, the freeing of the copyright system from mere technicalities which tend to forfeit rights for inadequate reasons, the recognition in the law itself of the present *status* of copyright as determined by judicial interpretations, the adoption into our law of useful features found in the copyright systems of other countries, are all *desiderata* for our domestic code, and the appointment by Congress of a Commission of experts to report a revised and comprehensive system, at an ensuing session or to a later Congress, would be most desirable.

The relations between authors and publishers is not properly within the scope of such a code— a fact overlooked by the advocates of what is called " the royalty system." The law, whether as to copyright or other matters, should afford a basis of certainty for business, but it cannot wisely interfere with freedom of contract between the parties to a business transaction. " The royalty plan," whether for domestic or international copyright, proposes that the law shall permit any person to publish the work of any author, on payment to him of a specified royalty, say of ten or five per cent, or a fixed sum per copy, on each copy sold. In reply to the criticism that the author would thus be put at the mercy of irresponsible persons, unless the Government undertook an elaborate system of accounting and guarantee to the author as its ward, the suggestion has been made that the royalty should be paid by means of stamps affixed to each copy published, sold by the aut or to the publisher—a system actually in practice in the shoe business, under the royalty scheme of the McKay Sewing-Machine Company. The answer to both is that the author is now at liberty to make such arrangements, by contract with one publisher or with many, and that a law to compel him to adopt any one plan of marketing his wares would interfere with his freedom of choice and his natural return. The reason that an author chooses one publisher instead of many is the simple one that the original cost of making and advertising a book is, in this way, reduced to one outlay instead of multiplied in many, and that this cost is minimized by being distributed over the largest possible edition. It is the practice of any successful publisher to plan for such an edition as will command the widest sale, and so distribute the original cost over as many copies as possible, and when a copyright book proves to be of such general demand that different styles of editions can be sold, such editions are in fact made by the same publisher. " The royalty plan" would only protect the public against the unwisdom of publishers whose mistakes are presently corrected by business failure or by the transfer of his books by the author to more enterprising houses.

The relations between author and publisher are simply those between principal and agent, or, where an author sells " outright," between buyer and seller. The " outright" price of a book is purely a matter of bargain, and no general rule applies. The author may reserve the " renewal " for his own benefit, or contract to renew as part of the original bargain. In the case where the publisher acts as agent for the author, the arrangement may be one of several different kinds. Either the author or the publisher may bargain to defray the cost of setting the type or making " plates," in which last case the plates usually remain the property of the party paying for them. An allowance of about ten per cent on the actual manufacturing cost of plates is a fair charge of the publisher for his oversight of them. Either the author or the publisher may bargain to defray the cost of making the edition (paper, press-work, and binding), and of the advertising, usually a large item, and like expenses. The remaining profits may be equally divided, which is the " half profits" system used in England. Or a definite percentage, usually calculated on the retail price (excluding

the price of fancy bindings), may be paid the author—usually in America fifteen or twenty per cent when the author pays for the book and takes the risk ; ten per cent on general, and five per cent on school and subscription books when the publisher does these. Or the author may arrange to pay the publisher a definite commission of ten or twenty per cent, as selling agent, and take all risk. An author's copyright is reckoned almost invariably not on copies printed, but on copies sold, and accounted for yearly or half-yearly. The " half-profits" system is apt to lead to much misunderstanding as to the actual expenses (e.g., general office expenses of a publisher,) to be deducted before profits are reckoned, and the American ten per cent system is, on the whole, most satisfactory. The publisher does not, as is sometimes naïvely assumed, get the other ninety per cent as profit ; he gets the difference between the returns from the trade or public on copies actually sold—averaging perhaps two thirds of the " retail price," on which the author's ten per cent (really thus fifteen per cent) is reckoned—and the cost of making the entire edition and of advertising and marketing the book. The author, in any event, gets a return proportioned to the success of his book. If its sales are small, the publisher makes a loss if large, the publisher makes a profit increasing proportionately with each extra thousand sold.

It is by means of this profit on successful books that the publisher is able to take risks with new books and new authors. It has been said that of five books, three fail, one covers its cost, the fifth must pay a profit to cover the rest. The element of risk in the book business is, in fact, very large ; if the author complains that his successful book ought not to pay for others' unsuccessful books, he can get over the difficulty by taking the risk himself, and making corresponding terms with a publisher. On a dollar cloth-bound book, it may usually be roughly estimated that the cost is 30 cents, the trade discount 30 cents (covering the bookseller's expenses, risk, and profit), the author's royalty 10 cents ; out of the remaining 30 cents the publisher covers expenses, risk, and profit. On the average, he nets probably less than the 10 cents of the author, and the system is essentially on an equitable basis. The publisher's larger returns come from the fact that he handles more books than any one author writes. The publisher has usually in bargaining with the author the advantage of larger experience and superior business ability, and of the fact that the author seeks him rather than he the author ; but no law can better the author in these respects. As a matter of practice, the better publishing houses treat with new authors on the same terms as with old, and have a form of contract on which transactions are based. It is usually understood in these contracts that a book remains with the publisher so long as he keeps it in the market ; if an author wishes to retain control of his book, that should be specified. The true secret, in fact, of satisfactory relations between author and publisher lies in a full understanding of the conditions of the arrangement in settling the terms of a contract, and these details of customary arrangements have here been given to correct the common confusion between copyright law and a business relation, which rests solely upon the common law of contracts.

In regard to international copyright, this country has yet to put itself on a par with other civilized nations, and blot out what has become a national disgrace. There are two great reasons for international copyright—the general principle of justice inciting us to pay foreign authors for the service they do us, and the unwisdom of discouraging home literature by subjecting home authors and home books to competition with absolutely unpaid labor. The plea against the first, that a nation legislates chiefly for its own citizens, is met by the second, as well as by the increasing disposition of civilized nations mutually to recognize and protect property of all kinds and of any owner. The reasons commonly advanced against international copyright are (1) that we have got on well without it, and may best leave things as they are, instead of "forcing the people to pay for what they can now have free ;" (2) that it would make books dearer, whereas American civilization depends on cheap education, which in turn depends on cheap books ; (3) that the benefit would be, not to the foreign author, but to the foreign publisher, who would foist on us English editions and take work from our mechanics ; (4) that the best foreign authors stimulate our own to greater efforts, so that they can supply the American market and drive out poor foreign books ; (5) that copyright gives a monopoly to a few authors against the interest of the many readers, and is kindred to patents, depriving new-comers of the benefit of what they might have invented for themselves.

The answers to these objections may be briefly outlined as follows : (1) " Things as they are" are against the present standard of international honesty, and against the interest of American authors. Moreover, people would not be "forced to pay for what they now have free," for international copyright would not be retroactive, and the cheap reprints from Shakespeare to Tennyson could still be had. (2) It would make the new books of foreign authors dearer, but by affording opportunity for wider sale of American books, it would tend to make them cheaper, distributing the original cost among larger editions. The novel-devourer, buying "the last new novel," now takes an English reprint at 10 or 20 cents instead of an American work at 50 cents or $1. Moreover, even in England, while three-volume novels, etc., are higher priced than here, the many lines of popular new books are often cheaper than here (*e. g.*, two shillings sixpence to our seventy-five cents), so that the question of relative prices has not the bearing alleged by the opponents of international copyright. The French copyright literature, with full copyright, is the cheapest in the world. American cheap education has come from cheap *school*-books, which are American and are already copyright. Further, "there is one thing better than a cheap book," as Mr. Lowell says, " and that is a book honestly come by ;" and, above all, American civilization depends on the honesty and justice of the people. (3) The foreign author would soon learn to bargain for his American market, and American editions would best meet American wants. The increased demand for American books would also operate to give our mechanics more to do. At worst, this objection would be met by the proposed manufacturing clause (which logically, however, has no more to do than the tariff with copyright), confining copyright to books printed here. Such a clause should not, however, prohibit the use of imported stereotype plates and electros of illustrations, since otherwise we should have to pay twice for doing work that can be done once for both countries, and should cut ourselves off from printing many illustrated books. The amount of type-setting involved is exaggerated—it is probably less than that of two or three of our daily papers together, and is largely the cheap work of women or machines. The manufacturing clause is advocated by some publishers for a term of years only, until foreign authors get into the habit of dealing for the American market separately. (4) American authors would still be "stimulated" by the best foreign authors, but they would no longer be disheartened by the underselling rivalry of poor books, (from unpaid labor, included by the cheap libraries to keep up their periodical character and thus keep themselves within the low postal rates. "Genius" will doubtless have its say, pay or no pay, but much useful literature comes from men who must earn their own bread and butter and support their families, and who are now underpaid or kept from authorship by the narrow market to which they are reduced. Moreover, although American authors now get British copyright by domestic law, that source of income might be taken away by change in British law, if we deny reciprocal rights to foreign authors. The author needs the widest market he can get, to give him similar return for his brain-work to that obtained by men in other intellectual or business pursuits. (5) The "few" authors have a right to ask from the "many" readers (even if it were 1 against 100,000,000) fair pay for the service which the reader is glad to enjoy. Moreover, copyright is not kindred to patents in the sense alleged. The first inventor of the telephone can prevent any one else patenting a telephone and utilizing the force of nature involved in it ; the author cannot do anything of the kind. No other author can be worse off because he has written. Copyright is a "monopoly" only as anything which a man produces and *owns* is a monopoly ; in this sense all property is monopoly, and the opposition to copyright becomes communism.

There has been a continuous growth in the United States, though displayed somewhat intermittently, of an active sentiment in favor of international copyright. For some years the question was less insistent, from the practical point of view, because of what was called "the courtesy of the trade," by which a publisher who was the first to reprint an English work was not disturbed by rival editions of that and succeeding works by the same author. Under this custom, the leading American publishers voluntarily made payments to foreign authors, in many cases the same ten per cent paid to American authors, and reaching in one case of "outright" purchase of "advance sheets" $5000, though there was no protection of law for the purchase.

American and English works then competed on much the same terms. In 1876 the cheap quarto "libraries" were started, reprinting an entire English novel, though on poor paper and often in dangerously poor type, for 10, 15, or 20 cents. They presently obtained the advantage, by regular issue (one "library" at one time issuing a book daily, others weekly) of the low postal rates for periodicals, of two cents a pound, and thus obtained a further advantage over American books. These quartos are gradually giving way to the "pocket edition," in more convenient shape, but not always in better print, at 20 or 25 cents. The normal price of these novels, in better type and print, under international copyright, would probably be 35 to 50 cents. The sales of corresponding American books has meanwhile definitely fallen.

The history of the movements for international copyright here show that there has been no continuous and well-defined policy on the part of the Government authorities, or of publishers, or of authors. While authors almost unanimously, and publishers generally, favor international copyright, the division lines as to method are not between authors and publishers, but between some authors and other authors, and between some publishers and other publishers. There are those, in both classes, who object to any bill which does not acknowledge to the full the inherent rights of authors, by extending the provisions of domestic copyright to any author of any country, without regard to other circumstances. There are others, at the other extreme, who oppose international copyright unless it is restricted to books manufactured in this country, issued simultaneously with their publication abroad, and of which the importation of other than the American copies is absolutely prohibited. But the number is steadily increasing of those willing to waive the abstract principle in favor of any moderate measure which shall be at least a first step of recognition, and which may justify by its results, even to the present opponents of international copyright, future steps of further progress. It is to be hoped that an International Copyright Union may, not many years hence, include all civilized nations on a mutual basis which shall do full justice to that class of producers who themselves do so much for the progress of the world.

THE following sections of the Revised Statutes and subsequent acts constitute the existing copyright law of the United States :

Revised Statute of the United States, being the Act of July 8, 1870, as contained in the Revised Statutes, Second Edition, 1878, page 957.

SECTION 4948. All records and other things relating to copyrights and required by law to be preserved, shall be under the control of the Librarian of Congress, and kept and preserved in the Library of Congress ; and the Librarian of Congress shall have the immediate care and supervision thereof, and, under the supervision of the joint committee of Congress on the Library, shall perform all acts and duties required by law touching copyrights.

SEC. 4949. The seal provided for the office of the Librarian of Congress shall be the seal thereof, and by it all records and papers issued from the office and to be used in evidence shall be authenticated.

SEC. 4950. The Librarian of Congress shall give a bond, with sureties, to the Treasurer of the United States, in the sum of five thousand dollars, with the condition that he will render to the proper officers of the Treasury a true account of all moneys received by virtue of his office.

SEC. 4951. The Librarian of Congress shall make an annual report to Congress of the number and description of copyright publications for which entries have been made during the year.

SEC. 4952. Any citizen of the United States or resident therein, who shall be the author, inventor, designer, or proprietor of any book, map, chart, dramatic or musical composition, engraving, cut, print,* or photograph or negative

* See Act of 1874, s. 3, *post*, p. 40.

thereof, or of a painting, drawing, chromo, statue, statuary, and of models or designs intended to be perfected as works of the fine arts, and the executors, administrators, or assigns of any such persons shall, upon complying with the provisions of this chapter, have the sole liberty of printing, reprinting, publishing, completing, copying, executing, finishing, and vending the same ; and, in the case of a dramatic composition, of publicly performing or representing it, or causing it to be performed or represented by others. And authors may reserve the right to dramatize or to translate their own works.

SEC. 4953. Copyrights shall be granted for the term of twenty-eight years from the time of recording the title thereof, in the manner hereinafter directed.

SEC. 4954. The author, inventor, or designer, if he be still living and a citizen of the United States or resident therein, or his widow or children, if he be dead, shall have the same exclusive right continued for the further term of fourteen years, upon recording the title of the work or description of the article so secured a second time, and complying with all other regulations in regard to original copyrights, within six months before the expiration of the first term. And such person shall, within two months from the date of said renewal, cause a copy of the record thereof to be published in one or more newspapers, printed in the United States, for the space of four weeks.

SEC. 4955. Copyrights shall be assignable in law, by any instrument of writing, and such assignment shall be recorded in the office of the Librarian of Congress within sixty days after its execution ; in default of which it shall be void as against any subsequent purchaser or mortgagee for a valuable consideration, without notice.

SEC. 4956. No person shall be entitled to a

copyright unless he shall, before publication, deliver at the office of the Librarian of Congress or deposit in the mail addressed to the Librarian of Congress, at Washington, District of Columbia, a printed copy of the title of the book or other article, or a description of the painting, drawing, chromo, statue, statuary, or a model or design for a work of the fine arts, for which he desires a copyright, nor unless he shall also, within ten days from the publication thereof, deliver at the office of the Librarian of Congress or deposit in the mail addressed to the Librarian of Congress, at Washington, District of Columbia, two copies of such copyright book or other article, or in case of a painting, drawing, statue, statuary, model, or design for a work of the fine arts, a photograph of the same.

SEC. 4957. The Librarian of Congress shall record the name of such copyright book or other article, forthwith, in a book to be kept for that purpose, in the words following : " Library of Congress, to wit : Be it remembered that on the day of , A. B., of , hath deposited in this office the title of a book (map, chart, or otherwise, as the case may be, or description of the article,) the title or description of which is in the following words, to wit ; (here insert the title or description,) the right whereof he claims as author, (originator, or proprietor, as the case may be,) in conformity with the laws of the United States respecting copyrights. C. D., Librarian of Congress." And he shall give a copy of the title or description, under the seal of the Librarian of Congress, to the proprietor whenever he shall require it.

SEC. 4958. The Librarian of Congress shall receive, from the persons to whom the services designated are rendered, the following fees :

First. For recording the title or description of any copyright book or other article, fifty cents.

Second. For every copy under seal of such record actually given to the person claiming the copyright, or his assigns, fifty cents.

Third. For recording any instrument of writing for the assignment of a copyright, fifteen cents for every one hundred words.*

Fourth. For every copy of an assignment, ten cents for every one hundred words.*

All fees so received shall be paid into the Treasury of the United States.

SEC. 4959. The proprietor of every copyright book or other article shall deliver at the office of the Librarian of Congress, or deposit in the mail addressed to the Librarian of Congress at Washington, District of Columbia, within ten days after its publication, two complete printed copies thereof, of the best edition issued, or description or photograph of such article as hereinbefore required, and a copy of every subsequent edition wherein any substantial changes shall be made.

SEC. 4960. For every failure on the part of the proprietor of any copyright to deliver or deposit in the mail either of the published copies, or description or photograph, required by sections four thousand nine hundred and fifty-six, and four thousand nine hundred and fifty-nine, the proprietor of the copyright shall be liable to a penalty of twenty-five dollars, to be recovered by the Librarian of Congress, in the name of the United States, in an action in the nature of an action of debt, in any district court of the United States within the jurisdiction of which the delinquent may reside or be found.

SEC. 4961. The postmaster to whom such copyright book, title, or other article is delivered, shall, if requested, give a receipt therefor ; and when so delivered he shall mail it to its destination.

SEC. 4962. No person shall maintain an action for the infringement of his copyright unless he shall give notice thereof by inserting in the several copies of every edition published, on the title-page or the page immediately following, if it be a book ; or if a map, chart, musical composition, print, cut, engraving, photograph, painting, drawing, chromo, statue, statuary, or model or design intended to be perfected and completed as a work of the fine arts, by inscribing upon some portion of the face or front thereof, or on the face of the substance on which the same shall be mounted, the following words, " Entered according to Act of Congress, in the year , by A. B., in the office of the Librarian of Congress, at Washington." *

SEC. 4963. Every person who shall insert or impress such notice, or words of the same purport, in or upon any book, map, chart, musical composition, print, cut, engraving, or photograph, or other article, for which he has not obtained a copyright, shall be liable to a penalty of one hundred dollars, recoverable one half for the person who shall sue for such penalty, and one half to the use of the United States.

---

* See Act of 1874, s. 2, *post*, p. 40.

* See Act of 1874, s. 1, *post*, p. 39.

Sec. 4964. Every person who, after the recording of the title of any book as provided by this chapter, shall within the term limited, and without the consent of the proprietor of the copyright first obtained in writing, signed in presence of two or more witnesses, print, publish, or import, or knowing the same to be so printed, published, or imported, shall sell or expose to sale any copy of such book, shall forfeit every copy thereof to such proprietor, and shall also forfeit and pay such damages as may be recovered in a civil action by such proprietor in any court of competent jurisdiction.

Sec. 4965. If any person, after the recording of the title of any map, chart, musical composition, print, cut, engraving, or photograph, or chromo, or of the description of any painting, drawing, statue, statuary, or model or design intended to be perfected and executed as a work of the fine arts, as provided by this chapter, shall, within the term limited, and without the consent of the proprietor of the copyright first obtained in writing, signed in presence of two or more witnesses, engrave, etch, work, copy, print, publish, or import, either in whole or in part, or by varying the main design with intent to evade the law, or, knowing the same to be so printed, published, or imported, shall sell or expose to sale any copy of such map or other article, as aforesaid, he shall forfeit to the proprietor all the plates on which the same shall be copied, and every sheet thereof, either copied or printed, and shall further forfeit one dollar for every sheet of the same found in his possession, either printing, printed, copied, published, imported, or exposed for sale ; and in case of a painting, statue, or statuary, he shall forfeit ten dollars for every copy of the same in his possession, or by him sold or exposed for sale ; one half thereof to the proprietor and the other half to the use of the United States.

Sec. 4966. Any person publicly performing or representing any dramatic composition for which a copyright has been obtained, without the consent of the proprietor thereof, or his heirs or assigns, shall be liable for damages therefor, such damages in all cases to be assessed at such sum, not less than one hundred dollars for the first, and fifty dollars for every subsequent performance, as to the court shall appear to be just.

Sec. 4967. Every person who shall print or publish any manuscript whatever, without the consent of the author or proprietor first obtained,

if such author or proprietor is a citizen of the United States, or resident therein, shall be liable to the author or proprietor for all damages occasioned by such injury.

Sec. 4968. No action shall be maintained in any case of forfeiture or penalty under the copyright laws, unless the same is commenced within two years after the cause of action has arisen.

Sec. 4969. In all actions arising under the laws respecting copyrights, the defendant may plead the general issue, and give the special matter in evidence.

Sec. 4970. The circuit courts, and district courts having the jurisdiction of circuit courts, shall have power, upon bill in equity, filed by any party aggrieved, to grant injunctions to prevent the violation of any right secured by the laws respecting copyrights, according to the course and principles of courts of equity, on such terms as the court may deem reasonable.

Sec. 4971. Nothing in this chapter shall be construed to prohibit the printing, publishing, importation, or sale of any book, map, chart, dramatic or musical composition, print, cut, engraving, or photograph, written, composed, or made by any person not a citizen of the United States nor resident therein.

Act of June 18, 1874. *An act to amend the law relating to patents, trade-marks, and copyrights, as contained in the Supplement to the Rev. Stat., v. 1, 1881, p. 40.*

Be it enacted by the Senate and House of Representatives of the United States of America in Congress assembled, [Section 1] That no person shall maintain an action for the infringement of his copyright unless he shall give notice thereof by inserting in the several copies of every edition published, on the title-page or the page immediately follow ing, if it be a book ; or if a map, chart, musical composition, print, cut, engraving, photograph, painting, drawing, chromo, statue, statuary, or model or design intended to be perfected and completed as a work of the fine arts, by inscribing upon some visible portion thereof, or of the substance on which the same shall be mounted, the following words, viz.: " Entered according to act of Congress, in the year ——, by A. B., in the office of the Librarian of Congress, at Washington ;" or, at his option the word " Copyright," together with the year the copyright was entered, and the name of the party by whom it was taken out ; thus —" Copyright, 18 –, by A. B."

SEC. 2. That for recording and certifying any instrument of writing for the assignment of a copyright, the Librarian of Congress shall receive from the persons to whom the service is rendered, one dollar ; and for every copy of an assignment, one dollar ; said fee to cover, in either case, a certificate of the record, under seal of the Librarian of Congress ; and all fees so received shall be paid into the Treasury of the United States.

SEC. 3. That in the construction of this act, the words " Engraving," " cut " and " print " shall be applied only to pictorial illustrations or works connected with the fine arts, and no prints or labels designed to be used for any other article of manufacture shall be entered under the copyright law, but may be registered in the Patent Office. And the Commissioner of Patents is hereby charged with the supervision and control of the entry or registry of such prints or labels, in conformity with the regulations provided by law as to copyright of prints, except that there shall be paid for recording the title of any print or label not a trade-mark, six dollars, which shall cover the expense of furnishing a copy of the record under the seal of the Commissioner of Patents, to the party entering the same.

SEC. 4. That all laws and parts of laws inconsistent with the foregoing provisions be and the same are hereby repealed.

SEC. 5. That this act shall take effect on and after the first day of August, eighteen hundred and seventy-four.

Approved, June 18, 1874.

Provisions of the Revised Statutes of the United States which, with section 4970 (ante, p. 39), govern Jurisdiction in Copyright Cases.

SEC. 629. The circuit courts shall have original jurisdiction as follows :

First. Of all suits of a civil nature at common law or in equity, where the matter in dispute, exclusive of costs, exceeds the sum or value of five hundred dollars, and an alien is a party, or the suit is between a citizen of the State where it is brought and a citizen of another State. . . .

*   *   *   *   *

Ninth. Of all suits at law or in equity arising under the patent or copyright laws of the United States.*

SEC. 699. A writ of error [to the Supreme Court of the United States] may be allowed to review any final judgment at law, and an appeal shall be allowed from any final decree in equity hereinafter mentioned, without regard to the sum or value in dispute :

First. Any final judgment at law or final decree in equity of any circuit court, or of any district court acting as a circuit court, or of the supreme court of the District of Columbia, or of any Territory, in any case touching patent-rights or copyrights.†

DIRECTIONS FOR SECURING COPYRIGHTS UNDER THE REVISED ACTS OF CONGRESS.

The following " Official Directions for Securing Copyright," in explanation of the law, are issued by the Librarian of Congress :

1. A *printed* copy of the title (besides the two copies to be deposited after publication) of the book, map, chart, dramatic or musical composition, engraving, cut, print, photograph, or a *description* of the painting, drawing, chromo, statue, statuary, or model or design for a work of the fine arts, for which copyright is desired, must be sent by mail or otherwise, *prepaid,* addressed

LIBRARIAN OF CONGRESS,
Washington, D. C.

This must be done before publication of the book or other article.

The *printed title* required may be a copy of the title-page of such publications as have title-pages. In other cases, the title must be printed expressly for copyright entry, with name of claimant of copyright. The style of type is immaterial, and the print of a type-writer will be

---

* U. S. Rev. Stat., p. 110, 111.

The Act of March 3. 1875, Supp. to Rev. Stat, v. 1, p. 173, provides that " the circuit courts of the United States shall have original cognizance, concurrent with the courts of the several States, of all suits of a civil nature at common law or in equity, where the matter in dispute exceeds, exclusive of costs, the sum or value of five hundred dollars, and arising under the Constitution or laws of the United States, or treaties made, or which shall be made, under their authority, or in which the United States are plaintiffs or petitioners, or in which there shall be a controversy between citizens of different States or a controversy between citizens of the same State claiming land under grants of different States, or a controversy between citizens of a State and foreign states, citizens, or subjects."

† U. S. Rev. Stat., p. 130.

accepted. But a separate title is required for each entry, and *each* title must be printed on paper as large as commercial note. The title of a *periodical* must include the date and number.

2. A fee of fifty cents, for recording the title of each book or other article, must be inclosed with the title as above, and fifty cents in addition (or one dollar in all) for each certificate of copyright under seal of the Librarian of Congress, which will be transmitted by early mail.

3. Within ten days after publication of each book or other article, two complete copies of the best edition issued must be sent, to perfect the copyright, with the address

Librarian of Congress,
Washington, D. C.

The postage must be prepaid, or else the publication inclosed in parcels covered by printed Penalty Labels, furnished by the Librarian, in which case they will come FREE by mail, according to rulings of the Post Office Department. Without the deposit of copies above required the copyright is void, and a penalty of $25 is incurred. No copy is required to be deposited elsewhere.

4. No copyright is valid unless notice is given by inserting in every copy published, on the title-page or the page following, if it be a book ; or, if a map, chart, musical composition, print, cut, engraving, photograph, painting, drawing, chromo, statue, statuary, or model or design intended to be perfected as a work of the fine arts, by inscribing upon some portion thereof, or on the substance on which the same is mounted, the following words, viz. : " *Entered according to act of Congress, in the year* ——, *by* ——, *in the office of the Librarian of Congress, at Washington,*" or, at the option of the person entering the copyright, the words : " *Copyright,* 18—, by ——."

The law imposes a penalty of $100 upon any person who has not obtained copyright who shall insert the notice, " *Entered according to act of Congress,*" or " *Copyright,*" etc., or words of the same import, in or upon any book or other article.

5. Any author may reserve the right to translate or to dramatize his own work. In this case, notice should be given by printing the words " *Right of translation reserved,*" or " *All rights reserved,*" below the notice of copyright entry, and notifying the Librarian of Congress of such reservation, to be entered upon the record.

Since the phrase *all rights reserved* refers exclusively to the author's right to dramatize or to translate, it has no bearing upon any publications except original works, and will not be entered upon the record in other cases.

6. The original term of copyright runs for twenty-eight years. *Within six months before* the end of that time, the author or designer, or his widow or children, may secure a renewal for the further term of fourteen years, making forty-two years in all. Applications for renewal must be accompanied by explicit statement of ownership, in the case of the author, or of relationship in the case of his heirs, and must state definitely the date and place of entry of the original copyright. Advertisement of renewal is to be made within two months of date of renewal certificate, in some newspaper, for four weeks.

7. The time within which any work entered for copyright may be issued from the press is not limited by any law or regulation, but depends upon the discretion of the proprietor. A copyright may be secured for a projected work as well as for a completed one.

8. A copyright is assignable in law by any instrument of writing, but such assignment must be recorded in the office of the Librarian of Congress within sixty days from its date. The fee for this record and certificate is $1, and for a certified copy of any record of assignment $1.

9. A copy of the record (or duplicate certificate) of any copyright entry will be furnished, under seal, at the rate of fifty cents each.

10. In the case of books published in more than one volume, or of periodicals, published in numbers, or of engravings, photographs, or other articles published with variations, a copyright is to be entered for each volume or part of a book, or number of a periodical, or variety, as to style, title, or inscription, of any other article. But a book published serially in a periodical, under the same general title, requires only one entry. To *complete* the copyright on such a work, two copies of each serial part, as well as of the complete work (if published separately), must be deposited.

11. To secure a copyright for a painting, statue, or model or design intended to be perfected as a work of the fine arts, so as to prevent infringement by copying, engraving, or vending such design, a definite description must accompany the application for copyright, and a photograph of the same, at least as large as " cabinet size," should be mailed to the Librarian of Con-

gress within ten days from the completion of the work or design.

12. Copyrights cannot be granted upon trade-marks, nor upon mere names of companies or articles, nor upon prints or labels intended to be used with any article of manufacture. If protection for such names or labels is desired, application must be made to the Patent Office, where they are registered at a fee of $6 for labels and $25 for trade-marks.

13. Citizens or residents of the United States only are entitled to copyright.

14. Every applicant for a copyright should state distinctly the full name and residence of the claimant, and whether the right is claimed as author, designer, or proprietor. No affidavit or formal application is required.

OFFICE OF THE LIBRARIAN OF CONGRESS,
Washington, 1885.

THE following are the dates and titles of the laws constituting the existing copyright law of Great Britain :

DOMESTIC COPYRIGHT.

8 *Geo.* 2. *c.* 13. An Act for the encouragement of the arts of designing, engraving, and etching historical and other prints by vesting the properties thereof in the inventors and engravers during the time therein mentioned.

7 *Geo.* 3. *c.* 38. An Act to amend and render more effectual an Act made in the eighth year of the reign of King George the Second for encouragement of the arts of designing, engraving, and etching historical and other prints ; and for vesting in and securing to Jane Hogarth, widow, the property in certain prints.

15 *Geo.* 3. *c.* 53. An Act for enabling the two universities in England, the four universities in Scotland, and the several colleges of Eton, Westminster, and Winchester, to hold in perpetuity their copyright in books given or bequeathed to the said universities and colleges for the advancement of useful learning and other purposes of education ; and for amending so much of an Act of the eighth year of the reign of Queen Anne as relates to the delivery of books to the warehouse keeper of the Stationers' Company for the use of the several libraries therein mentioned.

17 *Geo.* 3. *c.* 57. An Act for more effectually securing the property of prints to inventors and engravers by enabling them to sue for and recover penalties in certain cases.

54 *Geo.* 3. *c.* 56. An Act to amend and render more effectual an Act of His present Majesty for encouraging the art of making new models and casts of busts and other things therein mentioned, and for giving further encouragement to such arts.

3 *Will.* 4. *c.* 15. An Act to amend the laws relating to dramatic literary property.

5 & 6 *Will.* 4. *c.* 65. An Act for preventing the publication of lectures without consent.

6 & 7 *Will.* 4. *c.* 59. An Act to extend the protection of copyright in prints and engravings to Ireland.

5 & 6 *Vict.* *c.* 45. An Act to amend the law of copyright.

25 & 26 *Vict.* *c.* 68. An Act for amending the law relating to copyright in works of the fine arts, and for repressing the commission of fraud in the production and sale of such works.

38 & 39 *Vict.* *c.* 53, *in part.* An Act to give effect to an Act of the Parliament of the Dominion of Canada respecting copyright. *Section* 4 only repealed.

INTERNATIONAL COPYRIGHT.

7 & 8 *Vict.* *c.* 12. An Act to amend the law relating to international copyright.

15 & 16 *Vict.* *c.* 12, *in part.* An Act to enable Her Majesty to carry into effect a convention with France on the subject of copyright ; to extend and explain the International Copyright Acts ; and to explain the Acts relating to copyright in engravings. *Repeal not to extend to section* 14.

38 *Vict.* *c.* 12. An Act to amend the law relating to international copyright.

The following is the Digest of these laws, prepared by Sir James Stephen, Q.C., and presented in the Report of the Royal Copyright Commission, 1878, as the most authoritative statement of British copyright law :

ARTICLE 1.
Copyright in Private Documents.

The author or owner of any literary composition or work of art has a right, so long as it remains unpublished, to prevent the publication of any copy of it by any other person.

ARTICLE 2.
Effects of Limited Publication of Private Documents.

The publication of any such thing as is mentioned in the last article for a special and limited purpose, under any contract, or upon any trust express or implied, does not authorize the person to whom such thing is published to copy or reproduce it, except to the extent and for the purposes for which it has been lent or intrusted to him.

ARTICLE 3.
Letters.

A person who writes and sends a letter to another retains his copyright in such letter, except in so far as the particular circumstances of the case may give a right to publish such letter to the person addressed, or to his representatives, but the property in the material on which the letter is written passes to the person to whom it is sent, so as to entitle him to destroy or transfer it.

ARTICLE 4.
No other Copyright except by Statute.

There is (probably) no copyright after publication in any of the things mentioned in Article 1, except such copyright as is given by the express words of the statutes hereinafter referred to.

Publication in this article means in reference to books (as defined in the next article) publication for sale. It is doubtful whether in relation to works of art it has any other meaning. There is (it seems) no copyright in dramatic performances except by statute.

ARTICLE 5.
Book defined—Law of Copyright in Books.

In this chapter the word "book" means and includes every volume, part or division of a volume, pamphlet, sheet of letter-press, sheet of music, map, chart, or plan, separately published.

The word "copyright" means the sole and exclusive liberty of printing, or otherwise multiplying copies of any subject to which the word is applied.

When a book is published in the lifetime of its author, the copyright therein is the personal property of the author and his assigns from the date of such publication, for whichever may be

the longer of the two following terms, that is to say :

(1) A term of 42 years from publication.
(2) The life of the author, and a term of seven years, beginning from his death.

If the publication takes place after the author's death, the proprietor of the author's manuscript and his assigns have copyright in his book for a term of 42 years from its first publication.

If one person employs and pays another to write a book on the terms that the copyright therein shall belong to the employer, the employer has the same copyright therein as if he had been the author.

If the publisher or proprietor of any encyclopædia, review, magazine, or periodical work, or work published in parts or series, employs and pays persons to compose any volume, part, essay, article, or portion thereof, on the terms that the copyright therein shall belong to such publisher or proprietor, such publisher or proprietor has upon publication the same rights as if he were the author of the whole work (with the following exceptions) :

1. After 28 years from the first publication of any essay, article, or portion in any review, magazine, or other periodical work of a like nature [not being an encyclopædia], the right of publishing the same in a separate form reverts to the author for the remainder of the term for which his copyright would have endured if the same had been originally published by him elsewhere.

2. During the said term of 28 years the publisher or proprietor may not publish any such essay, article, or portion, separately or singly, without the consent of the author or his assigns.

The author of any such magazine as aforesaid may, by contract with any such publisher or proprietor, reserve the right of publishing any work, his composition, in a separate form, and if he does so he is entitled to copyright in such composition when so published for the same term as if such publication were the first publication, but without prejudice to the right of the publisher or proprietor to publish the same as part of such periodical work.

In order to provide against the suppression of books of importance to the public, the Judicial Committee of the Privy Council are empowered, on complaint that the proprietor of the copyright in any book after the death of its author has refused to republish or allow the republication of the same, and that by reason of such refusal such book may be withheld from the public, to grant a license to such complainant to publish such book in such manner and subject to such conditions as they think fit, and the complainant may publish such book accordingly.

The whole of this article is subject to the limitations contained in the subsequent articles of this chapter.

It applies—

1 To all books published after 1st July, 1842.
2 To all books published before that day in which copyright was then subsisting, unless such copyright was vested in any publisher or other person who acquired it for any consideration other than that of natural love or affection, in which case such copyright endures for the term then provided for by law, unless the author, if living on that day, or if he were then dead his personal representative, and (in either case) the proprietor of the copyright, registered before the expiration of the term of copyright to which they were then entitled, consent to accept the benefits of the Act 5 & 6 Vict. c. 45 in a form provided in a schedule therein.

ARTICLE 6.

Who may obtain Copyright in Books.

In order that copyright in a published book may be obtained under the provisions of Article 5, the book must in all cases be published in the United Kingdom. The author or other person seeking to entitle himself to copyright may be either—

(a) A natural born or naturalized subject of the Queen, in which case his place of residence at the time of the publication of the book is immaterial ; or

(b) A person who at the time of the publication of the book in which copyright is to be obtained owes local and temporary allegiance to Her Majesty by residing at that time in some part of Her Majesty's dominions.

It is probable, but not certain, that an alien friend who publishes a book in the United Kingdom while resident out of Her Majesty's dominions, acquires copyright throughout Her Majesty's dominions by such publication.

ARTICLE 7.

Previous and Contemporary Publication out of the United Kingdom.

No copyright in a book published in the United Kingdom can be obtained under Article 5, if the book has been previously published by the author in any foreign country, but the contemporaneous publication of a book in a foreign country and in the United Kingdom does not prevent the author from obtaining copyright in the United Kingdom.

It is uncertain whether an author obtains copyright by publishing a book in the United Kingdom, after a previous publication thereof in parts of Her Majesty's dominions out of the United Kingdom.

It is uncertain whether an author acquires copyright under Article 5 in any part of Her Majesty's dominions out of the United Kingdom (apart from any local law as to copyright which may be in force there) by the publication of a book in such part of Her Majesty's dominions.

ARTICLE 8.

No Copyright in immoral Publications.

No copyright can exist in anything in which copyright would otherwise exist if it is immoral, irreligious, seditious, or libellous, or if it professes to be what it is not, in such a manner as to be a fraud upon the purchasers thereof.

ARTICLE 9.

What is Infringement of Copyright in a Book, and what not—Fair Use of Books.

The owner of the copyright in a book is not entitled to prevent other persons from publishing the matter contained in it if they invent or collect it independently, nor to prevent them from making a fair use of its contents in the composition of other books.

The question, what is a fair use of a book, depends upon the circumstances of each particular case, but the following ways of using a book have been decided to be fair :

(a) Using the information or the ideas contained in it without copying its words or imitating them so as to produce what is substantially a copy.

(b) Making extracts (even if they are not acknowledged as such) appearing, under all the circumstances of the case, reasonable in quality, number, and length, regard being had to the object with which the extracts are made and to the subjects to which they relate.

(*c*.) Using one book on a given subject as a guide to authorities afterward independently consulted by the author of another book on the same subject.

(*d*.) Using one book on a given subject for the purpose of checking the results independently arrived at by the author of another book on the same subject.

An abridgment may be an original work if it is produced by a fair use of the original or originals from which it is abridged, but the republication of a considerable part of a book is an infringement of the copyright existing in it, although it may be called an abridgment, and although the order in which the republished parts are arranged may be altered.

ARTICLE 10.
Crown Copyright.

It is said that Her Majesty and her successors have the right of granting by patent from time to time to their printers an exclusive right to print the text of the authorized version of the Bible, of the Book of Common Prayer, and possibly the text of Acts of Parliament.

ARTICLE 11.
University Copyright.

The Universities of Oxford, Cambridge, Edinburgh, Glasgow, St. Andrew's, and Aberdeen, each college or house of learning at the universities of Oxford and Cambridge, Trinity College, Dublin, and the colleges of Eton, Westminster, and Winchester, have forever the sole liberty of printing and reprinting all such books as have been or hereafter may be bequeathed or given to them, or in trust for them, by the authors thereof, or by their representatives, unless they were given or bequeathed for any limited term.

ARTICLE 12.
How such Right forfeited.

The exclusive right mentioned in the last article lasts so long only as the books or copies belonging to the said universities or colleges are printed only at their own printing presses within the said universities or colleges respectively, and for their sole benefit and advantage.

If any university or college delegates, grants, leases, or sells its copyright or exclusive right of printing books granted by 15 Geo. 3. c. 53, or any part thereof, or allows or authorizes any person to print or reprint the same, the privilege granted by the said Act becomes void and of no effect, but the universities or colleges may sell the copyrights bequeathed to them as for the terms secured to authors by the 8 Anne c. 19.

ARTICLE 13.
Term of Copyright in Dramatic Pieces.

The author, or the assignee of the author, of any tragedy, comedy, play, opera, farce, or any other dramatic piece or entertainment or musical composition not printed and published by such author or assignee, has, as his own property, the sole liberty of representing or causing to be represented or performed, any such dramatic piece or musical composition at any place of dramatic entertainment whatever in Her Majesty's dominions (possibly in perpetuity, but more probably for) whichever is the longer of the two following terms, viz.—

(1) Forty-two years from the first public representation of such dramatic piece or musical composition.

(2) The life of the author and a further term of seven years beginning from his death.

The singing of a single song of a dramatic character in a dramatic manner may amount to a dramatic entertainment within the meaning of this article.

Any place at which a dramatic entertainment is given [? for profit] on any particular occasion is a place of dramatic entertainment within the meaning of this article.

ARTICLE 14.
Condition of Copyright in Dramatic Pieces.

The exclusive right of representing or performing a dramatic piece or musical composition cannot be gained if such dramatic piece or musical composition has been printed and published as a book before the first representation thereof.

Or, if it has been publicly represented or caused to be represented by the author or his assigns in any place out of Her Majesty's dominions before it was publicly represented in them, except under the International Copyright Act.

ARTICLE 15.

Copyright in and Representation of Dramas.

Copyright in a book containing or consisting of a dramatic piece or musical composition is a right distinct from the right to represent such dramatic piece or musical composition on the stage, and no assignment of the copyright of any such book conveys to the assignee the right of representing or performing such dramatic piece or musical composition unless an entry of such assignment is made in the registry book mentioned in Article 23, expressing the intention of the parties that such right should pass.

ARTICLE 16.

Representation of a Drama no Infringement of Copyright.

A dramatic piece or musical composition published as a book may (it seems probable) be publicly represented without the consent of the author or his assigns.

ARTICLE 17.

Dramatization of Novels.

The public representation of a dramatic piece constructed out of a novel is not an infringement of the copyright of the author of the novel or his assigns, but the printing and publication as a book of such dramatic piece so represented may be such an infringement.

If two persons independently of each other convert a novel into a dramatic piece, each has an exclusive right of representing his own dramatic piece, though one of them may be the author of the novel so dealt with and though the two pieces may have parts in common.

ARTICLE 18.

Infringement of Copyright in a Musical Composition.

Copyright in a musical composition is infringed when a substantial portion of the music in which copyright exists is reproduced either without any alteration or with such alterations as are required to adapt it to a different purpose or instrument, the alterations being of such a character that the substantial identity between the original and the altered version can be recognized by the ear.

ARTICLE 19.

Copyright in Lectures.

The author of any lecture, or his assign, has by statute the sole right of publishing any lecture, of the delivery of which notice in writing has been given to two justices living within five miles from the place where such lecture is delivered two days at least before it is delivered, unless such lecture is delivered in any university, public school, or college, or on any public foundation, or by any person in virtue of or according to any gift, endowment, or foundation.

The author of any lecture has [probably] at common law the same right as by statute, without giving such notice as is required by statute, but he cannot recover the penalties provided by the Act and specified in Article 35, for an infringement of his copyright.

ARTICLE 20.

Copyright in Sculpture.

Every person who makes or causes to be made any new and original sculpture, or model, or copy, or cast, . . .* has the sole right therein for the term of 14 years from first putting forth or publishing the same, provided that the proprietor causes his name, with the date, to be put on every such thing before it is published. If the proprietor be living at the end of the term of 14 years, his right returns to him for a further term of 14 years, unless he has divested himself thereof.

ARTICLE 21.

Copyright in Paintings and Photographs.

The author, being a British subject or resident within the dominions of Her Majesty, of any original painting, drawing or photograph, not having been sold before the 29th July, 1862, has the sole and exclusive right of copying, engraving, reproducing, and multiplying such painting or drawing, and the design thereof, or such photograph and the negative thereof, by any means or of any size, whether made in the Queen's dominions or not, for the term of his life and seven years after his death, but this right does not affect the right of any other person to represent any scene or object represented by any such painting.

If any painting or drawing, or the negative of any photograph, hereinbefore mentioned, is made by the author for or on behalf of any other person for a good or valuable consideration, such person is entitled to copyright therein.

If any such thing is, after the 29th July, 1862, for any such consideration transferred for the first time by the owner to any other person,

---

* Here is a reference to a note, scheduling the usual subjects of sculpture, but explaining that the section of the law here concerned "is a miracle of intricacy and verbosity" and involves much doubt.—F.D.

the owner may, by an agreement in writing signed at or before the time of such transfer by the transferee, reserve the copyright to himself, or he may, by an agreement in writing signed by himself or by his agent duly authorized, transfer the copyright to such transferee. (If no such agreement in writing is made, the copyright in such painting ceases to exist.)

ARTICLE 22.
Copyright in Engravings.

Every one has for 28 years from the first publishing thereof the sole right and liberty of multiplying, by any means whatever, copies of any print of whatever subject which he has—

(a) Invented or designed, graved, etched, or worked in mezzotinto or chiaro-oscuro ; or which he has—

(b) From his own work, design, or invention, caused or procured to be designed, engraved, etched, or worked in mezzotinto or chiaro-oscuro ; or which he has—

(c) Engraved, etched, or worked in mezzotinto or chiaro-oscuro, or caused to be engraved, etched, or worked from any picture, drawing, model, or sculpture, either ancient or modern :

Provided that such prints are truly engraved with the name of the proprietor on each plate and printed on every print.

Prints taken by lithography and other mechanical processes are now upon the same footing as engravings.

ARTICLE 23.
The Registration of Books.

A book of registry must be kept at Stationers' Hall, in which the proprietor of copyright in any book, or of the right of representation of any dramatic piece or musical composition, whether in manuscript or otherwise, may upon the payment of a fee of 5s. enter in the register the particulars stated in the form given in the foot-note.*

The proprietor of the copyright in any encyclopædia, review, magazine, or periodical work, or other work published in a series, is entitled to all the benefit of registration on entering in the book of registry the title of such work, the time of publishing the first volume or part, and the name and place of abode of the proprietor and publisher when the publisher is not also the proprietor.

Every such registered proprietor may assign his interest or any portion of his interest by making an entry in the said book of such assignment in the form given in the foot-note.†

Licenses affecting any such copyright may also be registered in the said register.

Any person aggrieved by any such entry may apply to the High Court, or any judge thereof, to have such entry expunged or varied, and the court may make such order for that purpose as it thinks just.

It is a misdemeanor to make or cause to be made any false entry in such book wilfully.

The officer in charge of the book is bound to give sealed and certified copies of the entries contained therein on payment of a fee of 5s., and such copies are *primâ facie* proof of the matters alleged therein.

The fee for the registration of university copyrights and for copies of them is 6d., and they may be inspected without fee.

ARTICLE 24.
Effect of Registration in case of Books.

No proprietor of copyright in any book can take any proceedings in respect of any infringement of his copyright unless he has, before com-

---

* (a) Original Entry of Proprietorship of Copyright of a Book.

Time of making the Entries.	Title of the Book.	Name of the Publisher and Place of Publication.	Name and Place of Abode of the Proprietor of the Copyright.	Date of First Publication.

† (b) Form of Entry of Assignment of Copyright in any Book previously registered.

Date of Entry.	Title of Book. Set out the Title and refer to the Page of the Registry Book in which the Original Entry of the Copyright thereof is made.	Assignor of Copyright.	Assignee of Copyright.

mencing such proceedings, caused an entry to be made in the said register under the last article.

The omission to make such entry does not affect the copyright in any book, but only the right to sue or proceed in respect of the infringement thereof.

ARTICLE 25.

Registration in respect of Dramatic Copyright.

The remedies which the proprietor of the sole liberty of representing any dramatic piece has under Article 32 are not prejudiced by an omission to make any entry respecting such exclusive right in the said register.

ARTICLE 26.

Registration of Copyright in Paintings, etc.

A book entitled the Register of Proprietors of Copyright in Paintings, Drawings, and Photographs, must be kept at the Hall of the Stationers' Company.

A memorandum of every copyright to which any person is entitled under Article 21, and of every subsequent assignment of any such copyright, must be entered therein ; such memorandum must contain a statement of :

(*a*) The date of such agreement or assignment ;

(*b*) The names of the parties thereto ;

(*c*) The name and place of abode of the person in whom such copyright is vested by virtue thereof, and of the author of the work ;

(*d*) A short description of the nature and subject of such work, and, if the person registering so desires, a sketch, outline, or photograph of the work in addition thereto.

No proprietor of any such copyright is entitled to the benefit of 25 & 26 Vict. c. 68 until such registration, and no action can be maintained, nor any penalty be recovered, in respect of anything done before registration ; but it is not essential to the validity of a registered assignment that previous assignments should be registered.

The three paragraphs of Article 23, relating to the correction of errors in the register, the making of false entries, and the giving of certificates, apply also the book in this article mentioned.

ARTICLE 27.

Penalties for infringing Copyright in Books.

Every one is liable to an action who, in any part of the British dominions—

(*a*) Prints or causes to be printed, either for sale or exportation, any book in which there is subsisting copyright, without the consent in writing of the proprietor ;

(*b*) Imports for sale or hire any such book so having been unlawfully printed from parts beyond the sea ;

(*c*) Knowingly sells, publishes, or exposes to sale or hire, or causes to be sold, published, or exposed to sale or hire, or has in his possession for sale or hire any book so unlawfully printed or imported.

The action must be brought in a Court of Record and within 12 months after the offence.

ARTICLE 28.

Special Penalty for unlawfully importing Copyright Books.

The following consequences are incurred by every one, except the proprietor of the copyright of any book, or some person authorized by him, who imports or brings, or causes to be imported or brought [for sale or hire], into the United Kingdom, or into any other part of the British dominions, any printed book in which there is copyright, first composed, written, or printed [and published] in any part of the United Kingdom, and reprinted in any country or place out of the British dominions ;

Or, who knowingly sells, publishes, or exposes to sale, or lets to hire, or has in his possession for sale or hire any such book, that is to say :

(*a*) Every such book is forfeited, and must be seized by every officer of Customs or Excise, and in that case must be destroyed by such officer.

(*b*) The person so offending must, upon conviction before two justices, be fined 10*l.* for every such offence, and double the value of every copy of any such book in respect of which he commits any such offence.

Provided that if the Legislature or proper legislative authorities in any British possession pass an Act or make an Ordinance, which, in the opinion of Her Majesty, is sufficient for the purpose of securing to British authors reasonable protection within such possessions, Her Majesty may approve of such Act, and issue an Order in Council declaring that so long as the provisions of such Act remain in force, the prohibition hereinbefore contained shall be suspended so far as regards such colony.

ARTICLE 29.
Pirated Copies forfeited to Registered Owner.

All copies of any book in which there is a duly registered copyright unlawfully printed or imported without the consent in writing under his hand of the registered proprietor of the copyright are deemed to be the property of the registered proprietor of such copyright, and he may sue for and recover the same, with damages for the detention thereof, from any person who detains them after a demand thereof in writing.

ARTICLE 30.
Copies of Books to be delivered for Public Libraries, and Penalties for non-delivery.

A copy of the first edition and of every subsequent edition containing additions and alterations of every book published in any part of the British dominions must be delivered at the British Museum between 10 A.M. and 4 P.M. on some week-day, other than Ash Wednesday, Good Friday, or Christmas Day, within a month after its publication, if it is published in London, within three months if it is published in the United Kingdom elsewhere than in London, and within 12 months if it is published in any other part of the British dominions.

It may be delivered to any person authorized by the Trustees of the British Museum to receive it, and such person must give a receipt in writing therefor.

Copies of every edition of every book published must, if demanded, be delivered to an officer of the Stationers' Company for each of the following libraries : the Bodleian Library, the Cambridge University Library, the Advocates Library at Edinburgh, and the Library of Trinity College, Dublin.

The demand, in writing, must be left at the place of abode of the publisher, within 12 months after the publication of the book, and the copies must be delivered within one month after such demand, either to the Stationers' Company or to the said libraries, or to any one authorized to receive the copies on their behalf.

The copy for the British Museum must be bound, stitched, or sewed together, and upon the best paper on which the book is printed.

The copies for the other libraries mentioned must be upon the paper of which the largest number of copies of the book or edition are printed for sale in the like condition as the copies prepared for sale by the publisher.

The copies must in each case include all maps and prints belonging thereto.

Any publisher making default in such delivery as is hereinbefore mentioned, is liable to a maximum penalty of 5*l.* and the value of the copy not delivered. This penalty may be recovered upon summary proceeding before two justices of the peace, or a stipendiary magistrate, at the suit of the librarian, or other officer properly authorized, of the library concerned.

ARTICLE 31.
Penalty for Offences against University Copyright.

Every one incurs the penalties hereinafter mentioned who does any of the following things with any book of which the copyright is vested in any university or college under Article 11 ; (that is to say,)

(*a*) Who prints, reprints, or imports, or causes to be printed, reprinted, or imported, any such book.

(*b*) Knowing the same to be so printed or reprinted, sells, publishes, or exposes to sale, or causes to be sold, published, or exposed to sale, any such book.

The penalties for the said offences are :

(*a*) The forfeiture of every sheet being part of such book to the university or college to which the copyright of such book belongs, which university or college must forthwith damask and make waste paper of them.

(*b*) One penny for every sheet found in the custody of such person printing or printed, published or exposed to sale, half to go to the Queen, and half to the informer.

None of the penalties aforesaid can be incurred—

Unless the title to the copyright of the book in respect of which the offence was committed was registered either before 24th June, 1775, or within two months after the time when the bequest or gift of the copyright of any book came to the knowledge of the vice-chancellor of any university or the head of any college or house of learning ;

Or unless the clerk of the Stationers' Company, being duly required to make the entry, refuses to do so, and the university advertises such refusal in the Gazette, in which case the clerk incurs a penalty of 20*l*. to the proprietors of the copyright.

The penalty must be sued for in the High Court.

ARTICLE 32.

Penalty for performing Dramatic Pieces.

Every person who, without the consent in writing of the author or other proprietor first obtained, represents or causes to be represented at any place of dramatic entertainment in the British dominions any dramatic piece or musical composition is liable to pay to the author or proprietor for every such representation an amount not less than 40*s.*, or the full amount of the benefit or advantage arising from such representation, or the injury or loss sustained by the plaintiff therefrom, whichever may be the greater damages.

The penalty may be recovered in any court having jurisdiction in such cases.

ARTICLE 33.

Penalty for Infringement of Copyright in Works of Art.

Every one (including the author, when he is not the proprietor) commits an offence who, without the consent of the proprietor of the copyright therein, does any of the following things with regard to any painting, drawing, or photograph in which copyright exists ; (that is to say,)

(*a*) Repeats, copies, colorably imitates, or otherwise multiplies, for sale, hire, exhibition, or distribution, any such work ; or the design thereof ;

(*b*) Causes or procures to be done anything mentioned in (*a*) :

(*c*) Sells, publishes, lets to hire, exhibits, or distributes, offers for any such purposes, imports into the United Kingdom any such repetition, copy, or other imitation of any such work or of the design thereof, knowing that it has been unlawfully made ;

(*d*) Causes or procures to be done, any of the things mentioned in (*c*) ;

(*e*) Fraudulently signs or otherwise affixes or fraudulently causes to be signed or otherwise affixed to or upon any painting, drawing, or photograph or the negative thereof, any name, initials, or monogram.

(*f*) Fraudulently sells, publishes, exhibits, or disposes of, or offers for sale, exhibition, or distribution, any painting, drawing, or photograph, or negative of a photograph, having thereon the name, initials, or monogram of a person who did not execute or make such work ;

(*g*) Fraudulently utters, disposes of, or puts off, or causes to be uttered or disposed of, any copy or colorable imitation of any painting, drawing, or photograph, or negative of a photograph, whether there is subsisting copyright therein or not, as having been made or executed by the author or makers of the original work from which such copy or imitation has been taken ;

(*h*) Makes or knowingly sells, publishes, or offers for sale, any painting, drawing, or photograph which after being sold or parted with by the author or maker thereof, has been altered by any other person by addition or otherwise, or any copy of such work so altered, or of any part thereof, as the unaltered work of such author or maker during his life and without his consent.

Every one who commits any of the offences (*a*), (*b*), (*c*), or (*d*) forfeits to the proprietor of the copyright for the time being a sum not exceeding 10*l.*, and all such repetitions, copies, and imitations made without such consent as aforesaid, and all negatives of photographs made for the purpose of obtaining such copies.

Every one who commits any of the offences (*e*), (*f*), (*g*), or (*h*) forfeits to the person aggrieved a sum not exceeding 10*l.*, or double the price, if any, at which all such copies, engravings, imitations, or altered works were held or offered for sale, and all such copies, engravings, imitations, and altered works are forfeited to the person whose name, initials, or monogram are fraudulently signed or affixed, or to whom such spurious or altered work is fraudulently or falsely ascribed ; provided that none of the last-mentioned penalties are incurred unless the person to whom such spurious or altered work is so fraudulently ascribed, or whose initials, name, or monogram is so fraudulently or falsely ascribed, was living at or within 20 years next before the time when the offence was committed.

The penalties hereinbefore specified are cumulative, and the person aggrieved by any of the acts before mentioned may recover damages in addition to such penalties, and may in any case recover and enforce the delivery to him of the things specified, and recover damages for their retention or conversion.

The penalties may be recovered either by action or before two justices or a stipendiary magistrate.

ARTICLE 34.
Importation of pirated Works of Art prohibited.

The importation into the United Kingdom of repetitions, copies, or imitations of paintings, drawings, or photographs wherein, or in the design whereof, there is an existing copyright under 25 & 26 Vict. c. 68, or of the design thereof, or of the negatives of photographs, is absolutely prohibited, except by the consent of the proprietor of the copyright or his agent authorized in writing.

ARTICLE 35.
Penalty for pirating Lectures.

Every person commits an offence who, having obtained or made a copy of any lecture, prints or otherwise copies and publishes the same, or causes it to be so dealt with without the leave of the author or his assigns ;

Or, who, knowing it to have been printed or copied or published without such consent, sells, publishes, or exposes it to sale or causes it to be so dealt with ;

Every person who commits such offence forfeits such printed or copied lectures, together with one penny for every sheet thereof found in his custody, half to the Queen and half to the informer.

The printing and publishing of any lecture in any newspaper without leave is an offence within the meaning of this article.

This section does not apply to the publication of lectures which have been printed and published as books at the time of such publication.

The penalty must be sued for in the High Court.

ARTICLE 36.
Penalty for pirating Sculptures.

Every person is liable to an action for damages who makes or imports, or causes to be made or imported, or exposed to sale, or otherwise disposed, anything of which the copyright is protected by the 54 Geo. c. 56.

This article does not apply to any person who purchases the right or property of anything protected by the said Act of the proprietor by a deed in writing, signed by him with his own hand in the presence of and attested by two credible witnesses.

ARTICLE 37.
Penalty for pirating Prints and Engravings.

Every person commits an offence who, without the consent of the proprietor in writing, signed by him and attested by two witnesses—

(*a*) In any manner copies and sells, or causes or procures to be copied and sold, in whole or in part, any copyright print ; or

(*b*) Prints, reprints, or imports for sale any such print, or causes or procures any such print to be so dealt with ; or

(*c*) Knowing the same to be so printed or reprinted without the consent of the proprietors publishes, sells, exposes to sale, or otherwise disposes of any such print, or causes or procures it to be so dealt with.

Every person committing any such offence is liable to an action for damages in respect thereof, and forfeits to the proprietor, who must forthwith destroy and damask the same, the plate on which any such print is copied, and every sheet being part of such print, or whereon such print is copied, and also five shillings for every sheet found in his custody in respect of which any such offence is committed, half to the Queen and half to the informer.

The penalty must be sued for in the High Court within six months after the offence.

ARTICLE 38.
International Copyright may be granted in certain Cases.

Copyright in books, dramatic pieces and musical compositions, paintings, drawings, and photographs, sculptures, engravings, and prints, first published in foreign countries, may be granted to the authors of such works, in the manner, to the extent, and on the terms hereinafter mentioned, if what Her Majesty regards as due protection has been secured by the foreign country in which such works are first published for the benefit of persons interested in similar works first published in Her Majesty's dominions.

ARTICLE 39.

Orders in Council as to International Copyright.

Her Majesty may by Order in Council (stating as the ground for issuing the same that such protection as aforesaid h.is been secured as aforesaid) direct that the authors of all or any of the things mentioned in the last Article, being first published in any such foreign country as is mentioned in that Article, shall have copyright therein in Her Majesty's dominions for a term, to be specified in the Order, not exceeding the term of copyright which authors of things of the same kind first published in the United Kingdom are entitled by law at the date of the Order.

The terms so to be specified and the terms for registration and delivery of copies of books as hereinafter mentioned may be different for works first published in different foreign countries. and for different classes of such works.

ARTICLE 40.

Term of International Copyright.

The authors of the works specified in the Order are entitled to copyright therein as follows—

Under 5 & 6 Vict. c. 45, and the other Acts relating to copyright in books, except the sections relating to the deposit of copies in certain libraries, if the works specified in the Order are books ;

Under the Engraving Copyright Acts, the Sculpture Copyright Acts, or the Paintings Copyright Act respectively, if the works specified in the Order are prints, engravings, articles of sculpture, pictures, drawings, or photographs ;

Under the Dramatic Copyright Acts, provided that such copyright does not extend to prevent fair imitations or adaptations to the English stage of any dramatic piece or musical composition published in any foreign country, if the works specified in the Order are dramatic pieces or musical compositions, unless the order directs that it shall extend to them.

Subject in each case to such limitations as to the duration of the right as may be specified in the Order, and subject also to the provisions hereinafter contained.

ARTICLE 41.

No Work Copyright without Registration.

No author of any such work as is referred to in this chapter is entitled to any benefit under the provisions contained in it, unless such work is registered, and a copy of the first edition and of every subsequent edition containing additions or alterations, but of no other editions of it, is delivered at the Hall of the Stationers' Company, within a time to be specified in the Order of Council, and in the manner prescribed in the schedule in the footnote hereto.*

* SCHEDULE.

The register must show, if the work is—		Name and place of abode	Name and place of abode	Time and place of first
A book .... The title............		of author (unless the book is anonymous, 7 & 8 Vict. c. 12. s. 7).	of proprietor of copyright.	publication.
Dramatic piece or musical composition printed.	Do.	Do..	Do................	Do. and time and place of first representation or performance.
Dramatic piece or musical composition in MS.	Do.	Do...........	Do.	Do.
Print......	Do.	Do. of inventor, designer, or engraver.	Do.....	Do. First publication in foreign country.
Sculpture...............	Descriptive title	Do. of maker......	Do................	Do.
Painting, drawing, or photograph.	Short description of nature and subject of work, and a sketch outline or photograph thereof, if the person registering pleases.	Name and abode of author.	Do.	

The three paragraphs preceding the last paragraph of Article 23 apply to such entries.

The copy so delivered must within one month of its delivery be deposited in the British Museum by the officer of the Stationers' Company.

ARTICLE 42.
No International Copyright in Newspaper Articles.

Articles of political discussion published in any newspaper, or periodical, in any foreign country may, if the source from which the same are taken is acknowledged, be republished or translated in any newspaper or periodical in this country, notwithstanding anything hereinbefore or hereinafter contained.

Articles on other subjects so published may be dealt with in the same manner on the same condition, unless the author has signified his intention of preserving the copyright therein, and the right of translating the same, in some conspicuous part of the newspaper or periodical in which the same was first published, in which case such publication is to be regarded as a book within the meaning of Article.

ARTICLE 43.
Translations of Foreign Books.

Her Majesty may by Order in Council direct that the authors of books published, and of dramatic pieces first publicly represented, in the foreign countries referred to in Article 38, may, for a period not exceeding five years from the publication of an authorized translation thereof, prevent the publication in the British dominions of any unauthorized translation thereof, and, in the case of dramatic pieces, the public representation of any such translation.

Upon the publication of such Order the law in force for the time being for preventing the infringement of copyright, and the sole right of representing dramatic pieces, in the British dominions applies to the prevention of the publication of such unauthorized translation.

Provided that no such Order prevents fair imitations or adaptations to the English stage of any dramatic piece or musical composition published in any foreign country.

But Her Majesty may by Order in Council direct that this proviso shall not apply to the dramatic pieces protected under the original Order in Council.

If a book is published in parts, each part is regarded, for the purposes of this article, as a separate book.

ARTICLE 44.
Conditions of International Copyright in Translations.

No author, and no personal representative of any author, is entitled to the benefit of the provisions of the last preceding article unless he complies with the following requisitions :

1. The original work from which the translation is to be made must be registered, and a copy thereof deposited in the United Kingdom, in the manner required for original works by the said International Copyright Act, within three calendar months of its first publication in the foreign country :

2. The author must notify on the title-page of the original work, or, if it is published in parts, on the title-page of the first part, or, if there is no title-page, on some conspicuous part of the work, that it is his intention to reserve the right of translating it :

3. The translation sanctioned by the author, or a part thereof, must be published either in the country mentioned in the Order in Council by virtue of which it is to be protected, or in the British dominions, not later than one year after the registration and deposit in the United Kingdom of the original work, and the whole of such translation must be published within three years of such registration and deposit :

4. Such translation must be registered, and a copy thereof deposited in the United Kingdom, within a time to be mentioned in that behalf in the Order by which it is protected, and in the manner provided by the said International Copyright Act for the registration and deposit of original works :

5. In the case of books published in parts, each part of the original work must be registered and deposited in this country, in the manner required by the said International Copyright Act, within three months after the first publication thereof in the foreign country :

6. In the case of dramatic pieces the translation sanctioned by the author must be published within three calendar months of the registration of the original work :

7. The above requisitions apply to articles originally published in newspapers or periodicals, if the same be afterward published in a separate form, but not to such articles as originally published.

ARTICLE 45.

Importation of Pirated Works.

The importation into any part of the British dominions of copies of any work of literature or art, the copyright in which is protected by the provisions of this chapter, and of unauthorized translations thereof, is absolutely prohibited, unless the registered proprietor of the copyright therein, or his agent authorized in writing, consents, and the provisions of Article 28 apply to the importation of such copies into any part of the British dominions.

A Memorial

of

American Authors.

THE undersigned American citizens who earn their living in whole or in part by their pen, and who are put at disadvantage in their own country by the publication of foreign books without payment to the author, so that American books are undersold in the American market, to the detriment of American literature, urge the passage by Congress of an International Copyright Law, which will protect the rights of authors, and will enable American writers to ask from foreign nations the justice we shall then no longer deny on our own part.

Henry Abbey.

Lyman Abbott

Charles Kendall Adams

Henry C. Adams.

Herbert B. Adams

Oscar Fay Adams.

Louisa May Alcott

Edward Atkinson

Leon[d] W. Bacon.

Hubert H Bancroft.

Charles Barnard

Amelia E Barr

Henry Ward Beecher

Edward Bellamy

William Henry Bishop.

Hjalmar H Boyesen

R. R. Bowker.

Francis F Browne

Oliver B Bunce

H.C. Bunner

Frances Hodgson Burnett

Edwin Lassetter Bynner

G.W. Cable

Lizzie W. Champney

S.L. Clemens (Mark Twain.)

Titus Munson Coan

Robert Collyer

Clarence Cook

George Willis Cooke

J. Esten Cooke.

A. Cleveland Coxe

George William Curtis.

Charles de Kay

Eugene L. Didier.

John Dimitry.

Nathan Haskell Dole

Maurice Francis Egan.

Edw. Eggleston.

George Cary Eggleston

Richard T. Ely.

Edgar Fawcett.

Charles Gayarré

Richard Watson Gilder

Arthur Gilman

James R. Gilmore
("Edmund Kirke")

Washington Gladden

Parke Godwin

Robert Grant

F. V. Greene

Edward Irsey

Wm Elliot Griffis

Hattie Tyng Griswold

W. M. Griswold

Louise Imogen Guiney.

John Habberton.

Edward E. Hale

E. Hale

William A. Hammond

Marion Harland

Joel Chandler Harris

Miriam Coles Harris.

Wm. T. Harris

James A. Harrison.

J. M. Hart

Bret Harte

Thos. Wentworth Higginson

Edward S Holden

Oliver Wendell Holmes.

James K. Hosmer

W. D. Howells.

Ernest Ingersoll

Helen Jackson (H. H.)

Sarah O. Jewett

Rossiter Johnson.

Ellen Olney Kirk

Thos. W. Knox

Martha J. Lamb

George Parsons Lathrop

Henry Cabot Lodge

Benson J. Lossing

J. R. Lowell.

Hamilton W. Mabie

James McCosh

John Bach McMaster.

Albert Matthews

Brander Matthews

Edwin D. Mead

Donald G. Mitchell

T. T. Munger

Simon Newcomb

R Stebr Newton

. Chas Ledyard Norton .

Grace A. Oliver

John Boyle O'Reilly

Francis Parkman

James Parton

P. Y. Pember.

Thomas S. Perry.

Ben: Perley Poore

David L. Pindgich

Isaac L. Rice

J. T. Rothrock

Philip Schaff

James Schouler

Horace E. Scudder

Eugene Schuyler

Isaac Sharpless

Albert Shaw.

George William Sheldon

E. V. Smalley

Ainsworth R. Spofford

Edmund C. Stedman

Frederic J. Stimson.

Frank R. Stockton

R. H. Stoddard

Maurice Thompson

Moses Coit Tyler.

Francis H. Underwood

William Hayes Ward

Susan Hayes Ward

Chas. Dudley Warner

David A. Wells

Horace White

William D. Whitney

John G. Whittier

Constance Fenimore Woolson

John Burroughs

Rose Elizabeth Cleveland

Mary Mapes Dodge

Henry George

W. Hamilton Gibson

Anna Katharine Green

George Walton Green

Harry Harland (Sidney Luska)

John Hay

Henry F Keenan

Mary N. Murfree
(Charles Egbert Craddock)

Harriet Prescott Spofford

Walt Whitman

Adeline D.T. Whitney.

The undersigned, an American citizen,
urges the passage by Congress of an International Copyright Law, which will protect
the rights of authors and will enable
American writers to ask the same act of
justice from foreign nations.

George Bancroft

BIBLIOGRAPHY OF LITERARY PROPERTY

BEING A CATALOGUE OF BOOKS AND ARTICLES RELATING TO LITERARY
PROPERTY (COPYRIGHT, INTERNATIONAL COPYRIGHT
AND KINDRED SUBJECTS)

BY

THORVALD SOLBERG,

ASSISTANT IN THE LIBRARY OF CONGRESS, WASHINGTON, D. C.

TO

Charles Solberg,

AS A SLIGHT TOKEN

OF

THE WARMEST FILIAL LOVE AND RESPECT.

COMPILER'S NOTE.

In bringing to a close an undertaking which has involved a greater amount of tedious labor than any one who has not attempted a similar task can realize, it is a pleasure to make a public acknowledgment of the encouragement and helpful courtesy received from those who have had an interest in the progress of the work. First among these was Mr. FREDERICK LEYPOLDT, whose interest was of the warmest nature from the start. His earnestness led him to find time even in his busy life to write frequent, and sometimes lengthy, letters discussing the smallest details of preparation and printing with a patience which was remarkable. These letters were full of friendly encouragement, and constant in stimulating the endeavor to make the result as perfect as possible. Considerations of economy or convenience were never allowed to interfere, but the constant direction was, "take your own time about it, and make it as complete in every respect as you know how." Much of his interest in this bibliography was doubtless due to his earnest belief that an author's intellectual property should have both national and international recognition and protection, and any effort which directed attention to the subject he deemed of value.

To J. A. L. WHITTIER, Esq., of Boston, sincere thanks are tendered for his generous kindness in sending a number of rare books from his own library to be examined and catalogued ; and to Mr. CHARLES C. SOULE, of the same city, for aid in obtaining and verifying titles. Thanks are also due to EATON S. DRONE, Esq., whose numerous and varied writings upon the subject of copyright occupy so much space in this catalogue, for his hearty co-operation, which has secured to one portion of the list a completeness otherwise impossible.

And last, but not least, most sincere acknowledgment is made to Mr. A. GROWOLL, of the *Publishers' Weekly* office, for his unvarying courtesy and patience from beginning to end ; and this, notwithstanding that he has occupied the trying position of mediator between the compiler and the sorely-tried printer. It is to Mr. GROWOLL's unremitting and critical oversight, also, that the beauty and uniformity of typography (so difficult to secure in a catalogue) are due. Every line of the work has had the benefit of his careful revision.

THORVALD SOLBERG.

WASHINGTON, 1885.

BIBLIOGRAPHY OF LITERARY PROPERTY.

THE English baptismal names in the following catalogue have been abbreviated as follows : Augustus A:, Benjamin B:, Charles C:, David D:, Edward E:, Frederick F:, George G:, Henry H:, Isaac I:, John J:, Karl K:, Louis L:, Mark M:, Nicholas N:, Otto O:, Peter P:, Richard R:, Samuel S:, Thomas T:, William W:. For uniformity's sake, the rule of non-capitalizing is followed in both English and foreign titles.

A. (J. K.) Literary property. [By Joseph Kinnicutt Angell?] *In* "American jurist." v. 10. 8°. Boston, 1833, p. 62–81.

A. (M.) Brief observations on the copy-right bill, attempting to prove its injustice towards authors. *In* "The Pamphleteer." v. 18. 8°. London, A. J. Valpy, 1821, p. 523–528.

ABBOTT (B: Vaughan). Obtaining copyright. *In* "The Literary world." 4°. Boston, April 26, 1879, p. 137, 138.

—— Progress of copyright law. *In* "The Popular science monthly." v. 20. 8°. New York, no. 3, Jan. 1882, p. 340–347.

—— Recent advance in the law of intellectual property. *In* "The Popular science monthly," v. 19. 8°. New York, no. 3, July 1881, p. 372–378.

ADAM (G. Mercer). Copyright in Canada. *In* "The Athenæum." 4°. London, no. 2646, July 13, 1878, p. 47, 48.

ADAMS (W: Bridges). The political economy of copyright. *In* "The Fortnightly review." v. 2. 8°. London, Sept. 1, 1865, p. 227–239.

ADDISON (C: Greenstreet). Wrongs and their remedies, being a treatise on the law of torts. 2d ed. 8°. London, V. & R. Stevens, sons, & Haynes, 1864.
Contains : Infringement of statutory copyright, p. 36–41. *Also in the same :* 3d ed. by F. S. P. Wolferstan. 8°. London, Stevens & sons, 1870, p. 39–45. *Also in the same :* 4th ed. by Wolferstan. 8°. London, Stevens & sons, 1873, p. 41–47. *Also in the same :* 4th Eng. ed. by Wolferstan. American notes by James M. Dudley and Edwin Baylies. 8°. New York, Banks & Brothers, 1876, v. 1, p. 51–59. *Also in the same :* A treatise on the law of torts. Reprinted from the last Lond. ed. with full Am. notes by H. G. Wood. 8°. New York, J. Cockcroft & co., 1876, v. 1, p. 68–78.

ADDRESS (An) to the parliament of Great Britain on copy-right. 1813. *See* Duppa (R:)

ALEXANDER & GREEN. N. Y. supreme court. George Haven Putnam and others against Walter F. Pollard and others. Plaintiffs' brief on motion for injunction. 74 p. 8°, New York, Evening post, 1880.

ALISON (Sir Archibald). The copyright question. [*Anon.*] *In* "Blackwood's Edinburgh magazine." v. 51. 8°. No. 315, Jan. 1842, p. 107–121.

—— *Same. In* Essays by A. Alison. v. 2. 8°. Edinburgh and London, W. Blackwood & sons, 1850, p. 419–446.

ALLEN (Grant). The ethics of copyright. *In*

"Macmillan's magazine." v. 43. 8°. London, no. 254, Dec. 1880, p. 153–160. *Notice in* "The Academy." v. 18. 4°. London, no. 449, Dec. 11, 1880, p. 424.

ALLEN (Grant). Landowning and copyright. *In* "Fraser's magazine." 8°. London, no. 609, Sept. 1880,p. 343–356.

ALLEN (W: F.) International copyright. *In* "Lippincott's magazine." v. 25. 8°. Philadelphia, no. 145, Jan. 1880, p. 102–108.

AMERICAN copyright. [*Anon.* New York, Aug. 1847.] *In* "Blackwood's Edinburgh magazine." v. 62. 8°. no. 385, Nov. 1847, p. 534–546.

AMERICAN COPYRIGHT CLUB. An address to the people of the United States in behalf of the club, adopted at New York, Oct. 18, 1843. [Signed by W: Cullen Bryant, Francis L. Hawks and Cornelius Mathews.] 20 p. 8°. New York, 1843.

AMERICAN (The) view of the copyright question. 1868. *See* White (R: Grant).

ANDERS (Joseph, freiherr von). Beiträge zur lehre vom litterarischen und artistischen urheberrecht. About xix, 298 p. 8°. Innsbruck, Wagner, 1881.

ANDRAL (Charles Guillaume Paul). D'un projet de loi organique sur la propriété littéraire et artistique. About 16 p. 8°. Paris, Guiraudet, 1855.

ANDREWS (E: L.) Brief on behalf of authors and publishers in favor of international copyright before Joint committee of the Senate and House of Representatives of the U. S. Dillaway & Andrews, of counsel. 1 p. l. 7 p. 8°. Washington, Gibson Brothers, 1882. *Anon. notice* [by Simon Newcomb] in "The North American review." v. 114. 8°. Boston, no. 235, April, 1872, p. 432–435.

ANGELL (Joseph Kinnicutt). *See* A. (J. K.)

ANNALES de la propriété industrielle artistique et littéraire. Journal de législation, doctrine et jurisprudence françaises et étrangères en matière de brevets d'invention, littérature, [etc.] Rédigé par mm. J. Pataille, A. Huguet, Éd. Calmels et Perrot de Chaumeux. 1855–1867. 13 v. 8°. Paris, 1856–68.

ANNUAIRE de la librairie. 1867–1878. 12°. Paris. *Note.* Each volume contains : Résumé de la législation relative aux droits de propriété littéraire et artistique. By Auguste Henri Jules Delalain, aided in année 1878 by Paul Delalain.

ANNUAIRE de législation étrangère publié par la Société de législation comparée. 1er-7me année. 8°. Paris, Cotillon & ce., 1872-78.

Contains : 1re année [1870-72], p. 205-223, Germany ; Loi du 11 juin 1870 concernant le droit d'auteur sur les écrits, dessins, compositions musicales et œuvres dramatiques ; traduction et notes de Paul Gide.—5me année 1875, p. 564-567, Italy ; Loi du 10 août 1875 sur les droits d'auteur ; notice et traduction par Léopold Gravier.—p. 802, 803, Norway ; Loi du 22 mai 1875 sur l'autorisation des représentations dramatiques et autres : notice par Pierre Dareste.—6me année 1876, p. 88-134, Germany ; Loi du 9-11 jan. 1876 concernant le droit d'auteur [etc.] ; notice, traduction et notes par André Morillot.—p. 609-618, Norway ; Loi du 8 juin 1876 sur la protection du droit vulgairement nommé propriété littéraire ; notice, traduction et notes par Pierre Dareste.—p. 753-755, Canada ; Acte du 26 oct. 1875, concernant la propriété littéraire et artistique ; analyse par m. Valabrèque.—7me année 1877, p. 653-657 Norway ; Loi du 12 mai 1877 sur la protection de la propriété artistique [and] Loi sur la protection des photographs ; notice et traductions par G. Cogordan.—p. 658-663, Sweden ; Loi sur la propriété littéraire, du 10 août 1877 ; notice, traduction et notes par Pierre Dareste.

APPLETON (C: E: Cutts Birchall). American efforts after international copyright. *In* " The Fortnightly review." v. 27. 8°. London, no. 122, Feb. 1, 1877, p. 237-256.

—— *Same. In* Appleton (J: Hoblyn) *and* Sayce (Archibald H:) Dr. Appleton : his life and literary relics. 8°. London, Trübner & co., 1881, p. 245-280.

Review by Moy Thomas in " The Athenæum." 4°. London, no. 2571, Feb. 3, 1877, p. 155-157.—*Review in* " The Popular science monthly." v. 10. 8°. New York, no. 60, April 1877, Editor's table, p. 746-748.—*Notice in* " Scribner's monthly." v. 14. 8°. New York, no. 1, May 1877, p. 108, 109.

APPLETON (W: H.) International copyright. [With reply by F: R: Daldy.] *In* " American literary gazette." v. 18. 8°. Philadelphia, no. 2, Nov. 15, 1871, p. 39-41.

—— Letters on international copyright. 24 p. 8°. New York, D. Appleton & co., 1872.

AREOPAGITICA secunda ; or, speech of the shade of John Milton, on sergeant Talfourd's copyright extension bill. [*Anon.*] 8°. London, 1838.

ARNOLD (Matthew). Copyright. *In* " The Fortnightly review." v. 33. 8°. London, no. 159, n. s. March 1, 1880, p. 319-334.

—— *Same. In* " The Eclectic magazine," n. s. v. 31. 8°. New York, no. 5, May 1880, p. 513-524.

——*Same. In* Harper & Brothers. [Memorandums in regard to international copyright. 8°. New York, 1880], p. 41-55.

—— *Same. In* " The Library magazine." v. 3. 16°. New York, 1880, p. 632-648.

—— *Same. In* " The Publishers' weekly." v. 17. 8°. New York, no. 427, March 10, 1880, p. 296, 297.

Notice in " The Popular science monthly." v. 17. 8°. New York, no. 1, May 1880, Editor's table, p. 121-124.

—— *See also* The Publishers' weekly.

ARTISTIC copyright. [*Anon.*] *In* " The Spectator." v. 51. fol. London, no. 2613, July 27, 1878, p. 947, 948.

ARTISTIC copyright. [*Anon.*] *In* " The Westminster review." v. 113, n, s. v. 57. 8°. London, April 1880, p. 355-365.

ASSOCIATION pour la défense de la propriété littéraire et artistique. La propriété littéraire au dix-huitième siècle. Recueil de pièces et de documents, avec une introduction et des notices par mm. Édouard Laboulaye et Georges Guiffrey. About xxxii, 632 p. 8°. Paris, L. Hachette & ce., 1860.

Review by Émile Pierre Levasseur in " Journal des économistes." 2e série. v. 28. 8°. Paris, 1860, p. 456-460.

—— La propriété littéraire et artistique. About 32 p. 8°. Paris, L. Hachette & ce., 1862.

—— *Same.* De l'application du droit commun à la propriété littéraire et artistique. 2e éd. About 32 p. 8°. Paris, L. Hachette & ce., 1862.

—— *See also* Diderot (Denis).

ATLANTIC monthly. 8°. Boston.

Contains : v. 20. 1867, p. 430-451. Int. cop. By James Parton.—v. 29. 1872, p. 387, 388. [Int. cop. Anon. by Arthur G: Sedgwick.]—v. 41. 1878, p. 393, 394. Literary plunderers.—v. 42. 1878, p. 370, 371. Cheap reprints.—v. 43. 1879, p. 217-230. Int. cop. By judicial decision. By Arthur G: Sedgwick.—v. 44. 1879, p. 269-271. Review of: A treatise on the law of property in intellectual productions. By Eaton S. Drone.

AUGER (Louis Simon). Observations sur la nature de la propriété littéraire. About 8 p. 4°. Paris, Pillet aîné, 1826.

AUTHORS' rights before publication, 1875. *See* Drone (Eaton Sylvester).

B. (A.) De la propriété littéraire. 1833. *See* Boullée (Aimé Auguste).

BAIRD (H: Carey). International copyright. *In* " American literary gazette." v. 18. 8°. Philadelphia, no. 5, Jan. 1, 1872, p. 68-70.

—— *See also* The Publishers' weekly.

BALL (James). Copyright. 12°. London, Butterworths, 1877. [Popular monthly law tracts, no. 1. May, 1877.]

BARTHE (Félix). Progetto di legge sulla proprietà letteraria presentato alla camera dei pari di Francia dal signor Barthe. About 28 p. 8°. Firenze, G. P. Vieusseux, 1839.

BATBIE (Anselme Polycarpe). Introduction générale au droit public et administratif. 8°. Paris, Cotillon, 1861.

Contains : Propriété littéraire et artistique, p. 463-475.

BAUDOUIN (Alexandre). Note sur la propriété littéraire, et des moyens d'en assurer la jouissance aux auteurs dans les principaux états de l'Europe, sans nuire aux intérêts matériels des peuples et sans nécessiter des lois prohibitives. [*Anon.*] About 18 p. 8°. Bruxelles, Berthot, 1836.

Note. A second, corrected edition was published the same year and is pronounced the best ed.

BAUDRY (Jules). Propriété littéraire. Premières observations. [*Also*] Nouvelles observations. 8 p. 12°. [Paris, Crapelet, 1850.]

BEAUCÉ (—). Légitimité de la propriété en faits d'ouvrages de l'esprit ou du genre. About 24 p. 8°. Paris, Gueffier, 1818.

BEAUME (Alexandre). Code général de la propriété industrielle, littéraire et artistique. 1854. *See* Blanc (Étienne) *and* Beaume.

BEAUME (Alexandre) *and* HUARD (Adrien). Dialogue des morts sur la propriété littéraire. About 46 p. 8°. Paris, Castel, 1862.

BERGER (Carl Albert Ferdinand). Beiträge zur lehre vom büchernachdruck. 8°. Leipzig, G. Wigand, 1841.

BERTAULD (Charles Alfred). De la nature du droit des auteurs sur leurs œuvres. *In* " Revue critique de législation et de jurisprudence." v. 22. 8°. Paris, 1863, p. 385-399.

BEUCHAT (Adrien Jean Quentin). Réflexions sur les lois concernant la propriété littéraire. About 8 p. 8°. Paris, Pillet aîné, 1817.

BIANCHINI (Edoardo). Intorno alla proprietà letteraria ed artistica. Saggio. v. 1. About 232 p., 16°. Siena, tip. Moschini, 1869.

BIELITZ (Gustaf Alexander). Versuch, die von dem verlagsrechte geltenden grundsätze aus deren analogie und deren positiven gesetze abzuleiten. 8°. Dresden, Grimmer, 1799.

BLACK (W:) *see* The Publishers' weekly.

BLACKSTONE (Sir W:) Commentaries on the laws of England. 4°. Oxford, Clarendon press, 1766.
Contains: Literary property, (Book 2, chap. 26, sec. 8), p. 405-407.
Also in the same: [Am. ed.] by T: M. Cooley. v. 1. 8°. Chicago, Callaghan & Cockcroft, 1871, p. 405-407.
Also in the same: Adapted to the present state of the law by Robert Malcolm Kerr. v. 2. 4th ed. 8°. London, J. Murray, 1876, p. 359-363.

BLAINE (Delabere Roberton). Literary and musical copyright. *In* " Fraser's magazine." v. 81, n. s. v. 1. 8°. London, no. 2, Feb. 1870, p. 278-284.

—— On international copyright in works of literature, music and the fine arts. *In* National association for the promotion of social science. Transactions. 1862. 8°. London, J. W. Parker & son, 1863, p. 866-869.

—— On the laws of artistic copyright, and their defects. 8°. London, J. Murray, 1853.

—— Suggestions on the copyright (works of art) bill. 8°. About 25 p. London, Hardwicke, 1861.

BLANC (Étienne). Observations adressées par les artistes à la chambre des députés, sur la nouvelle loi relative à la propriété intellectuelle. 8°. Paris, Terzuolo, 1839.

—— Traité de la contrefaçon, et de sa poursuite en justice. About 640 p. 8°. Paris, chez l'auteur, 1837.

—— *Same.* 8°. Paris, Raymond, 1838.

—— *Same.* 4me éd. About 840 p. 8°. Paris, Plon, 1855.

—— *and* BEAUME (Alexandre). Code général de la propriété industrielle, littéraire et artistique, comprenant les législations de tous les pays et les traités internationaux sur les inventions brevetées, les œuvres de littérature [etc.] About 620 p. 8°. Paris, Cosse, 1854.
Review by Augustin Charles Renouard in " Journal des économistes." 2e série. v. 4. 8°. Paris, 1854, p. 34-43.

BLATCHFORD (S:) Copyright. [Decision in the case of Augustin Daly *vs.* H; D. Palmer.

Circuit court of the United States for the southern district of New York. Dec. 1868.] *In* " The American law review." v. 3. 8°. Boston, no. 3, April, 1869, p. 453-467.

BLATCHFORD (S:) *Same. In* Reports of cases in the circuit court. By S: Blatchford. v. 6. 8°. New York, Baker, Voorhis & co., 1870, p. 256-271.

BOHN (H: G:) The question of unreciprocated foreign copyright in Great Britain. Report of speeches at a meeting at Hanover square rooms, July 1, 1851. 8°. London, Bohn, 1851.

BONNEVILLE DE MARSANGY (Louis). *See* Jordão Paiva Manso (Levy Maria).

BOOSEY *vs.* PURDAY. Assumed copyright in foreign authors. Judgment given in the court of exchequer Westminster hall, June 5, 1849. 16 p. 8°. London, F. Elsworth, [1849.]

BOSSANGE (Hector). Opinion nouvelle sur la propriété littéraire. About 40 p. 8°. Paris, imp. de Rignoux, 1836.

BOSWELL (James). The decision of the court of session upon the question of literary property, in the cause of J: Hinton of London, pursuer ; against Alexander Donaldson and J: Wood, in Edinburgh, and James Meuros in Kilmarnock, defenders. 4°. Edinburgh, 1774.
Anon. review in " The Monthly review." v. 51. 8°. London, Aug. 1774, p. 90-94.

BOULLÉE (Aimé Auguste). De la propriété littéraire et du plagiat. Par A. B. [*Anon.*]. About 8 p. 8°. Bourg, Bottier, 1833.

BOWKER (R: Rogers). *See* The Publishers' weekly.

BOZZO BAGNERA (Giovanni Battista). Sulla perpetua proprietà letteraria ed artistica : studio. About 58 p. 16°. Palermo, tip. Volpes, 1871.

—— *Same.* 2a ed. 12°. Milano, C. Barbini, 1871.

BREULIER (Adolphe). De la propriété littéraire. Réfutation de l'Exposé des motifs du projet de loi sur la propriété littéraire. About 16 p. 8°. Paris, Delamotte, 1839.

—— Du droit de perpétuité de la propriété intellectuelle. About 140 p. 8°. Paris, Durand, 1855.

—— Réponse au mémoire de m. [Levy Maria] Jordão sur la propriété littéraire chez les Romains. *In* " Revue critique de législation et de jurisprudence." v. 21. 8°. Paris, 1862, p. 85-91.

BRIEF observations on the copy-right bill. 1821. *See* A. (M.)

BRISTED (C: Astor). International copyright. *In* " The Galaxy." v. 10. 8°. New York, no. 6, Dec. 1870, p. 811-818.

BRITISH copyright in foreign compositions. *See* English copyright in foreign compositions.

BRITISH international copyright law. [*Anon.*] *In* " American jurist." v. 21. 8°. Boston, 1839, p. 478-484.

BRITTON (J:) The rights of literature; or, an inquiry into the policy and justice of the claims of certain public libraries on all the publishers and authors of the United Kingdom, for eleven copies of every new publication. About vii, 80 p. 8°. London, 1814.

Notice by T. E. Jones in : A descriptive account of the literary works of J: Britton. Being a 2d part of his auto-biography. By T. E. Jones. 8°. London, 1849, p. 190-197.

BROWNE (Irving). Copyright in private letters. Chap. vi. of Humorous phases of the law. [*Anon.*] *In* "Albany law journal." v. 2. fol. Albany, Aug. 20, 1870, p. 131-135.

BRUNET (Jean Baptiste). Constitution de la propriété intellectuelle ; 1er vol. About 174 p. 18°. Paris, Walder, 1858.

—— *Same.* Résumé. About 30 p. 12°. Paris, Walder, 1858.

BRUSSELS. *See* Congrès de la propriété littéraire et artistique à Bruxelles, 1858.

BRYANT (W: Cullen). *See* American copyright club ; *also* Copyright (The) association.

BRYDGES (Sir S: Egerton). Answer to the Further statement by the syndics of the University of Cambridge. 7 p. 8°. [London, Barnard & Farley, 1818.]

—— Reasons for a farther amendment of the act 54 Geo. III. c. 156, being an act to amend the copyright act of queen Anne. 48 p. 8°. London, Nichols, son, & Bentley, 1817.

——. *Same.* Another impression. 47 p. 8°. London, Nichols, son, & Bentley, 1817.

—— *Same.* *In* "The Pamphleteer." v 10. 8°. London, A. J. Valpy, 1817, p. 492-507.

—— A summary statement of the great grievance imposed on authors and publishers by the late copyright act. iv, 22 p. 8°. London, for Longmans, 1818.

—— A vindication of the pending bill for the amendment of the copyright act, from the misrepresentations and unjust comments of the syndics of the University library, at Cambridge. 32 p. 8°. London, for Longmans, 1818.

BUCKINGHAM (James Silk). Copyright laws. Speech of S. I. Buckingham in the house of commons, April 1836. About 18 p. 8°. London, Manning & Smithson, 1836.

BUMP (Orlando Franklin). The law of patents, trade-marks and copy-rights : consisting of the sections of the revised statutes of the United States, with notes under each section, referring to the decisions of the courts. xl, 493 p. 8°. New York, Baker, Voorhis & co., 1877. [Copyrights, p. 351-378.]

BUNCE (Oliver Bell). *See* Drone (Eaton Sylvester).

BURKE (P:) Copyright law and the press. 8° London, S. Low, 1855.

—— The law of international copyright between England and France, in literature, the drama, music, and the fine arts, analysed

and explained. The whole in English and French. xii, 158 p. 12°. London, S. Low & son, 1852.

Note. Has also French title: Loi international entre l'Angleterre et la France sur la propriété des ouvrages littéraires [etc.]

BURKE (P:) The present state of the law of copyright, with a view to its amendment. About 18 p. 8°. London, 1863.

—— A treatise on the law of copyright in literature, the drama, music, engraving, and sculpture ; including the recent [English] statutes on the subject. 1 p. l. v-xii, 128 p. 12°. London, J. Richards & co., 1842.

Anon. review in "The Jurist." v. 6, part 2. 8°. London, no. 311, Dec. 24, 1842, p. 511, 512.

—— A supplement to Godson's practical treatise on the law of patents for inventions, and of copyright in literature, [etc.] viii, 236 p. 8°. London, W. Benning & co., 1851.

BURNETT (Frances Eliza Hodgson). *See* The Publishers' weekly.

BURROW (Sir James). *See* Millar (Andrew) *vs.* Taylor (Robert).

C. *see* COURTNEY (Leonard H:)

C. Copyright in sermons. [*Anon.*] *In* "The Law magazine." v. 25. 8°. London, May, 1841, p. 249-270.

C. (T. H.) International copyright. *See* Carter (Timothy Harrington).

CALLET (Auguste). De la propriété littéraire. Un procès contre m. le duc de Noailles et consorts, ou Fin de l'histoire de la marquise de Montagu. About 164 p. 8°. Paris, M. Lévy frères, 1865.

CALMELS (Antoine Édouard). De la contrefaçon des inventions brevetées, des modèles et des dessins de fabrique, des œuvres littéraires et artistiques, législation et jurisprudence. About 20 p. 8°. Paris, Roret, 1852.

Review by Victor Lesage in "Revue critique de législation et de jurisprudence." v. 3. 3me année. 8°. Paris, 1853, p. 192.

—— De la propriété des œuvres de l'esprit et des dangers qu'elle recèle. *In* "Revue contemporaine." v. 26. 8°. Paris, Mars, 1862, p. 127-151.

—— *Same.* 8°. Paris, 1862.

—— De la propriété et de la contrefaçon des œuvres de l'intelligence. About 876 p. 8°. Paris, Cosse, 1856.

Review by Joseph Garnier in "Journal des économistes." 2e série. v. 26. 8°. Paris, 1860, p. 143, 144.

—— Observations sur le chapitre 8, concernant la répression des contrefaçons et autres délits en matière de propriété littéraire et artistique, [etc.] adressées à m. Levy-Maria Jordão. About 55 p. 8°. Paris, Hennuyer, 1862.

—— *See also* Annales de la propriété littéraire.

CAMBRIDGE (University of). *See* University of Cambridge, *England.*

CAMPBELL (J:) Considerations and arguments proving the inexpediency of an international

copyright law. 24 p. 8°. New York, W. E.
Dean, 1844.
Reviewed by W: Gilmore Simms in "The Southern
literary messenger." v. 10. 8°. Richmond, Aug. 1844, p.
461-469.

CANADA. *See* Annuaire de législation étrangère
1876, p. 753-755.

CANADIAN copyrights. [*Anon.*] *In* "The Saturday review." v. 39. fol. London, no. 1014,
April 3, 1875, p. 441, 442.

CAPEN (Nahum). Memorial of N. Capen, of
Boston, on the subject of international copy-
right. Jan. 15-19, 1844. 10 p. *In* United
States. Executive documents, 28th congress,
1st session. v. 3. 8°. [Washington, Blair &
Rives, 1844.] Doc. no. 61.

—— *Same.* 12 p. 8°. [Washington, 1844.]

—— *Same.* 1 p. l. 12 p. 8°. [Boston, no date.]

CAPPELLEMANS (Victor). De la propriété littéraire et artistique en Belgique et en France.
18°. Bruxelles, Delevingne & Callewaert,
1854.
Notice by Léon Mégret in "Revue contemporaine."
v. 17. 8°. Paris, 1854, p. 668.

CAPUANO (Luigi). Della proprietà letteraria.
In "Annali di diritto teorico pratico." Anno
2. v. 4. 8°. Napoli, 1858, fasc. 4-5.

CAREY (H: C:) The international copyright
question considered, with special reference to
the interests of American authors, American
printers and publishers, and American readers. 30 p. 8°. Philadelphia, H. C. Baird,
1872.

—— Letters on international copyright. 72 p.
1 slip erratum. 8°. Philadelphia, A. Hart,
1853.

—— *Same.* 2d ed. 88 p. 8°. New York,
Hurd & Houghton, 1868.
Anon. review: International copyright, in "The
American law register." v. 2. 8°. Philadelphia, [no. 3],
Jan. 1854, p. 129-144.
Anon. notice in "The Nation." v. 6. 4°. New York,
no. 138, Feb. 20, 1868, p. 147, 148.
Anon. review in "Putnam's magazine." v. 3, 8°.
New York, no. 13, Jan. 1854, p. 96-103.

—— *Same.* Briefe über schriftstellerisches
eigenthum. Nach dem amerikanischen
original übersetzt. About vi, 93 p. 8°. Berlin,
Eichhoff, 1866.

CARLYLE (T:) Petition on the copy-right bill.
In Critical and miscellaneous essays, by T:
Carlyle. v. 4. 12°. Boston, J. Munroe & co.,
1839, p. 382-384.

—— *Also in the same :* 3d. ed. v. 4. 12°. London, Chapman & Hall, 1847, p. 195-197.

—— *Also in the same :* v. 5. 8°. London,
Chapman & Hall, 1869. p. 425-429, and summary, p. 444.
Summary, p. 444: "Assuring to each man the just
recompense of his labour, the business of all Legislation
and Government among men. To have written a gen-
uine enduring book, not a sufficient reason for the forfeiture of the Law's protection. Why, then, should ex-
traneous persons be allowed to steal from the poor
book-writer the poor market-price of his labour?"

CARMICHAEL (C: H: E:) Trade marks and
copyright. How can the international difficulty with regard to trade marks and copy-

right, caused by recent judgments of the
supreme court of the United States, best be
met? *In* National association for the promotion of social science. Transactions. 1880.
8°. London, Longmans, 1881, p. 154-164.

CARMICHAEL (C: II: E:) What action should be
taken on the report of the royal commission
on copyright? *In* National association for
the promotion of social science. Transactions. 1879. 8°. London, Longmans, 1880,
p. 195-204.

—— *Same :* Copyright law and the report of
the royal commission. *In* "The Law magazine and review." 4th series. v. 5. 8°. London, Nov. 1879, p. 68-78.

CARTE (T:) Further reasons addressed to parliament for rendering more effectual an act of
queen Anne relating to vesting in authors the
right of copies, by R. H. [*Anon.*] 8°. London,
1737.

CARTER (Timothy Harrington). International
copyright with Great Britain. [Signed T. H.
C.] 7 p. 8°. [*Boston*, 187-].

CASATI (Charles). Un projet de loi sur la propriété littéraire et artistique. *In* "Revue
pratique de droit français." 8°. Paris, fév.
1862.

—— *Same.* 8°. Paris, Marescq aîné, 1862.

CASE (The) of authors by profession or trade
stated. 1758. *See* Ralph (James).

CASE (The) stated between the public libraries
and the booksellers. [*Anon.*] 32 p. 8°. London, J. Moyes, 1813.

—— *Same.* [*Anon.*] *In* "The Pamphleteer." v.
2. 8°. London, A. J. Valpy, 1813, p. 343-368.
Note. Halkett and Laing, *Anonymous and pseudonymous literature,* ascribe this work to James Cochrane on
the authority of the Bodleian library. I do not find it in
the catalogues of this library, nor do I find any trace of a
bookseller named James Cochrane. The work is evidently by a bookseller or publisher, and the Library of
Congress copy has "J. G. Cochrane" in MS. on title-page ;
this John George Cochrane was a well-known publisher
at the time and possibly the author.

CASES (The) of the appellants and respondents
in the cause of literary property, before the
house of lords : wherein the decree of lord
chancellor Apsley was reversed, 26 Feb. 1774.
With the arguments of the counsel, the opinions of the judges, notes, references, and observations. By a gentleman of the Inner
temple. [*Anon.*] 4°. London, Bew, 1774.
Anon. notice in "The Monthly review." v. 51. 8°.
London, Sept. 1774, p. 202-209.

CASES of Walcot *v.* Walker ; Southey *v.* Sherwood ; Murray *v.* Benbow, and Lawrence *v.*
Smith, [*Anon.*] *In* "The Quarterly review."
v. 27. 8°. London, no. 53, April 1822, p.
123-138.

CASTILLE (Charles Hippolyte). Discours sur la
propriété littéraire. *In* "Le travail intellectuel." 8°. Paris, 1847, no. du 15 octobre.

CAVALLOTTI (Felice). Della proprietà letteraria
ed artistica e sua proprietà, lettera al deputato
Antonio Billia. About 80 p. 8°. Milano, E.
Politti, 1871.

CELLIEZ (Henry). Proposition d'un vœu à exprimer par le congrès littéraire international de Paris 1878, relativement au droit des auteurs sur leurs œuvres publiées en pays étranger. About 15 p. 8°. Paris, Chaix & ce. 1878.

CENTURY (The) magazine. *See* Scribner's monthly.

CHAMBERLIN (Franklin). American commercial law. 8°. Hartford, O. D. Case & co., 1869.
Contains : Copyright, p. 879-887.
Also in the same : 8°. Hartford, O. D. Case & co., 1875, p. 879-887.

CHAMBERS (William) *and* CHAMBERS (Robert). Brief objections to mr. Talfourd's new copyright bill. 8°. Edinburgh, 1838.

CHAMPAGNAC (Gustave de). Étude sur la propriété littéraire et artistique ; [précédée d'une lettre de m. le vicomte A. de La Guéronnière.] About xi, 176 p. 12°. Paris, E. Dentu, 1860.

CHAMPEIN (Marie François Stanislas). Commission de la propriété littéraire : réflexions présentées à la commission, en sa séance du 27 fév. 1826. About 12 p. 4°. Paris, Pillet aîné, 1826.
Note. Edition of 30 copies. Reissued same year ed. of 50 copies.

CHAMPETIER DE RIBES (Camille). Notes, addressées au comité d'organisation du congrès de la propriété artistique. About 16 p. 18°. Paris, imp. ve Renou, Maulde & Cock, 1878.

CHAPPELL (F: Patey) *and* SHOARD (J:) A handybook of the law of copyright, comprising literary, dramatic and musical copyright, and copyright in engravings, sculpture and works of art : with appendix containing statutes and forms. x, 159 p. 16°. London, H. Sweet, 1863.

CHARPENTIER (Gervais). De la prétendue propriété littéraire et artistique. About 31 p. 8°. Paris, chez l'auteur, 1862.
Note. From " Revue nationale." 10-25 fév. 1862.

CHATAIN (Marcel). De la propriété littéraire. About 186 p. 8°. Paris, Cotillon & cie, 1881.

CHAUFFOUR (Victor). Loi réglant les droits sur les productions littéraires et les œuvres d'art en Saxe. [Dissertation.] *In* " Revue de législation et de jurisprudence." v. 20. 8°. Paris, 1844, p. 176-189.

CHEVALIER (Michel). Les brevets d'invention contraires à la liberté du travail. *In* " Journal des économistes." 4e série. v. 2. 8° *Paris*, 1878, p. 171-225.

—— *Same* About 103 p. 8°. Paris, Guillaumin & ce, 1878.

CHRISTIAN (E:) A vindication of the right of the universities of Great Britain to a copy of every new publication. About 36 p. 8°. Cambridge, 1807.

—— *Same.* 2d ed., much enlarged by the judgment of the court of king's bench, and gen-

eral observations. 2 p. l. 159 p. 8°. Cambridge, J. Smith, 1814.

CHRISTIAN (E:) A vindication of the right of the universities of the United kingdom to a copy of every new publication. 3d ed. 2 p. l. 199 p. 8°. Cambridge, J. Smith, 1818.

—— *Same.* [Reply to the reviews in " British review," v. 13, 1819, and " Quarterly review," v. 21. 1819.] 4 p. 8°.
Published with Charges delivered to grand juries in the Isle of Ely. By E:.Christian. 2d ed. London, for T. Clarke & Sons, 1819.

CHRISTIE (W: Dougal). A plea for perpetual copyright. 8°. London, 1840.

CLAIMS of public libraries to the gratuitous delivery of books. [*Anon.*] *In* " The British review." v. 13. 8°. London, 1819, no. 25, p. 226-247.

CLAPIER (Alexandre). Du droit de propriété à propos de la loi du 14 juillet 1866, sur les droits d'auteur. About 37 p. 8°. Marseille, Barlatier-Feissat et Demonchy, 1867.

CLAY (H:) *see* United States. Report of the select committee, 1837.

CLÉMENT (Paul). Du droit des auteurs sur leurs œuvres. Dissertation juridique lue, le 17 déc. 1866, à la séance de rentrée des conférences des avocats stagiaires. About 28 p. 8°. Grenoble, Maisonville & fils, 1867.

CLEVELAND (H: Russell). Copy-right of foreign books. *In* " The North American review." v. 44. 8°. Boston, Jan. 1837, p. 133-137.

CLUNET (Édouard). Concordance des résolutions du Congrès de la propriété artistique, tenu à Paris en 1878, avec les dispositions déjà admises sur la matière dans : les congrès internationaux ; les traités internationaux conclus par la France ; les lois positives des principaux pays. 8°. Paris, imp. national, 1879.
Anon. notice in " The Law magazine and review." 4th series. v. 5. 8°. London, no. 18, Feb. 1880, p. 203, 204. *Anon, notice in* " Le Livre." 1ère année. Bibliographie moderne, tome 2. 8°. Paris, 8e livraison, 10 août, 1880, p. 100.

COCHUT (André). Du projet de loi sur la propriété littéraire et la contrefaçon. *In* " Revue des deux mondes." v. 17. 4e série. 8°. Paris, 1839, p. 388-402.

COLLET (Émile) *and* LESENNE (Charles). A propos d'André Chénier. Étude sur la propriété des œuvres posthumes, suivie de l'opinion de mm. Pataille, Caraby et Huard. About 184 p. 18°. Paris, Charpentier, 1879.
Anon. notice in " Journal du droit international privé," 1879. 8°. Paris, nos. 3-4, p. 228.

COLLINS (W: Wilkie). Considerations on the copyright question. Addressed to an American friend. *In* " The International review." v. 8. 8°. New York, no. 6, June 1880, p. 609-618.

—— *Same.* 8°. London, Trübner, 1880.
Notice in " Harper's new monthly magazine." v. 61. 8°. New York, no. 363, Aug. 1880, Editor's easy chair, p. 469, 470. *Notice in* " The Popular science monthly." v. 17. 8°. New York, no. 4, Aug. 1880, Editor's table, p. 554-557.

COMETTANT (Oscar) La propriété intellectuelle au point de vue de la morale et du progrès. About 56 p. 12°. Paris, Guillaumin & ce, 1857.

—— *Same.* 2e éd., revue et augmentée. About 108 p. 12°. Paris, Guillaumin & ce, 1858.

—— *Same.* 3e éd., revue et augmentée. About 252 p. 12°. Paris, Guillaumin & ce, 1862.

COMMUNITY of copy-right between the United States and Great Britain. [*Anon.*] *In* "The Knickerbocker." v. 6. 8°. New York, no. 4, Oct. 1835, p. 285–289.

COMTE (François Charles Louis). Traité de la propriété. 2 v. 8°. Paris, Chamerot, 1834. *Contains :* Des fondements et de la nature de la propriété littéraire. chap. 31.

CONANT (Stillman S.) International copyright. I. An American view [by Conant.] II. An Englishman's view of the foregoing. [Signed C. *i.e.* Leonard H: Courtney.] *In* "Macmillan's magazine." v. 40. 8°. London, no. 236, June 1879, p. 151–166.

—— *Same :* With rejoinder by S. S. Conant, from The Academy. *In* Harper & Brothers. [Memorandums in regard to international copyright. 8°. New York, 1880], p. 17–40. *Notice in* "The Academy." v. 15. 4°. London, no. 370, n. s. June 7, 1879. p. 497. *Anon. notice in* "The Nation," v. 29. 4°. New York, no. 751, Nov. 20, 1879, p. 340, 341. *Notice in* "The Popular science monthly." v. 16. 8°. New York, no. 5, March 1880, Editor's table, p. 697, 698.

—— International copyright and "Macmillan's magazine." [Reply to "C," *i.e.* L. H. Courtney. New York, June 25, 1879.] *In* "The Academy." v. 16. 4°. London, no. 380, n. s. Aug. 16, 1879, p. 125, 126.

——*Same. In* "The Publishers' weekly." v. 16. 8°. New York, no. 402, Sept. 27, '79, p. 387, 388.

CONGRÈS de la propriété littéraire et artistique à Bruxelles. 1858. Circulaire et programme [etc.] *In* "Journal des économistes." 2e série. v. 19. 8°. Paris, 1858, p. 144–150.

—— Compte rendu des travaux du Congrès de Bruxelles. About 36 p. 8°. Paris, Pillet fils aîné, 1858.

—— *In* "Journal des économistes." 2e série. v. 20. 8°. Paris, 1858 : Congrès de la propriété littéraire. [Compte rendu, signed "Un membre du Congrès,"] p. 78–102 :—Société d'économie politique—Compte rendu du Congrès de la propriété littéraire. Discussion sur la nature de cette propriété, p. 134–153, 284–313, 442–470.

—— [Proceedings and reports etc.] *In* "Journal général de l'imprimerie et de la librairie." [Bibliographie de la France.] 2e série tome 2. année 1858. 2e partie : Chronique. 8°. Paris, 1858, p. 25, 61, 124, 130, 137, 146, 165, 173, 188, 207, 217, 218, 221, 229, 233, 241, 245, 257, 266, 273, 277, 282, 291, 297.

—— La propriété intellectuelle. Le Congrès de Bruxelles. *In* Vapereau (Louis Gustave). L'année littéraire et dramatique. (1858.) 12°. Paris, L. Hachette & cie, 1859, p. 471–479.

—— *See also* Foucher (Victor), *and* Romberg (Édouard).

CONGRÈS international de la propriété artistique tenu à Paris, pendant l'exposition universelle, en 1878 [19–29 Sept.] Compte-rendu analytique des séances. Résolutions votées par le Congrès. [etc.] 63 p. 4°. Paris, 1878.

CONGRÈS littéraire international de Paris, 1878. Présidence de Victor Hugo. Comptes rendus in extenso et documents. 8° Paris, 1879. *Anon. notice* signed F. G. in "Le Livre," 1 ère année. Bibliographie moderne, tome 2. 8°. Paris, 9e livraison, 10 Sept. 1880, p. 162.

CONKLING (Alfred). Opinion upon the question of copyright in manuscripts, in the case of Little and company against Hall, Gould and Banks, respecting the fourth volume of Comstock's reports. 33 p. 8°. Albany, J. Munsell, 1852. *Anon. review :* The opinion of judge Conkling, in Little and others vs. Gould and others, in "The United States monthly law magazine." v. 3. 8°. New York, nos. 5 and 6, May and June, 1851, p. 592–599.

CONSIDERATIONS on the nature and origin of literary property. 1767. *See* Maclaurin (J:, lord Dreghorn).

CONWAY (Moncure Daniel). *See* The Publishers' weekly.

COOK (J: T.) *See* Underhill (Arthur).

COPINGER (Walter Arthur). The law of copyright, in works of literature and art : together with international and foreign copyright, with the statutes, and references to the English and American decisions. xxii, 3, 266, cxlix p. 8°. London, Stevens & Haynes, 1870.

—— *Same.* 2d ed. xxxix, 918 p. 8°. London, Stevens & Haynes, 1881. *Anon. notice in* "The American law review." v. 5. 8°. Boston, no. 2, Jan. 1871, p. 337, 338. *Anon. notice in* "The Athenæum." 4°. London, no. 2248, Nov. 26, 1870, p. 682. *Anon. review in* "The Law magazine and review." 4th series. v. 6. 8°. London, no. 22, Feb. 1881, p. 202–204.

COPY before publication. The proprietary right of an author or his assigns over literary productions unprinted by authority derived from him. Crowe *v.* Aiken. Dec. 31, 1869. [*Anon.*] *In* "The American law review." v. 4. 8°. Boston, no. 3, April 1870, p. 450–458.

COPYRIGHT. [*Anon* review.] *In* "The Literary gazette." v. 2. 4°. London, no. 66, April 25, 1818, p. 257–259.

COPYRIGHT and morality. [*Anon.*] *In* "The Popular science monthly." v. 14. 8°. New York, no. 82, Feb. 1879, p. 530–533.

COPYRIGHT (The) acts consolidation [*sic*] bill, 1857. *In* "The Jurist." N. s. v. 3, part 2. 8°. London, no. 134, Aug. 1, 1857, p. 311–316.

COPYRIGHT (The) association for the protection and advancement of literature and art. International copyright. Meeting of authors and publishers, at the rooms of the New York historical society, April 9, 1868 and organization of the International copyright association. [Edited by Edmund Clarence Stedman.] 46 p. 8°. New York, 1868. *Anon. notice in* "The Nation " v. 6. 4°. New York, no. 153, June 4, 1868, p. 452, 453.

——*See also* Bristed (C: Astor).

COPYRIGHT (The) consolidation and amendment bill, 1879, in its relation to the fine arts. [*Anon.*] *In* "The Athenæum." 1880. 4°. London. I.—no. 2723, p. 25, 26. II.—no. 2725, p. 94, 95. III.—no. 2728, p. 189, 190. IV.—no 2730, p. 255, 256.

COPYRIGHT in China. *In* "Chambers's Journal." 8°. Edinburgh, August 1, 1881.

COPYRIGHT in dramatic performances. [*Anon.*] *In* "The Jurist." N. s. v. 6, part 2. 8°. London, no. 266, Feb. 11, 1860, p. 46, 47.

COPYRIGHT in Italy. [*Anon.*] *In* "The Foreign quarterly review." v. 26. 8°. London, no. 52, Jan. 1841, p. 289-311.

——*Same* abridged. *In* "The American eclectic." v. 1. 8°. New York, 1841, p. 370, 371.

COPYRIGHT in private letters. *See* Browne (Irving.)

COPYRIGHT in sermons 1841. *See* C.

COPYRIGHT (The) law. [*Anon.*] *In* "The United States monthly law magazine." v. 3. 8°. New York, no. 4, April 1851, p. 396-401.

Note. In favor of granting to authors a perpetual copyright.

COPYRIGHT, national and international, from the point of view of one who has been a publisher. [*Anon.*] 8°. London, E. Stanford, 1879.

Anon. notice in "The Academy." v. 15. 4°. London, no. 367 n. s. May 17, 1879, p. 433.

COPYRIGHT, national and international. 1879. *See* Marston (E:)

COPYRIGHT (The) question. [*Anon. review.*] *In* "The Quarterly review." v. 69. 8°. London, no. 137, Dec. 1841, p. 186-227.

——*Same* abridged. *In* "The American eclectic." v. 3. 8°. New York, no. 8, March 1842, p. 376-380.

COPYRIGHT (The) question. [*Anon.*] *In* "The Westminster review." N. s. v. 60. 8°. London, no. 2, Oct. 1881, p. 392-403.

COPYRIGHT (The) question. 1842. *See* Alison (Sir Archibald).

COPYRIGHT reform in Belgium, Spain and England. [*Anon.*] *In* "The Law magazine and review." 4th series. v. 3. 8°. London, no. 12, Aug. 1878, p. 427-459.

CORYTON (J:) Stageright, a compendium of the law relating to dramatic authors, musical composers, and lecturers as regards the public representation of their works, etc. viii, 100, lii p. 8°. London, D. Nutt, 1873.

COURTNEY (Leonard H:) *See* Conant (Stillman S.)

COX (Rowland). *See* The Publishers' Weekly.

CRAWFORD (G: Morland). Copyright in law reports. The case of Saunders *v.* Smith. 8°. London, 1839.

CURMER (Henri Léon). La propriété intellectuelle est un droit. À m. J. T. de Saint-Germain [*i.e.* Jules Romain Tardieu. *Anon.*,

and in verse.] About 20 p. 8°. Paris, E. Dentu, 1858.

CURMER (Henri Léon). La propriété littéraire et artistique. About 16 p. 8°. Paris, E. Dentu, 1862.

CURTIS (G: Ticknor). [Opinion in the case of Ticknor & Fields *vs.* Bunce & Huntington: — "Home ballads by our home poets."] *In* "American literary gazette." v. 5. 8°. Philadelphia, no. 10, Sept. 15, 1865, p. 210, 211.

——A treatise on the law of copyright in books, dramatic and musical compositions, letters and other manuscripts, engravings and sculpture, as enacted and administered in England and America ; with some notices of the history of literary property. xi, 450 p. 8°. Boston, C. C. Little & J. Brown, 1847.

Anon. review in "The Jurist." v. 12, part 2. 8°. London, no. 597, June 17, 1848, p. 238-240.

Anon. review in "The Literary world." v. 3. 4°. New York, no. 53, Feb. 5, 1848, p. 1-3.

Anon. review [by Cornelius Conway Felton.] in "The North American review." v. 67. 8°. Boston, no. 140, July 1848, p. 161-173.

——*See also.* The Publishers' weekly.

CURTIS (G: W:) *See* Harper's new monthly magazine. *Also,* The Publishers' weekly.

CUSHING (Luther Stearns). Analysis of Kant's doctrine of the rights of authors. *In* "American jurist." v. 22. 12°. Boston, 1840, p. 84-92.

——*See also* Lieber (Francis).—Nicklin (Philip Houlbrooke).—Renouard (Augustin Charles).

CYCLOPÆDIA of political science. Edited by J: J. Lalor. v. 1. 8°. Chicago, Rand, McNally & Co., 1881.

Contains: Rights of authors. By J. C. Bluntschli, p. 182, 183. Copyright. By H. D. Macleod, p. 642-648.

D. (E.) Cheap literature. *In* "The Southern literary messenger". v. 10. 8°. Richmond, no. 1, Jan. 1844, p. 33-39.

D. (J.) Le droit de traduction. [*Anon.*] *In* "Journal général de l'imprimerie et de la librairie". [Bibliographie de la France.] 2e série. v. 2. 2e partie : Chronique. 8°. Paris, 1858, pp. 193-196, 198-206, 209-217.

Note. By Auguste Henri Jules Delalain ?

——*Same.* [*Anon.*] About 23 p. 8°. Paris, Pillet fils aîné, 1858.

D. (J. B.) *See* Dabney (J: Blair).

DABNEY (J: Blair). Reply to E. D. and Mr. [W: Gilmore] Simms. [By J. B. D. *Anon.*] *In* "The Southern literary messenger." v.10. 8°. Richmond, 1844. April, p. 193-199. May, p. 289-296.

DALDY (F: R:) *See* Appleton (W: H.)

DALLOZ (Victor Alexis Désiré) *and* DALLOZ (Armand). Jurisprudence générale. Répertoire méthodique et alphabétique de législation de doctrine et de jurisprudence. Nouv. éd. v. 38. 4°. Paris, 1857.

Contains: Propriété littéraire et artistique, p. 441-524.

DAMBACH (Otto). Die gesetzgebung des norddeutschen Bundes betreffend das urheberrecht an schriftwerken, abbildungen, musikalischen kompositionen und dramatischen werken erläutert. About iv, 298 p. 8°. Berlin, T. C. F. Enslin, 1871.

DAMBACH (Otto). Gutachten des königlichen preussischen literarischen sachverständigenvereins über nachdruck und nachbildung aus den jahren 1864–73. About xviii, 168 p. 8°. Leipzig, 1874. [Publicationen des Börsenvereins der deutschen buchhändler. I.]

——Die preussische nachdrucksgesetzgebung. 1863. *See* Heydemann (Ludwig Eduard) and Dambach.

——Wider den nachdruck! Aussprüche berühmter deutscher gelehrten, schriftsteller, dichter etc. älterer und neuerer zeit über nachdruck und nachbildung. About v, 29 p. 8°. Berlin, Springer, 1872.

DANIEL DE FOLLEVILLE (Louis André). De la propriété littéraire et artistique. About 35 p. 8°. Paris, Durand & Pedone-Lauriel, 1877. *Note.* Originally published in "La France judiciaire," 16me avril, 1877.

DE LA PROPRIÉTÉ INTELLECTUELLE ; études par mm. Frédéric Passy, Victor Modeste et P. Paillottet, avec une préface par Jules Simon. About xxv, 347 p. 12°. Paris, E. Dentu, 1859. *Review* by Léon Walras in "Journal des économistes." 2e série. v. 24. 8°. Paris, 1859, p. 392–407.

DE LA PROPRIÉTÉ LITTÉRAIRE, 1833. *See* Boullée (Aimé Auguste).

DE LA PROPRIÉTÉ LITTÉRAIRE ; par un illettré. [*Anon.*] About 19 p. 8°. Paris, A. René, 1864.

DE LA SITUATION actuelle de la librairie et particulièrement des contrefaçons de la librairie française dans le nord de l'Europe. [*Anon.*] *In* "Revue britannique". v. 26. 4e série. 8°. Paris, 1840, p. 52–97.

DE AUGUSTINIS (Matteo). Della proprietà letteraria e de'suoi giusti confini. About 20 p. 8°. Napoli, [dalla tipografia Flautina], 1838.

DEFERT (Henry). Procédure en matière de contrefaçon. 1879. *See* Pelletier (Michel) *and* Defert.

DELALAIN (Auguste Henri Jules). Historique de la propriété des brevets d'imprimeur. About 15 p. 8°. Paris, J. Delalain, 1869.

—— *Same.* 2e éd., revue et augmentée. About 63 p. 8°. Paris, J. Delalain & fils, 1869.

—— Législation de la propriété littéraire, collationnée sur les textes officiels, avec notes interprétatives. About 24 p. 12°. Paris, Delalain, 1852.

—— *Same.* 2e éd. About 28 p. 12°. Paris, Delalain, 1852.

—— *Same.* About 36 p. 12°. Paris, Delalain, 1854.

—— *Same :* Législation de la propriété littéraire et artistique, recueillie et annotée. About 56 p. 8°. Paris, Delalain, 1855. *Note.* Only 100 copies printed in colors for distribution at the Universal Exposition.

—— *Same.* 6e tirage, revue et corrigé. About 40 p. 12°. Paris, Delalain, 1855.

DELALAIN (Auguste Henri Jules). Législation de la propriété littéraire et artistique, suivie des conventions internationales. Nouv. éd., revue et augmentée. About 248 p. 8°. Paris, J. Delalain, 1858.

—— *Same :* Suivie d'un résumé du droit international français et de la législation des pays étrangers. xi, 120 p. 8°. Paris, Delalain, 1862.

—— *Same :* Nouvelle législation de la propriété littéraire et artistique, accompagnée de notes explicatives et suivie d'un résumé de la législation des pays étrangers. 6e éd. About x, 84 p. 8°. Paris, J. Delalain & fils, 1868.

—— Législation française et belge de la propriété littéraire et artistique, suivie de la convention conclue entre la France et la Belgique, et accompagnée de notes explicatives. About 76 p. 12°. Paris, J. Delalain, 1854.

—— *Same.* Nouv. éd. 8°. Paris, Delalain, 1858.

—— Recueil des conventions conclues par la France pour la reconnaissance de la propriété littéraire et artistique. About xlvii, 336 p. 12°. Paris, J. Delalain & fils, 1865.

—— *Same.* 2e éd. 12°. Paris, J. Delalain & fils, 1866.

—— *Same.* 3e éd. About lii, 379 p. 12°. Paris. J. Delalain & fils, 1867.

—— *See also* Annuaire de la librairie.

DELALAIN (Paul). *See* Annuaire de la librairie.

DELALANDE (E.) Étude sur la propriété littéraire et artistique. 8°. Paris, Marescq aîné, 1880. *Note.* Originally published in "Revue pratique de droit français." v. 48, nos. 5–8. *Anon. notice* by F. W. [Fernand Worms?] in "Le Livre." 2me année. Bibliographie moderne. 8°. Paris, 7e liv. 10 juillet 1881, p 417.

DELORME (Charles). Traité pratique de droit industriel [etc.], 1855. *See* Rendu (Ambroise).

DENKSCHRIFT über den büchernachdruck ; zugleich bittschrift um bewirkung eines deutschen reichsgesetzes gegen denselben. [*Anon.*] 4°. Leipzig, Kummer, 1815.

DENTU *contra* DREYFOUS. Ein interessanter pressprozess vor dem zuchtpolizei-gericht zu Paris in sachen der übersetzung des buches von Moritz Busch : Graf Bismarck und seine leute. About 23 p. 8°. Leipzig, W. Friedrich, 1880.

DES MOULINS (Charles). De la propriété littéraire en matière de nomenclature scientifique. 24 p. 8°. Bordeaux, G. Gounouilhou, 1854.

DESPRÉS (Jean Baptiste Denis). Du droit de propriété dans ses rapports avec la littérature et les arts. About 52 p. 8°. Paris, Pillet aîné, 1825.

DICEY (E:) The copyright question. *In* "The Fortnightly review." v. 25. 8°. London, no. 109, Jan. 1, 1876, p. 126–140.

DICTIONNAIRE du notariat par les notaires et jurisconsultes rédacteurs du journal des

notaires et des avocats.　4me éd.　v. 10.　8°.
Paris, 1861.
Contains : Propriété littéraire et artistique, p. 297-307.

DIDEROT (Denis).　Lettre sur le commerce de
la librairie ; publiée pour la première fois
par le comité de l'association pour la défense
de la propriété littéraire et artistique, avec introduction par Georges Guiffrey.　About iv,
86 p.　8°.　Paris, L. Hachette & cie, 1861.

DIDIER (Eugene Lemoine).　Congress and international copyright.　*In* " Scribner's magazine."　v. 20.　8°.　New York, no. 1, May 1880,
p. 132-138.

DIDOT (Ambroise Firmin).　Note sur la propriété littéraire, et sur la répression des contrefaçons faites à l'étranger, particulièrement
en Belgique.　15 p.　8°.　Paris, Didot frères
& cie, [1836.]

DIRITTI (I) D'AUTORE sulle opere librarie, artis-
tiche, musicali e sulle rappresentazioni delle
opere sceniche.　Anno 1°.　n. 1.　(1. gennaio,
1870).　24 p. 4°.　Firenze, tipografia dell' associazione, 1870.

DISRAELI (I:)　The case of authors stated, including the history of literary property.　*In*
The Calamities of authors.　By I. D'Israeli.
v. 1.　8°.　London, 1812.

—— *Same.* *In* " The Quarterly review."　v. 8.
8°.　London, no. 15, Sept. 1812, p. 109-114.

—— *Same.* *In* Miscellanies of literature by I.
D'Israeli.　8°.　London, E. Moxon, 1840, p.
54-57.

—— *Same.* *In* The Calamities and quarrels of
authors.　By I. Disraeli.　New ed., edited
by B. Disraeli.　12°.　London, Routledge,
Warnes & Routledge, 1859, p. 15-21.

DOGNÉE (Eugène).　De la propriété littéraire,
rapport au Congrès littéraire international.
About 12 p. 8°.　Paris, Chaix & ce, 1878·

DREGHORN (J: Maclaurin, lord).　*See* Maclaurin.

DREWRY (C: Stewart).　A treatise on the law
of injunctions.　8°.　London. S. Sweet, 1841.
Contains : Injunctions to restrain infringement of copyright, p. 191-219.
Also in the same.　8°.　Philadelphia, J. S. Littell, 1842.
[The Law library.　Edited by T: I. Wharton.　v. 36], p.
137-153.

—— Supplement to the law of injunctions.　8°.
Philadelphia, T. & J. W. Johnson, 1854.　[The
Law library.　v. 79.]
Contains : Copyright, p. 34-39.

DRONE (Eaton Sylvester).　American copyright
[by E. S. Drone] and Connecticut [by W. G.
Abbot].　28 p.　12°.　Boston, Little, Brown,
& co., 1877.　[Copyright, p. 3-12.]

—— Authors' rights before publication.—The
representation of manuscript plays.　[*Anon.*]
In 'The American law review."　v. 9.　8°.
Boston, no. 2, Jan. 1875, p. 236-251.
Notice by Amos Kidder Fiske in " Boston daily Globe,"
Jan. 5, 1875.

—— Copyright.　[*Anon.*]　*In* The American
cyclopædia.　v. 5.　8°.　New York, D. Appleton & co., 1874, p. 335-337.

—— Copyright.　[*Anon.*]　*In* Appletons' an-

nual cyclopædia.　1878.　N. s. v. 3.　8°.　New
York, 1879, p. 223-227.

DRONE (Eaton Sylvester).　Copyright.　*See* Robertson (Edmund) *and* Drone.

—— Foreign dramatists under American laws.
In "Scribner's monthly,"　v. 11.　8°.　New
York, no. 1, Nov. 1875, p. 90-97.　And p.
136.
Notice in "The Evening Post," New York, Oct. 15,
1875.
Notice in "The Nation."　v. 21. 4°.　New York, no.
540, Nov. 4, 1875, p. 293, 294.
Notice by G: Ripley in " New-York Tribune," Nov. 9,
1875.

—— International copyright.　*In* "Appletons'
journal."　v. 12. 4°.　New York, no. 296, Nov.
21, 1874, p. 659-661.

—— Is copyright perpetual ?　An examination
of the origin and nature of literary property.
[*Anon.*]　*In* "The American law review."　v.
10.　8°.　Boston, no. 1, Oct. 1875, pp. 16-38.
Notices.—By Amos Kidder Fiske in " Boston daily
Globe," Oct. 12, 1875.—In " Brooklyn Eagle," Feb. 24,
1876.—In " The Evening Post," New York, Oct. 11, 1875.
—In " The Nation," v. 21. 4°.　New York, no. 540, Nov.
4, 1875, p. 293, 294.—In " New-York Tribune," Oct. 12,
1875.—By G: Ripley in " New-York Tribune," Oct. 15,
1875.—In " The Publishers' weekly." v. 8. 8°.　New York,
no. 196, Oct. 16, 1875, p. 642.—In " The World," New
York, Oct. 15, 1875.

—— The law of literature and art in England
and America.—How near are we to international copyright ?　[*Anon.*]　*In* " The American law review."　v. 9.　8°.　Boston, no. 1,
Oct. 1874, p. 1-17.
Notices.—In " Albany law journal," v. 10. Oct. 17, 1874,
p. 255.—By Alexander Young in " Boston daily Globe,"
Oct. 10, 1874.—By Amos Kidder Fiske in " Boston daily
globe," Oct. 12, 1874.—*Anon.* in " The Churchman," N.
s. v. 8. New York, Oct. 31, 1874, p. 348.—In " The
Evening Post," New York, Oct. 19, 1874.—By C: Ripley
in " New-York Tribune," Oct. 16, 1874.—In " The Press,"
Philadelphia, Oct. 9, 1874.—In " Zanesville daily Courier,"
Oct. 23, 1874.

—— Property in letters.　*In* " The Albany law
journal."　v. 13.　4°.　June 10, 1876, p. 411, 412.
Notice in "The Evening Post," New York, June 12,
1876.

—— A treatise on the law of property in intellectual productions in Great Britain and the
United States.　Embracing copyright in works
of literature and art, and playright in dramatic and musical compositions.　liv pp. 1 l.
774 p.　8°.　Boston, Little, Brown, & co.,
1879.
Anon. notice in " The Academy," v. 15. 4°. London,
no. 356 n. s. March 1, 1879, p. 185, 186.—*Notices* in " The
Albany law journal," v. 19. 4°. 1879, Feb. 8, p. 119 ; April
12, p. 288, 289.—*Anon. review* by Oliver Bell Bunce in
" Appletons' journal," N. s. v. 6. 8°. New York, no. 34,
April 1879, p. 372-374.—*Anon. notice* in " The Athenæum," 4°. London, no. 2686, March 8, 1879, p. 311.—
Anon. review in " The Atlantic monthly," v. 44. 8°. Boston, no. 262, Aug. 1879, p. 269-271.—*Anon. review* in " The
Central law journal," v. 8. 4°. St. Louis, Feb. 21, 1879,
p. 159, 160.—*Anon. review* by James L. High in " The
Chicago Tribune," Feb. 22, 1879.—*Notice* in " Harper's
magazine," v. 58. 8°. New York, no. 343, May 1879, Editor's easy chair, p. 939.—*Anon. review* in " The International review," v. 6. 8°. New York, no. 6, June 1879, p.
699-702.—*Anon. notice* in " Journal du droit international
privé," 1879. 8°. Paris, nos. 5-6, p. 326. *Anon. notice*
in " The Law magazine," 4th series, v. 5. 8°. London,
no. 234. Nov. 1879, p. 93, 94.—*Anon. notice* by Arthur G:
Sedgwick in " The Nation," v. 28. 4°. New York, no. 722,
May 1, 1879, p. 303, 304.—*Anon. review* in " The Popu-

lar science monthly," v. 14. 8°. New York, no. 83, March 1879, p. 679, 680.—*A non. review* in "Scribner's monthly," v. 17. 8°. New York, no. 6, April 1879, p. 911.—*Review* by James O. Pierce in " The Southern law review," N. s. v. 5. 8°. St. Louis, no. 3, Aug. 1879, p. 420-436.

Minor notices: In " The Bookseller," London, July 3, 1879, p. 596.—In " Boston daily Advertiser," Jan. 29, 1879.—In " Boston Post," Jan. 24, 1879.—In " Boston Saturday Evening Gazette," March 9, 1879.—In " Boston weekly Courier," Feb. 22, 1879.—In " The Chicago Legal News," v. 11. Feb. 8, 1879, p. 171.—In " The Chicago Times," Feb. 15, 1879.—*A non.* by Lucius P. Marsh in " The Cincinnati Commercial," March 1, 1879.—By N: Longworth in " Cincinnati Gazette," Feb. 22, 1879.—In " The Courier-Journal," Louisville, Nov. 20, 1879.—By Roscellus S. Guernsey in " The daily Register," New York, March 20, 1879.—In " The Evening Post," New York, Feb. 4, 1879.—By S: T. Spear in " The Independent," New York, Feb. 13, 1879.—In " The Law Times," v. 67 fol. London, Oct. 18, 1879, p. 409.—In " New York Herald," Feb. 3, 1879.—In " The New York Sun," May 25, 1879.—By Amos Kidder Fiske in " The New-York Times," Feb. 5, 1879.—By G: Ripley in " New York Tribune," Jan. 31, 1879.—The same in " The Publishers' Weekly," v. 15. 8°. New York, no. 369, Feb. 8, 1879, p. 167-169.— In " The Press," Philadelphia, Feb. 14, 1879.—In " The Times," Philadelphia, Jan 24. 1879.—In " St. Louis Post Dispatch," March 22, 1879.—In " The Saturday review," v. 47. fol. London, March 22, 1879, p. 378.—In " The Virginia Law Journal." v.3. 8°. Richmond, no. 3, March 1879, p. 192.—In " The Western Jurist," v. 13. 8°. Des Moines, no. 4, April 1879, p. 185, 186.—By Lucius P. Marsh in " Zanesville daily Courier," Feb. 5, 1879.

DRONE (Eaton Sylvester). Writers' rights in letters after transmission. *In* " Sloan's Legal & financial register." v. 3. 8°. New York, no. 3, July 1875, p. 16-22.

Note. Mr. Drone has contributed editorials, reviews, and other articles upon Copyright to the following papers : " The New York Herald :" Dec. 22, 1874, Int. cop. An exposition of the law as it stands.—Dec. 31, 1879, " The Pirates of Penzance" at the Paignton Royal Bijou.—Jan. 28, 1880, Piracy of the " Pirates."—March 19, 1880, M. Arnold on cop.—April 13, 1880, Copyrighting letters.— April 23, 1880, Cop. in foreign works.—May 31, 1880, Complaints of British painters.—s. d. W. Collins on the cop. ques.—Aug. 29, 1880, Cop. in the Bible.—Oct. 4, 1880, Int. cop —Oct. 17, 1880, Dramatists' rights to their plays. —Oct. 25, 1880, A new phase of the cop. discussion.— Dec. 13, 1880, Justice to foreign authors.—Jan. 10, 1881, Controversies about foreign plays.—March 11. 1881, A British publisher's [C: Ja. Longman's] view of int. cop. —March 23, 1881, [Notice of R: G. White's The Am. view of the cop. ques.].—April 5, 1881, The treaty making power.—June 22, 1881, An interesting ques. [Cop. in Ingersoll's lectures].—July 26, 1881, A new idea in copyright.—Aug. 7, 1881, Foreign dramatists under American laws.—Sept. 19, 1881, Legalized piracy.—Sept. 22, 1881, Piracy by memory. " The New York Sun :" June 19, 1878, The proposed changes in the English cop. law.—Jan. 5, 1879, Rights in foreign plays.—Nov. 2, 1879, Cop. in England. " The New-York Times :" June 16, 1878, The British cop. system.—July 21, 1878, The royal cop. comm. and foreign authors.—July 28, 1878, The Paris literary cong.— Aug. 25, 1878, Authors and money.—Oct. 31, 1878, Piratical dramatization.—Dec. 15, 1878, Literature and law.— March 24, 1879, Int. cop.—Sept. 17, 1879, The English cop. bill.—Nov. 21, 1879, [Literary property].—Jan. 2, 1880, [Encyclopædia Britannica case].—Feb. 18, 1880, [British cop. comm.].—March 12, 1880, [Cop. in systems of book-keeping ; C: Selden's case].—March 21, 1880, Anglo-American cop. again. [Notice of M. Arnold on cop.].—June 3, 1880, [W. Collins on cop.].—June 9, 1880, [Rosenbach v. Dreyfuss]. " The New York daily Tribune:" Nov. 5, 1875, [Review of Ja. A. Morgan's The law of literature].—Jan. 8, 1876, Property in telegraphic news.

—— *See also* Morgan (James Appleton), *and* White (R: Grant).

DUCOS (Florentin). Essai sur la propriété littéraire. About 18 p. 8°. Paris, Everat, 1825.

DUPPA (R:) An address to the parliament of Great Britain, on the claims of authors to their own copy-right. 2d ed. [*Anon.*] 1 p. l. 58 p. 8°. London, Longmans, 1813.

—— *Same.* 3d ed. ; not published. [*Anon.*] *In* " The Pamphleteer." v. 2. 8°. London, A. J. Valpy, 1813, p. 169-202.

DUVERGIER (Jean Baptiste Marie). Du droit international en matière de propriété littéraire. *In* " Annales de la propriété industrielle artistique et littéraire." Année 1860. 8°. Paris, 1860, p. 33—.

—— Projet de loi proposé à la sous-commission. *In* France. *Ministère d'état.* (*Commission de la propriété littéraire et artisque*). Rapports à l'empereur. 4°. Paris, 1863, p. 71-79 and 125-164.

DWIGHT (Theodore W:) Literary property. *In* Johnson's new universal cyclopædia. v. 3. 8°. New York, A. J. Johnson & son, 1877, p. 62-65.

EGGLESTON (E:) The blessings of piracy. *In* " The Century magazine " (Scribner's monthly). v. 23, n. s. v. 1. 8°. New York, no. 6, April 1882, p. 942-945.

—— *See also* The Publishers' Weekly.

EGGLESTON (G:C.) *See* The Publishers' Weekly.

EISENLOHR (Ch. F. M.) Das literarisch-artistische eigenthum und verlagsrecht mit rücksicht auf die gesetzgebungen. About x, 119 p. 8°. Schwerin, Stiller, 1855.

—— Sammlung der gesetze und internationalen verträge zum schutze des literarisch-artistischen eigenthums in Deutschland, Frankreich und England. About viii, 294 p. 8°. Heidelberg, Bangel & Schmitt, 1856.

—— *Same.* Nachtrag. About viii, 96 p. 8°. Heidelberg, Bangel & Schmitt, 1857.

ELIOT (C: W.) *See* The Publishers' Weekly.

ELLSWORTH (W: Wolcott). A copy-right manual : designed for men of business, authors, scholars, and members of the legal profession. 48 p. 12°. Boston, O. Ellsworth, 1862.

ENDEMANN (Wilhelm). Das gesetz betreffend das urheberrecht an schriftwerken [etc.] vom 11. Juni 1870. Mit den vertiägen zum schutz des geistigen eigenthums zwischen Deutschland und Italien, der Schweiz, England, Frankreich und Belgien. About 152 p. 8°. Berlin, Kortkampf, 1871.

ENFANTIN (Prosper). Le crédit intellectuel. About 32 p. 8°. Paris, E. Dentu, 1866.

ENFIELD (W:) Observations on literary property. 4°. London, Johnson, 1774. *Anon. review in* " The Monthly review," v. 51. 8°. London, Nov. 1774, p. 357-360.

ENGLISH copyright in foreign compositions. [*Anon.*] *In* " The Jurist." v. 18, part 2. 1854. 8°. London, no. 922, p. 311-313 ; no. 923, p. 326-329.

—— *Same.* British copyright in foreign compositions (first published after July 1, 1842), shewn to be unaffected by the decision in Jeffreys v. Boosey. Reprinted from " The Jurist." [*Anon.*] 8°. London, 1854.

—— *See also* S. (G.)

ENQUIRY (An) into the nature and origin of literary property. [*Anon.*] About 39 p. 8°. London, Flexney, 1762.

Note. Halkett and Laing *Anonymous and pseudonymous literature,* ascribe this work to William Warburton on the authority of the Dyce Catalogue v. 2, p. 406 where it is put under Warburton with this statement " ' By the Bp. of Gloucester.'—MS." It is, however, not included in Warburton's Works, while there is printed in v. 12 an article on literary property that was originally published anonymously in 1747. *See* Warburton.

ÉPÎTRES d'un étranger. — La première aux hommes de lettres sur la propriété littéraire. 2e éd. [*Anon.*] 8°. Paris, E. Dentu, 1859.

ESCRICHE (Joaquin). Diccionario razonado de legislacion y jurisprudencia. 3a ed. 2 v. fol. Madrid, Libreria de la señora viuda e hijos de d. A. Calleja, editores, 1847.
Contains : Autor. v. 1, p. 377-385.—Propiedad literaria. v. 2, p. 767-769.

ESCUDIER (Léon). Les pirates de la littérature et de la musique. 8°. Paris, E. Dentu, 1862.

ESPINASSE (I:) A treatise on the law of actions on statutes, remedial as well as penal, in general ; and on the statutes respecting copyright. 8°. London, 1824.

EVANS (W: D:) A general view of the decisions of [W: Murray] lord Mansfield, in civil causes. 2 v. 4°. London, for J. Butterworth, [1803.]
Contains : Literary property, v. 1, p. 363-404.

FARRER (T: H:) The principle of copyright. *In* "The Fortnightly review". v. 30, or v. 24, n. s. 8°. London, no. 181 or 144 n. s., Dec. 1, 1878, p. 836-858.

FELTON (Cornelius Conway). *See* Curtis (G: Ticknor).

FEW (A) words on international copyright. [*Anon.* notice of copyright treaty between France and Great Britain. 1851.] *In* "The Edinburgh review." v. 95. 8°. no. 193, Jan. 1852, p. 145-152.

FEW (A) words on the copyright question, shewing it to be one of public interest ; with some objections to sergeant Talfourd's bill. [*Anon.*] 8°. London, 1839.

FIELD (D: Dudley). Draft. Outlines of an international code. 8°. New York, Diossy & co., 1872.
Contains : Title xix. Copyrights, p, 274-280.

FISCHER (Robert). Gesetz betreffend das urheberrecht an schriftwerken [etc.] vom 11. Juni 1870. Nach den amtlichen materialien erläutert. About xvi, 52 p. 8°. Gera, Griesbach, 1870.
—— *Same.* 2 aufl. About xvi, 52 p. 8°. Gera, Griesbach, 1872.

FISHER (Robert Alexander). A digest of the reported cases [courts of Great Britain] 1756 to 1870. 5 v. 8°. London, H: Sweet, 1870.
Contains : Copyright, v. 6, col. 1863-1901. v. 5, col. 9338-9345.
—— *Same.* [Annual digest.] 1868-1877. 10 v. 8°. London. H: Sweet, 1869-78.
Contains : Copyright, 1868, p. 46-48 : 1869, col. 99-102 : 1870, col. 93, 94 : 1871, col. 86-88 : 1872, col. 79, 80 : 1873, col. 91 : 1874, col. 82, 83 : 1875, col. 87, 88 : 1876, col. 98, 99 : 1877, col. 88, 89.

FISHER (Robert Alexander). A digest of the reported English cases relating to patents, trade marks and copyrights. Edited and brought down to the present time, by H: Hooper. xvi p. 2 l. 196 p. 8°. Cincinnati, R. Clarke & co.; New York, Baker, Voorhis & co., 1872. [Copyright cases, 1 l. and p. 139-196.

FISHER (T:) Petition presented in 1814 to the commons of the United Kingdom. [And letter on copyright.] *In* "The Gentleman's magazine." v. 87, part 1. 8°. London, June 1817, p. 489-492.
—— *Same. In* Reasons for a farther amendment of the act 54 Geo. III. c. 156. By Sir Egerton Brydges. 8°. London, 1817, p. 44-48.

FISKE (Amos Kidder). *See* Drone (Eaton Sylvester).

FIX (Théodore). De la contrefaçon des livres français en Belgique. Extrait de la Revue mensuelle d'économie politique. 21 p. 8°. Paris, imp. de Bourgogne et Martinet, 1836.

FLINIAUX (Charles). Essai sur le droit des auteurs français et étrangers en France, et des auteurs français en pays étrangers. About 40 p. 8°. Paris, E. Thorin, 1879.
Anon. notice in " Journal du droit international privé," 1879, 8°. Paris, nos. 5-6, p. 328.—*Anon. notice in* " The Law magazine and review," 4th series, v. 5. 8°. London, no. 235, Feb. 1880, p. 208, 209.
—— Législation et jurisprudence concernant la propriété littéraire et artistique. About viii, 220 p. 8°. Bruxelles, Decq ; Paris, E. Thorin, 1867.
—— *Same.* 2e éd. About 225 p. 8°. Paris, E. Thorin, 1878.
Review by Charles Lyon-Caen in " Revue critique de législation et de jurisprudence," nouv. séries. v. 7. 8°. Paris, 1878, p. 607, 608.
—— La propriété industrielle et la propriété littéraire et artistique en France et à l'étranger. Législation et jurisprudence françaises, législations étrangères et conventions internationales. About 430 p. 12°. Tours, imp. Rouillé-Ladevèze ; Paris, librairie Delagrave, 1879.
Notice by Adalbert Frout de Fontpertuis in " Journal des économistes," 4e série. v. 6. 8°. Paris, no. 18, 15 juin 1879, p. 454, 455.

FLOURENS (Abel). Origine et développement en France de la législation sur les droits d'auteur. Commentaire de la loi de 1866. 8°. Paris, F. Pichon, 1874.

FOLLEVILLE (Daniel de). *See* Daniel de Folleville.

FONSCOLOMBE (Henri de). Essai sur la propriété littéraire. 8°. Paris, Marescq, 1880.

FONTPERTUIS (Adalbert Frout de). *See* Fliniaux (Charles). La propriété industrielle et la propriété littéraire.

FOUCHER (Victor). De la propriété littéraire et de la contrefaçon. 8°. Paris, 1837.
Note. Originally published in " Revue étrangère et française de législation et d'œconomie politique." v. 4. 8°. Paris, 1837, p. 321—, 361—, 506—, 573—.

FOUCHER (Victor). Le Congrès de la propriété littéraire et artistique à Bruxelles. [1858]. *In* " Revue contemporaine." 7ème année, 2e série. v. 5. 8°. Paris, 1858, p. 812–853.

—— *Same.* About 136 p. 12°. Paris, M. Lévy frères, 1858.

FRAGE (Die) des literarischen eigenthums. [*Anon.*] *In* " Unsere zeit. Deutsche revue der gegenwart." Neue folge. 2ter jahrgang. 1ste hälfte. 8°. Leipzig, 1866, p. 801–823.

FRANCE. *Commission de la propriété littéraire.* Collection des procès-verbaux. About 348 p. 4°. Paris, Pillet aîné, 1826.

—— Rapport de la commission chargée de preparer un projet de loi sur la propriété littéraire. 8°. Paris, 1826.
Anon. notice with translation of the report: French law of literary property. *In* " The Jurist." v. 1. 8°. London, March 1827, p. 113–120.

—— *See also* Auger (Louis Simon).—Champein (Marie François Stanislas).—Lally Tollendal (Trophine Gérard, marquis de).—Lemercier (Népomucène Louis).—Portalis (Le comte Joseph Marie).

—— *Ministère d'état.* (*Commission de la propriété littéraire et artistique.*) Décrets, discours de s. exc. le ministre d'état. Législation. Documents. About 44 p. 4°. Paris, imp. Panckoucke & cie, 1862.

—— —— Rapports à l'empereur. Décrets. Collection des procès-verbaux. Documents. 286 p. 1 l. 4°. Paris, imprimerie impériale, 1863.

FRASER (James). A handy-book of patent and copyright law English and foreign for the use of inventors, patentees, authors, and publishers. xvi, 242 p. 12°. London, S. Low, Son, & co., 1860. [Copyright, p. 168–228.]
Anon. notice in " The Jurist." N. s. v. 7, part 2. 8°. London, no. 322, March 9, 1861, p. 97.

FRESQUET (Raymond de). *See* Nion (Alfred).

FRIEDLÄNDER (Max). Der einheimische und ausländische rechtsschutz gegen nachdruck und nachbildung. Rechtswissenschaftliche und für den praktischen gebrauch bestimmte darstellung der heutigen gesetzgebung und des internationalen rechts zum schutz schriftstellerischer und künstlerischer erzeugnisse. About xv, 227 p. 8°. Leipzig, Brockhaus, 1857.

FROUDE (James Anthony). The copyright commission. [*Anon.*] *In* " The Edinburgh review." v. 148. 8°. Edinburgh, no. 304, Oct. 1878, p. 295–343.

FURTHER reasons addressed to parliament [etc.] 1737. *See* Carte (T:)

GAMBIER (Ernest). On piracy of artistic copyright. 8°. London, W. Tegg, 1863.
Anon. notice in " The Art-journal." N. s. v. 2, 4°. London, June 1, 1863, p. 128.—*Anon. review in* " The Athenæum." 4°. London, no. 1862, July 4, 1863, p. 16, 17.

GARNIER (Joseph). *See* Calmels (Antoine Édouard).

GASTAMBIDE (Joseph Adrien). Historique et théorie de la propriété des auteurs. 132 p. 8°. Paris, Cosse & Marchal, 1862.

—— Traité théorique et pratique des contrefaçons en tous genres, ou de la propriété en matière de littérature, théâtre, musique, peinture, dessin, etc. viii, 496 p. 8°. Paris, Legrand & Descauriet, 1837.
Review by Louis Nigon de Berty in " Revue étrangère et française de législation et d'œconomie politique." v. 4. 8°. Paris, 1837, p. 835–*seq.*

GAY (Jules). Ce qu'on appelle la propiété littéraire est nuisible aux auteurs, aux éditeurs et au public. 8°. Paris, J. Gay, 1862.

GERBER (Karl Friedrich von). Ueber die natur d. rechte d. schriftstellers und verlegers. *In* " Jahrbücher für die dogmatik d. heutigen römischen und deutschen privatrechts. Herausgegeben von R. Jhering." v. 3. 8°. Jena.

GERHARD (Frederick). Will the people of the United States be benefited by an international copyright law, or, will such a law be an injury to them ? 27 p. 8°. New York, 1868.
Note. The author thinks an international copyright law would not be a benefit, but an injury to the people of the United States.

GERMANY. Bericht der 6. kommission über den gesetz-entwurf, betreffend das geistige urheberrecht an schriftwerken u. s. w. nebst zusammenstellung der präsidial-vorlagen mit den von der kommission gefassten beschlussen. About 27 p. fol. Berlin, Kortkampf, 1870. [Aktenstücke des Reichstags. Session 1870, nr. 7.]

—— Entwurf eines gesetzes betreffend, a. das urheberrecht von schriftwerken, abbildungen &c. b. schutz der photographien gegen unbefugte nachbildung mit motiven. About 25 p. fol. Berlin, Kortkampf, 1870. [Aktenstücke des Reichstags. Session 1870, nr. 3.]

—— Gesetz, betreffend das urheberrecht an schriftwerken, abbildungen, musikalischen kompositionen und dramatischen werken. Vom 11. Juni 1870. *In* Bundes-Gesetzblatt des Norddeutschen bundes. 1870. 4°. Berlin, No. 19, p. 339–353.

—— *Same.* About 15 p. 8°. Berlin, von Decker, 1870.

—— *Same.* About 24 p. 16°. Berlin, Kortkampf, 1870.

—— *Same :* Nach den amtlichen materialien erläutert und mit ausführl. alphabet. sachregister versehen, für den praktischen handgebrauch herausgegeben von Robert Fischer. About xvi, 52 p. 8°. Gera, Griesbach, 1870.

—— *Same :* 2. Aufl. About xvi, 52 p. 8°. Gera, Griesbach, 1872.

—— *Same :* Mit den verträgen zum schutz des geistigen eigenthums zwischen Deutschland und Italien, der Schweiz, England, Frankreich und Belgien. Von Wilhelm Endemann. About 152 p. 8°. Berlin, Kortkampf, 1871.

—— *Same :* Erläutert von Otto Dambach. About iv, 298 p. 8°. Berlin, T. C. F. Enslin, 1871.

GERMANY. *Same :* Systematisch dargestellt von Rudolf Klostermann. About iii, 74 p. 8°. Berlin, Guttendag, 1871.

—— *Same :* Loi du 11 juin 1870 concernant le droit d'auteur. Traduction et notes de Paul Gide. *In* Annuaire de législation étrangère. 1870-1871. 8°. Paris, 1872, p. 205-223.

—— Loi du 9 Jan.—11 Jan. 1876 concernant le droit d'auteur. Notice, traduction et notes par André Morillot. *In* Annuaire de législation étrangère. 1876. 8°. Paris, 1877. p. 88-134.

GERMOND DE LAVIGNE (Léopold Alfred Gabriel). La protection de la propriété littéraire à l'étranger. Conférence faite au Cercle de la librairie, le 18 mars 1881. About 24 p. 8°. Paris, *Pillet et Dumoulin*, 1881.

GIDE (Paul). *See* Germany. Loi du 11 juin 1870 concernant le droit d'auteur.

GILDER (R: Watson). *See* Scribner's monthly.

GODKIN (Edwin Lawrence). *See* Nation (The).

GODSON (R) A practical treatise on the law of patents for inventions and of copyright ; with an introductory book on monopolies ; illustrated with notes of the principal cases. xxxiv p. 1 l. 452 p. 8°. London, for J. Butterworth & Son, 1823.

—— *Same :* With an abstract of the laws in force in foreign countries. 2d ed. xxxv, 496, 118 p. 8°. London, Saunders & Benning, 1840.

—— *Same :* 2d ed., to which is added a supplement, containing the law to the present time. 1 p. l. [xxxv], 496, 94 p. viii, 158 p. 8°. London, W. Benning & Co., 1844.

—— *Same :* Supplement, with an abstract of the laws in force in America, Spain, Austria, Netherlands, and France. 8°, London, 1832.

—— *Same :* A supplement to the 2d edition of A practical treatise on the law of patents for inventions and of copyright. viii, 158 p. 8°. London, W. Benning & Co., 1844.

—— De la propriété littéraire et du droit de copie en général, ou du droit de propriété dans ses rapports avec la littérature et les arts en Angleterre. Traduction de l'Anglais, par Théodore Regnault. 8°. Paris, Warée, 1826.

—— *See also* Burke (P:) A supplement to Godson's practical treatise on patents and copyright. 1851.

GOEPEL (Ernst). Ueber begriff und wesen des urheberrechtes. Inaugural dissertation, Jena. 54 p. 12°. Altenburg, S. Geibel & co., 1881.

GOLTDAMMER (Dr. —). Ueber die strafbare nachbildung von kunstwerken. About 43 p. 8°. Berlin, von Decker, 1864. [Aus Archiv für preussisches strafrecht besonders abgedruckt.]

GOUJET (Charles) *and* MERGER (C. B.) Dictionnaire de droit commercial. 2e éd., mise en harmonie avec la législation nouvelle jusqu'au 30 mars 1852. v. 4. 8° Paris, A. Marescq, and Cotillon, 1852.

Contains : Propriété artistique, p. 298-323. Propriété littéraire, p. 363-411.

GOUJON (Alexandre Marie). Essai sur la garantie des propriétés littéraires. 8°. Paris, Goujon, 1801.

GOURNOT (Achille Louis). Du principe des droits d'auteur et de la perpétuité. 2 p. l. 48 p. 8°. Paris, E. Dentu, 1862.

GOVI (Gilberto). Della proprietà intellettuale, considerazioni di G. Govi. About 16 p. 8°. Firenze, tip. Cellini, 1867.

GRÄFF (Er. Mor.) Versuch einer erläuternden darstellung des eigenthums der eigenthumsrechte des schriftstellers und des verlegers und ihrer gegenseitigen rechte und verbindlichkeiten. 8°. Leipzig, Wienbrack, 1794.

GRAHAM (Catherine Sawbridge). *See* Macaulay (Mrs. Catherine Sawbridge).

GREAT BRITAIN. Acts relating to copy right in books, 8 Ann. [1708-9] c. 19. 15 Geo. 3. [1774-5] c. 53. 41 Geo. 3. [1800-1] c. 107. 28 p. 12°. London, G. Eyre & A. Strahan, 1812.

—— Acts relating to literary and artistic copyright. *In* The Statutes. Revised ed. 15 v. sm. fol. London, 1871-78.

Summary : v. 2. An act for the encouragement of the arts of designing, engraving, and etching historical and other prints, by vesting the properties thereof in the inventors and engravers. 8 Geo. II. 1734-5, chap. 13, p. 399, 400. An act to amend and render more effectual an act made in 8 Geo. II. for encouragement of the arts of designing, engraving, and etching prints. 7 Geo. III. 1766-7, chap. 38, p. 707, 708.—v. 3. An act for enabling the two universities in England, the four universities in Scotland and the several colleges of Eton, Westminster and Winchester, to hold in perpetuity their copy right in books. 15 Geo. III. 1774-5, chap. 53, p. 81-84. An act for more effectually securing the property of prints to inventors and engravers, by enabling them to sue for and recover penalties in certain cases. 17 Geo. III. 1776-7, chap. 57, p. 130, 131.—v. 5. An act to amend and render more effectual an act of his present majesty for encouraging the art of making new models and casts of busts and other things therein mentioned. 54 Geo. III., 18th May 1814, chap. 56, p. 291, 292.—v. 7. An act to amend the laws relating to dramatic literary property. 3 & 4 Will. IV., 10th June 1833, chap. 15, p. 355, 356. An act for preventing the publication of lectures without consent. 5 & 6 Will. IV., 9th Sept. 1835, chap 65, p. 898, 899. An act to extend the protection of copyright in prints and engravings to Ireland. 6 & 7 Will. IV., 13th Aug. 1836, chap. 59, p. 1055, 1056. An act to repeal so much of an act of the 54 Geo. III. respecting copyrights, as requires the delivery of a copy of every published book to the libraries of Sion college, the four universities of Scotland, and of the King's Inns in Dublin. 6 & 7 Will. IV., 20th Aug. 1836, chap. 110, p. 1175, 1176.—v. 8. An act to amend the law of copyright. 5 & 6 Vict., 1st July 1842, chap. 45, p. 1152-1162. *Abstract in* "The Jurist." v. 6, part 2. 8°. London, no. 291, Aug. 6, 1842, p. 278-281.—v. 9. An act to amend the law relating to international copyright. 7 & 8 Vict., 10th May, 1844, chap. 12, p. 224-232. —v. 10. An act to amend the law relating to the protection in the colonies of works entitled to copyright in the United Kingdom. 10 & 11 Vict., 22d July, 1847, chap. 95, p. 275, 276.—v. 11. An act to enable her majesty to carry into effect a convention with France on the subject of copyright ; to extend and explain the international copyright acts ; and to explain the acts relating to copyright in engravings. 15 & 16 Vict., 28th May 1852, chap. 12, p. 283-287.—v. 14. An act for amending the law relating to copyright in works of the fine arts, and for repressing the commission of fraud in the production and sale of such works. 25 & 26 Vict., 29th July 1862, chap. 68, p. 162-

167. *Same in* " The Journal of the Society of arts." v.
10. sm. 4°. London, no. 507, Aug. 8, 1862, p. 592–594.

GREAT BRITAIN. *Same.* *In* " The Law reports.
The public general statutes. v. 1–17. 8°.
London, 1866–81.
   Summary : v. 10. An act to amend the law relating to
international copyright. 38 Vict., 13th May 1875, chap.
12, p. 133, 134. An act to give effect to an act of the Parliament of the dominion of Canada respecting copyright.
38 & 39 Vict., 2d Aug. 1875, chap. 53, p. 338–345. An act
to amend the copyright of designs act. [Copyright in
sculpture.] 38 & 39 Vict., 13th Aug. 1875, chap. 93, p.
1042–1044.—v. 11. An act to consolidate the customs laws.
39 & 40 Vict., 24th July 1876, chap. 36. sections 42, 44, 45
& 152 : Importation of foreign reprints of copyright books,
p. 181, 183 & 210.

—— Extracts from the evidence taken before
the select committee of the House of Commons, on the copyright acts, in April and May,
1818. 16 p. 8°. London, Strahan & Spottiswoode, [1818.]

—— *Same.* 22 p. 8°. [London, Barnard & Farley, 1818.]

—— Legislative documents relating to literary
and artistic copyright. 1800–1880. *In* Parliamentary papers : Bills ; Reports from com-
mittees ; Accounts and papers. fol. London,
1800–80.
   Note.—Papers, etc., relating to the copyright of designs
have been omitted.
   Summary : A bill for securing the copyright of printed
books to authors or their assigns. Parliamentary papers,
v. 1. Session 1801, no. 112.
   A bill for securing copies of books to universities, and
copyrights to authors. Par. pap. v. 1. Sess. 1808, no.
314 and 321.
   A bill to amend the several acts for securing copyrights.
Par. pap. v. 2. Sess. 1813–1814, no. 184, 214, 307 and 321.
   A bill to amend an act passed in the 54th year of the
reign of his present majesty, intituled, " An act to
amend the several acts for the encouragement of learning,
by securing the copies and copyright of printed books to
the authors of such books, or their assigns." Ordered,
by the House of Commons, to be printed, 16 March, 1818.
2 p. 1 l. Par. pap. v. 1 : Bills. Sess. 27 Jan.–10 June
1818, no. 126.
   A bill to alter and extend the provisions of the 54th
George third, cap. 156, with respect to dramatic writings.
Ordered, by the H. of C., to be printed, 24 Feb. 1830.
6 p. Par. pap. v. 2 : Bills v. 2. Sess. 5 Feb.–23 July 1830,
no. 78.
   A bill to authorize the purchase of the rights of literary
property enjoyed by the King's and Marischal colleges in
Aberdeen. Ordered, by the H. of C., to be printed, 1
Aug. 1832. 4 p. Par. pap. v. 1 : Bills v. 1. Sess. 6 Dec.
1831–16 Aug. 1832, no. 670.
   A bill to amend the laws relating to dramatic literary
property. Ordered, by the H. of C., to be printed, 13
March 1833. 4 p. Par. pap. v. 2 : Bills v. 2. Sess. 2
Jan.–29 Aug. 1833, no. 73.
   A bill, intituled, an act for preventing the publication
of lectures without consent. Ordered, by the H. of C.,
to be printed, 20 Aug. 1835. 2 p. 1 l. Par. pap. v. 3 :
Bills v. 3. Sess 19 Feb.–10 Sep. 1835, no. 546.
   A bill to repeal so much of an act of the fifty-fourth year
of king George the third, commonly called " The copyright act," as requires the gratuitous delivery of eleven
copies of every published book to eleven of the public libraries of the kingdom, in the said act named, and to
provide other means for the encouragement of learning.
(Prepared and brought in by mr. Buckingham, colonel
Thompson and mr. Ewart.) Ordered, by the H. of C., to
be printed, 10 May 1836. 4 p. Par. pap. v. 2 : Bills v. 2.
Sess. 4 Feb.–20 Aug. 1836, no. 252.—*Same.* As amended
by the committee. Ordered, by the H. of C., to be print-
ed, 14 July 1836. 2 pp. 1 l. Par. pap. v. 2 : Bills v. 2.
Sess. 4 Feb.–20 Aug. 1836, no. 441.
   A bill to extend the protection of copyright in prints and
engravings to Ireland. (Prepared and brought in by mr.
Buckingham and mr. Aglionby.) Ordered, by the H. of
C., to be printed, 14 June 1836. 2 p. Par. pap. v. 2 :
Bills v. 2. Sess. 4 Feb.–20 Aug. 1836, no. 333.—*Same* As

amended by the committee. Ordered, by the H. of C.,
to be printed, 11 July 1836. 2 p. Par. pap. v. 2 : Bills v.
2. Sess. 4 Feb.–20 Aug. 1836, no. 431.
   A bill to consolidate and amend the laws relating to
copyright in printed books, musical compositions, acted
dramas and engravings, to provide remedies for the violation thereof, and to extend the term of its duration. (Prepared and brought in by mr. serjeant Talfourd, mr. chancellor of the exchequer, lord viscount Mahon, and sir
Robert Harry Inglis.) Ordered, by the H. of C., to be
printed, 6 June 1837. 16 p. Par. pap. v. 1 : Bills v. 1.
Sess. 31 July 1837, no. 380.
   A bill to amend the law relating to copyright. (Prepared and brought in by mr. serjeant Talfourd, lord viscount Mahon, sir Robert Inglis, and mr. chancellor of the
exchequer. Ordered, by the H. of C., to be printed, 27
Feb. 1838. 14 p. 1 l. Par. pap. v. 1 : Bills v. 1. Sess.
15 Nov. 1837–16 Aug. 1838, no. 164.—*Same.* As amended
by the committee. Ordered, by the H. of C., to be
printed, 6 June 1838. 18 p. Par. pap. v. 1 : Bills v. 1.
Sess. 15 Nov. 1837–16 Aug. 1838, no. 461.—*Notice in*
" Tait's Edinburgh magazine." v. 5, n. s. 8°. Edinburgh,
no. 53, May 1838, p. 332–334.
   A bill for securing to authors, in certain cases, the benefit of international copyright. (Prepared and brought in
by mr. Poulett Thomson and lord John Russell.) Ordered,
by the H. of C., to be printed, 11 April 1838. 6 p. Par.
pap. v. 1 : Bills v. 1. Sess. 15 Nov. 1837–16 Aug. 1838,
no. 295.—*Same.* As amended by the committee. Ordered,
by the H. of C., to be printed, 8 June 1838. 6 p. Par.
pap. v. 1 : Bills v. 1. Sess. 15 Nov. 1837–16 Aug. 1838,
no. 509.
   A bill to amend the law of copyright. (Prepared and
brought in by mr. serjeant Talfourd, mr. chancellor of the
exchequer, sir Robert Harry Inglis, and lord viscount
Mahon.) Ordered, by the H. of C., to be printed, 12 Feb.
1839. 18 p. Par. pap. v. 1 : Bills v. 1. Sess. 5 Feb.–27
Aug. 1839, no. 19.
   A bill to amend the law of copyright. (Prepared and
brought in by mr. serjeant Talfourd, sir Robert Harry Inglis, lord viscount Mahon, and mr. Gladstone.) Ordered,
by the H. of C., to be printed, 11 Feb. 1840. 16 p. 1 l.
Par. pap. v. 1 : Bills v. 1. Sess. 16 Jan.–11 Aug. 1840,
no. 61.—*Same.* Ordered, by the H. of C., to be printed,
29 Jan. 1841. 16 p. 1 l. Par. pap. v. 1 : Bills v. 1.
Sess. 26 Jan.–22 June 1841, no. 6.
   A bill for the registering of copyrights and assignments
thereof, and for the better securing the property therein.
(Prepared and brought in by mr. Godson and mr. Bulkeley
Hughes.) Ordered, by the H. of C., to be printed, 8
Feb. 1842. 4 p. 1 l. Par. pap. v. 1 : Bills v. 1. Sess.
Feb.–12 Aug. 1842, no. 9.—*Anon. review in* " The Jurist."
v. 6, part 2. 8°. London, 1842, no. 267, Feb. 19, p. 49, 50:
no 271, March 19, p. 89–91: no. 276, April 23, p. 141, 142.
   A bill to amend the law of copyright. (Prepared and
brought in by viscount Mahon, sir Robert Harry Inglis,
mr. Gladstone, and mr. Charles Howard.) Ordered, by
the H. of C., to be printed, 4 March 1842. 16 p. 1 l.
Par. pap. v. 1 : Bills v. 1. Sess. 3 Feb.–12 Aug. 1842, no
79.—*Same* As amended by the committee. Ordered, by
the H. of C., to be printed, 23 March 1842. 18 p. Par.
pap. v. 1 : Bills v. 1. Sess. 3 Feb.–12 Aug. 1842, no. 139.
—*Same* As amended by the committee, and on re-commit-
ment. Ordered, by the H. of C., to be printed, 21 April
1842. 16 p. Par. pap. v. 1 : Bills v. 1. Sess. 3 Feb.–12
Aug. 1842, no. 194.—*Same.* Amendments made by the
lords. Ordered, by the H. of C., to be printed, 27 June
1842. 4 p. Par. pap. v. 1 : Bills v. 1. Sess. 3 Feb.–12
Aug. 1842, no 370.
   A bill to amend the law relating to international copyright. (Prepared and brought in by mr. Greene, mr.
Gladstone, and mr. Bingham Baring.) Ordered, by the
H. of C., to be printed, 12 March 1844. 11 p. 1 l. Par.
pap. v. 1 : Bills v. 1. Sess. 1 Feb.–5 Sept. 1844, no. 101.
   A bil' to amend the law relating to the protection in the
colonies of works entitled to copyright in the United
Kingdom. (Prepared and brought in by mr. Milner Gibson and mr. Parker.) Ordered, by the H. of C., to be
printed, 1 July 1847. 2 p. 1. l. Par. pap. v. 1 : Bills v. 1.
Sess. 19 Jan.–23 July 1847, no. 598.
   A bill to enable her majesty to carry into effect a convention with France on the subject of copyright ; to
extend the international copyright act ; and to explain
the acts relating to copyright in engravings. (Prepared
and brought in by mr. Labouchere and mr. attorney
general.) Ordered, by the H. of C., to be printed, 18
Feb. 1852. 1 p. 1. 8 p. Par. pap. v. 1 : Bills v. 1. Sess.
3 Feb.–1 July 1852, no. 85.

A bill for consolidating the laws relating to copyright in works of literature and art. (Prepared and brought in by mr. Wilson and the chancellor of the exchequer.) Ordered, by the H. of C., to be printed, 20 July 1857. 1 p. l. 22 p. Par. pap. v. 1 : Bills v. 1. Sess. 30 April-28 Aug. 1857, no 142.—*Criticism in* " The Jurist." N. s. v. 3, part 2. 8°. London, no. 134, Aug 1, 1857, p. 311-316.

A bill for amending the law relating to copyright in works of the fine arts, and for repressing the commission of fraud in the production and sale of such works. (Prepared and brought in by mr. Massey, mr. attorney general, sir George Lewis, and mr. solicitor general.) Ordered, by the H. of C., to be printed, 15 April 1861. 1 p. l. 12 p. Par. pap. v. 1 : Bills v. 1. Sess. 5 Feb.-6 Aug. 1861, no. 104.—*Same* (Prepared by mr. Massey, mr. solicitor general, and mr. attorney general) Ordered, by the H. of C., to be printed, 27 Feb. 1862. 8 p. Par. pap. v. 1 : Bills v. 1. Sess. 6 Feb.-7 Aug. 1862, no. 26.—*Same* As amended in committee. Ordered, by the H. of C., to be printed, 20 March 1862. 1 p. l. 6 p. 1 l. Par. pap. v. 1 : Bills v. 1. Sess. 5 Feb.-7 Aug. 1862, no. 53.—*Notices in* " The Athenæum" 4°, London, 1862, no. 1814, Aug. 2, p. 146, 147 : no. 1815, Aug. 9, p. 180 : no. 1829, Nov. 15, p. 630, 611.

A bill to consolidate and amend the acts relating to copyright in works of literature and the fine arts. (Prepared and brought in by mr. Stirling, and mr. Massey.) Ordered, by the H. of C., to be printed, 6 April 1864. 1 p. l. 24 p. 1 l. Par. pap. v. 1 : Bills v. 1. Sess. 4 Feb.-29 July 1864, no. 59.—*Same in* " The Jurist." N. s. v. 10, part 2. 8°. London, 1864, no. 485, April 23, p. 146-148 : no. 486, April 30, p. 156-160 : Editorial observations, no. 491, June 4, p. 211, 212.

A bill for amending the law relating to copyright, so far as regards the delivery of periodical publications at the British museum. (Prepared and brought in by mr. Ayrton and mr. chancellor of the exchequer. Ordered, by the H. of C., to be printed, 22 April 1869. 2 p. 1 l. Par. pap. v. 2 : Bills v. 2. Sess. 10 Dec. 1858-11 Aug. 1869, no. 93.

A bill to amend the law relating to international copyright. (Prepared and brought in by mr. Bourke and sir C. Adderley.) Ordered, by the H. of C., to be printed, 8 July 1874. 2 p. 1 l. Par. pap. v. 2 : Bills v. 2. Sess. 5 March-7 Aug. 1874, no. 197.

A bill intituled an act to give effect to an act of the Parliament of the Dominion of Canada respecting copyright. (Brought from the lords, 8 July 1875.) Ordered, by the H. of C., to be printed, 9 July 1875. 10 p. Par. pap. v. 1 : Bills v. 1. Sess. 5 Feb.-13 Aug. 1875, no. 246.

A bill to amend the law relating to international copyright. Par. pap. v. 3 : Bills v. 3. Sess. 5 Feb.-13 Aug. 1875, no 56.

A bill to consolidate and amend the law relating to copyright. (Prepared and brought in by lord John Manners, viscount Sandon, and mr. attorney general.) Ordered, by the H. of C., to be printed, 29 July 1879. iv, 34 p. 1 l. Par. pap. v. 2 : Bills v. 2. Sess. 5 Dec. 1878-15 Aug. 1879, no. 265.—*Review in* " The Athenæum," 1880, 4°. London. I.—no 2723, Jan. 3, p 25, 26. II.—no. 2725, Jan. 17, p. 94, 95. III.—no. 2728, Feb. 7, p. 189, 190. IV.—no 2730, Feb. 21, p. 255, 256.—*Notice in* " The Journal of the Society of Arts," v. 27. 8°. London, no. 1396, Aug. 22, 1879, p. 879, 880.

Convention between her majesty and the free Hanseatic city of Hamburg, for the establishment of international copyright. Signed at Hamburg, Aug. 16, 1853. 12 p. Par. pap. v. 72 : Accounts and papers v. 34. Sess. 31 Jan. 12 Aug. 1854, no. 37 or 1700.

Convention between her majesty and the French republic, for the establishment of international copyright. Signed at Paris, Nov. 3, 1851. 12 p. 1 l. Par. pap. v. 54 : Ac. and pap. v. 27. Sess. 3 Feb.-1 July 1852, no. 34 or 1432.

Convention between her majesty and the king of Hanover, for the establishment of international copyright. Signed at London, Aug. 4, 1847. 10 p. Par. pap. v. 65 : Ac. and pap. v. 27. Sess. 18 Nov. 1847-5 Sept. 1848, no. 200 or 889.—Accession of the grand duke of Oldenburg to the convention concluded Aug. 4, 1847, between Great Britain and Hanover, for the establishment of international copyright. Signed at Hanover, Dec. 28, 1847. 6 p. 1 l. Par. pap. v. 65 : Ac. and pap. v. 27. Sess. 18 Nov. 1847-5 Sept. 1848, no. 51 or 898.

Convention between her majesty and the king of Prussia, for the establishment of international copyright.

Signed at Berlin, May 13, 1846. 10 p. Par. pap. v. 52 : Ac. and pap. v. 28. Sess. 22 Jan.-28 Aug. 1846, no 93 or 715.—Accession of the duke of Anhalt to the convention concluded 13 May 1846, between Great Britain and Prussia, for the establishment of international copyright. Signed at Berlin, 8 Feb. 1853. Par. pap. v. 102 : Ac. and pap. v. 46. Sess. 4 Nov. 1852-20 Aug. 1853, no. 1598.—Accession of the duke of Brunswick to the convention concluded May 13, 1846, between Great Britain and Prussia. Signed at Berlin, March 30, 1847. 6 p. 1 l. Par. pap. v. 70 : Ac. and pap. v. 37. Sess. 19 Jan.-23 July 1847, no. 140 or 804.—Accession of the grand duke of Hesse to the conventions concluded May 13, 1846, and June 14, 1855, between Great Britain and Prussia. Signed at Berlin, Nov. 19, 1861. 1 p. l. 4 p. Par. pap. v. 63 : Ac. and pap. v. 35. Sess. 6 Feb.-7 Aug. 1862, no. 30 or 2908.—Accession of the king of Saxony to the convention concluded May 13, 1846, between Great Britain and Prussia. Signed at Berlin, Aug. 24, 1846. 6 p. 1 l. Par. pap. v. 70 : Ac. and pap. v. 37. Sess. 19 Jan.-23 July 1847, no. 17 or 770.—Accession of the states forming the Thuringian union, to the convention concluded May 13, 1846, between Great Britain and Prussia. Signed at Berlin, July 1, 1847. 8 p. Par. pap. v. 70 : Ac. and pap. v. 37. Sess. 19 Jan.-23 July 1847, no. 103 or 849.

Convention between her majesty and the king of Prussia, additional to the convention concluded at Berlin, May 13, 1846, for the establishment of international copyright. Signed at London, June 14, 1855. 8 p. Par. pap. v. 61 : Ac. and pap. v. 24. Sess. 31 Jan.-29 July 1856, no. 248 or 2013.

Convention between her majesty and the king of Sardinia, for the establishment of international copyright. Signed at Turin, Nov. 30, 1860. 1 p. l. 8 p. Par. pap. v. 67 : Ac. and pap. v. 34. Sess. 5 Feb.-6 Aug. 1861, no. 47 or 2758.

Convention between her majesty and the king of the Belgians, for the establishment of international copyright. Signed at London, Aug. 12, 1854. 1 p. l. 10 p. 1 l. Par. pap. v. 55 : Ac. and pap. v. 26. Sess. 12 Dec. 1854-14 Aug. 1855, no. 42 or 1872.

Convention between her majesty and the queen of Spain, for the establishment of international copyright. Signed at Madrid, July 7, 1857. 1 p. l. 8 p. 1 l. Par. pap. v. 60 : Ac. and pap. v. 28. Sess. 3 Dec. 1857-2 Aug. 1858, no. 260 or 2300.

Copies of or extracts from correspondence between the colonial office and any of the colonial governments on the subject of copyright ; and of colonial acts relating to copyright which have been allowed by her majesty. (Mr. Edward Jenkins.) Ordered, by the H. of C., to be printed, 13 April 1875. 30 p. 1 l. Par. pap. v. 51 : Ac. and pap. v. 10. Sess. 5 Feb.-13 Aug. 1875, no. 144.

Copies of two orders of her majesty in council, of 10th Jan. 1852, issued in furtherance of the copyright treaty with France. Ordered, by the H. of C., to be printed, 18 Feb. 1852. 4 p. Par. pap. v. 51 : Ac. and pap. v. 24. Sess. 3 Feb.-1 July 1852, no. 81.

Copies or extracts of correspondence between the colonial office, the board of trade, and the government of Canada, which preceded the passing of the act 10 & 11 Vict. c. 95 ; and, of any recent correspondence on the subject of that act and of proposals for amending or extending the same. (Sir Charles Adderley.) Ordered, by the H. of C., to be printed, 30 July 1872. viii, 80 p. Par. pap. v. 43 : Ac. and pap. v. 8. Sess. 6 Feb.-10 Aug. 1872, no. 339.

Copy of treasury minute, dated 17th July 1832 ; respecting the purchase of the rights of the University of Aberdeen to certain copies of books. Ordered, by the H. of C., to be printed, 28 July 1832. 2 p. Par. pap. v. 26. Sess. 6 Dec. 1831-16 Aug. 1832, no. 656.

Copyright commission. The royal commissions and the report of the commissioners. xc p. Par. pap. v. 24 : Reports from commissioners v. 6. Sess. 17 Jan.-16 Aug. 1878, no. c.-2036.

Contents : The commissions, p. iii-vi. Report : Home copyright, p. vii-xxx : Colonial copyright, p. xxx-xxxvi : International copyright, p. xxxvi-xliv : Dissent etc. p. xlv-lx. Digest of the law of copyright. By sir James Stephen, p. lxi-xc.

Notice by Moy Thomas in " The Academy," 4°. London, 1878. I.-v. 13, no. 321, June 29, p. 578, 579 : II.-v. 14, no. 323, July 13, p. 36-38 : III.-v. 14, no. 324, July 20, p. 61-63. *Anon. review* [by James Anthony Froude] in " The Edinburgh review." v. 148. 8°. Edinburgh, no. 304, Oct. 1878, p. 295-343. *Notice in* " The Nation." v. 27. 4°. New York, no. 680, July 11, 1878, p. 24, 25. *Review in* " The Popular science monthly." v. 13, 8°.

New York, no. 77, Sept. 1878, Editor's table, p. 618-620.
Anon. review in " The Saturday review," v. 45, fol.
London, no. 1183, June 29, 1878, p. 819, 820. *Anon notice in* " The Spectator." 4°. London, June 22, 1878,
p. 789, 790. *See also* Carmichael (C: H: E:)
Correspondence between the foreign office and her majesty's representatives abroad, and foreign representatives
in England, on the subject of copyright: 1872-75. 1 p. l.
38 p. 1 l. Par. pap. v. 78 : Ac. and pap. v. 37. Sess. 5
Feb.-13 Aug. 1875, no. c.-1285.
Correspondence respecting colonial copyright. 1 p. l.
30 p. Par. pap. v. 44 : Ac. and pap. v. 10. Sess. 5 March-
7 Aug. 1874, no. c.-1067.
Declaration cancelling section 3 of article IV. of the
copyright convention between Great Britain and France
of Nov. 3, 1851. Signed at London, Aug. 11, 1875. 2 l.
Par. pap. v. 82: Ac. and pap. v. 41. Sess. 5 Feb.-13 Aug.
1875, no. c.-1358.
Extracts of so much of the returns made by the universities of Oxford and Cambridge, (pursuant to the orders
of the 1st July 1817 and 20th Feb. last) as state, whether
any of the books claimed under the late copyright act
have been omitted to be placed in their respective libraries, and how otherwise disposed of. Ordered, by the
H. of C., to be printed, 6 March 1818. 6 p. 1 l. Par. pap.
v. 15: Ac. and pap. Sess. 27 Jan.-10 June, 1818, no.
98.
Minutes of evidence taken before the committee on acts
of 8 Anne, and 15 & 41 Geo. III. for the encouragement
of learning, by vesting the copies of printed books, in the
authors or purchasers of such copies. Ordered, by the H.
of C., to be printed, 20 July 1813. 33 p. 1 l. Par. pap.
v. 4 : Rep. from com. v. 2. Sess. 24 Nov.-22 July 1812-
1813; no. 341.—*Same.* Ordered, by the H. of C., to be
reprinted, 13 April 1818. 1 p. l. 33 p. Par. pap. v. 9:
Rep. from com. Sess. 27 Jan.-10 June 1818, no 177.
Minutes of evidence taken before the select committee
on the copyright acts of 8 Anne, c. 19 ; 15 Geo. III. c. 53 ;
41 Geo. III. c. 107 ; and 54 Geo. III. c. 116. Ordered, by
the H. of C., to be printed, 8 May 1818. 132 p. Par.
pap. v. 9: Rep. from com. Sess. 27 Jan.-10 June 1818,
no. 280.
Minutes of the evidence taken before the royal commission on copyright together with an appendix. v, 409 p.
Par. pap. v. 24 : Rep. from com. v. 6. Sess. 17 Jan.-16
Aug. 1878, no. c.-2036.-i.
Report from committee on acts of 8 Anne, and 15 & 41
Geo. III. for the encouragement of learning, by vesting
the copies of printed books, in the authors or purchasers
of such copies. Ordered, by the H. of C., to be printed,
17 June 1813. 2 p. 1 l. Par. pap. v. 4 : Rep. from com.
v 2. Sess. 24 Nov.-22 July, 1812-1813; no 292.
Report from the select committee on dramatic literature : with the minutes of evidence. Ordered, by the
H. of C., to be printed, 2 Aug. 1832. 250 p. 1 fol'd chart.
Par. pap. v. 7 : Rep. from com. v. 3. Sess. 6 Dec. 1831-
16 Aug. 1832, no. 679.—*Notice in* "The Legal observer."
v. 5. 8°. London, no. 107, Nov. 3, 1832, p. 6, 7.
Report from the select committee on the copyright acts
of 8 Anne, c. 19; 15 Geo. III. c. 53 ; 41 Geo. III. c. 107 ;
and 54 Geo. III. c. 116. Ordered, by the H. of C., to be
printed, 5 June 1818. 8 p. Par. pap. v. 9: Rep. from
com. Sess. 27 Jan.-10 June 1818, no. 402.
Report from the select committee on the copyright bill;
together with the proceedings of the committee, and minutes of evidence. Ordered, by the H. of C., to be printed,
29 June 1864. 10 p. 1 l. Par pap. v. 9 : Rep. from com.
v, 5. Sess. 4 Feb.-29 July 1864, no. 441.
Return of literary works and books of prints entered at
Stationers' Hall, 1709-1826. Ordered, by the H. of C.,
to be printed, 9 May 1827. Par. pap. v. 20: Ac. and
pap. v. 4. Sess. 21 Nov. 1826-2 July 1827, no. 322.
Return of the amount of wholesale prices of one copy
of each book entered at Stationers' Hall during the years
1833, 1834 and 1835. (Mr. Arthur Trevor.) Ordered, by
the H. of C., to be printed, 22 June 1836. 2 p. Par. pap.
v. 47 : Ac. and pap. v. 11. Sess. 4 Feb.-20 Aug. 1836,
no. 357.
Return of the colonies and British possessions in favour of which orders in council have been issued under
the act 10 & 11 Vict. c. 95, suspending the prohibition of
importation of reprints of British copyright works; also, of
the nature and terms of the provision made for securing
or protecting the rights of British authors in such colonies, &c. (Mr. Headlam.) Ordered, by the H. of C., to
be printed, 25 Aug. 1857. 4 p. Par. pap. v. 28 : Ac. and
pap. v. 4. Sess. 30 April-28 Aug. 1857, no. 303.
A return of the manner in which the books received

under the copyright act, 54 Geo. 3, c. 156, and stated by a
return made to an order of this house, dated 20th Feb.
1818, as not placed in the public library of the University
of Cambridge,—have been disposed of. Ordered, by the
H. of C., to be printed, 9 April 1818. 4 p. 1 l. Par.
pap. v. 15: Ac. and pap. Sess. 27 Jan.-10 June, 1818,
no. 168.
Return of the number of volumes received from Stationers' Hall by the British Museum, under the late copyright act ; from the 1st of Jan. to the 31st of Dec. 1817.
Ordered, by the H. of C., to be printed, 3 March 1818.
2 p. Par. pap. v. 15 : Ac. and pap. Sess. 27 Jan.-10 June,
1818, no. 81.
Return relating to the registration of works of literature,
&c. (Mr. Black.) Ordered, by the H. of C., to be
printed, 16 March 1864. 2 p. Par. pap. v. 50: Ac. and
pap. v. 19. Sess. 4 Feb.-29 July 1864, no. 129.

GRIESINGER (Ludwig Friedrich). Der büchernachdruck, aus dem gesichtspunkte des
rechts, der moral und politik betrachtet.
88 p. 16°. Stuttgart, A. F. Macklot, 1822.
—— *See also* Schmid (Karl Ernst).

GUAY (Marcel). De la propriété intellectuelle.
Études de législation comparée. États-Unis.
Dispositions de l'acte du 8 juillet 1870 rela-
tives aux droits de copie. 13 p. 1 l. 8°. Paris,
E. Duchemin, 1877.
—— De la propriété littéraire, dramatique et
artistique dans les divers états de l'Amérique
latine. Études de législation comparée. 1°.
Mexique. About 20 p. 8°. Paris, E. Duchemin, 1876.
—— — De la propriété littéraire, ou explication
de la loi française des 14-19 juillet 1866 sur les
droits des héritiers et des ayants cause des
auteurs. About 61 p. 8°. Paris, E. Duchemin,
1876.
—— De la répression de la contrefaçon en
matière de propriété littéraire, d'après la
science rationnelle et les législations positives. About 59 p. 8°. Paris, E. Dentu, 1877.

GUIDA pratica degli ufficj comunali per la
tutela dei diritti d'autore sulle rappresentazioni teatrali. [*Anon.*] 72 p. 8°. Milano,
N. Battezzati, 1870.

GUIFFREY (Georges). De l'unité à introduire
dans la législation internationale de la pro-
priété littéraire et artistique. About 12 p. 8°.
Paris, Guiraudet, 1855.
—— De la propriété intellectuelle au point de
vue du droit et de l'histoire. About 68 p. 8°.
Paris, Beaulé, 1862 (?)
—— La propriété littéraire au 18e siècle. 1860.
See Association pour la défense de la pro-
priété littéraire. *See also* Diderot (Denis).

GUILLOT (Adolphe). Examen du projet de loi
sur la propriété littéraire. 8°. Paris, Jousset,
1863.

H. (J. L.) *See* Drone (Eaton Sylvester).

H. (R.) Further reasons addressed to parliament [etc.] 1737. *See* Carte (T:)

HABBERTON (J:) *See* The Publishers' weekly.

HALE (E: Everett). *See* The Publishers' weekly.

HALLIWELL-PHILLIPS (James Orchard). Observations on some of the manuscript emenda-
tions of the text of Shakespeare, and are they
copyright? 16 p. 8°, London, J. R. Smith,
1853.

HAMMOND (W: A.) *See* The Publishers' weekly.

HANDY-BOOK (A) on the law of the drama and music : being an exposition of the law of dramatic copyright, copyright in musical compositions, dramatic copyright in music, and international copyright in the drama and music. [*Anon.*] viii, 79 p. 16°. London, T. H. Lacy, 1864.

HARGRAVE (Francis). An argument in defence of literary property. 2 p.l. 52 p. 12°. London, printed for the author, [1774].
Anon. review in "The Monthly review." v. 51. 8°. London, Sept. 1774, p. 209-213.

HARPER & BROTHERS. [Memorandums in regard to international copyright between the United States and Great Britain.] 16 p. 8°. [New York, 1879.]
Contents: I. A suggestion to the Department of State, p. 3, 4. II.-III. Convention proposed in 1870 by lord Clarendon, p. 5-11. IV. Bill proposed by W: H. Appleton, p. 12. V. Extracts from W: H. Appleton's letter to the "London Times," p. 12, 13. VI. Extracts from G: Haven Putnam's address on international copyright, p. 14-16.

—— *Same. In* "The Publishers' weekly." v. 15. 8°. New York, no. 374, March 15, 1879, p. 317-324.

—— *Same :* [Second issue.] 55 p. 8°. [New York, 1880.]
Contents: Memorandums, p. 3-16. International copyright. Papers relating thereto in Macmillan's magazine [by S. S. Conant and "C.," *i.e.* Leonard H: Courtney]. With rejoinder [by S. S. Conant], p. 17-40. Copyright by Matthew Arnold, p. 41-55.
Notice by Moy Thomas in "The Academy." v. 15. 4°. London, no. 361, n. s., April 5, 1879, p. 303, 304. *Anon. notice in* "The Athenæum." 4°. London, no. 2684, April 5, 1879, p. 439. *Notice in* "The Popular science monthly." v. 15. 8°. New York, no. 86, June 1879, Editor's table, p. 265-268.

—— *See also* Messrs. Harper and the international copyright question. [Letter in reply to Moy Thomas, by W. J. Sillman, and rejoinder by Moy Thomas.] *In* "The Academy." v. 15. 4°. London, no. 364, n. s., April 26, 1879, p. 371.

HARPER'S new monthly magazine. 8°. New York.
Contains: v. 46, 1873. International copyright. [*Anon.*], p. 906-911.—v. 58, 1879. [International copyright.] Editor's easy chair, p. 929-931.—v. 61, 1880. [Wilkie Collins on copyright.] Editor's easy chair, p. 469, 470.—v. 62, 1881. [International copyright with Great Britain.] Editor's easy chair, p. 946, 947.

HARUM (Peter). Die gegenwärtige österreichische pressgesetzgebung. Systematische darstellung und erläuterung der gesetzlichen bestimmungen über das autorrecht und der presspolizeigesetzgebung mit einer einleitenden abhandlung über das autorrecht im allgemeinen. About x, 350 p. 8°. Wien, Manz, 1857.

—— Die pressordnung vom 27. Mai 1852 nebst jenen bestimmungen des neuen allgemeinen strafgesetzes, welche auf druckschriften anwendung finden und den sonstigen noch in kraft bestehenden darauf bezuglichen verordnungen, insbesondere dem allerhöchste patente zum schutze des geistigen eigenthumes vom 19. October 1846. About vi, 77 p. 8°. Pesth, Geibel, 1852.

HASTINGS (G: Woodyatt). On copyright and trade marks. Cantor lecture, Monday, Jan. 15, 1866. *In* "The Journal of the Society of Arts." v. 14. 8°. London, no. 687, Jan. 19, 1866, p. 135-137.

HAUMAN (A.) De la réimpression en Belgique. 31 p. 8°. Bruxelles, Meline, Cans & comp., 1851.

HAWKS (Francis L.) *See* American copyright club.

HAY (J:) *See* The Publishers' weekly.

HEADLEY (J: Tyler). *See* The Publishers' weekly.

HEDDE (Philippe). Propriété littéraire, initiative, priorité, plagiat [etc.] About 16 p. 8°. Paris, Baillière, 1851.

HELPS (Sir Arthur). International copyright between Great Britain and America : a letter to Charles Eliot Norton, Esq. [*Anon.* Signed A British author.] *In* "Macmillan's magazine.' v. 20. 8°. London, no. 116, June 1869, p. 89-95.

—— *Same. In* "Every Saturday." v. 7. 8°. Boston, no. 180, June 12, 1869, p. 742-745.

HEN (Charles). La réimpression. Étude sur cette question considérée principalement au point de vue des intérêts belges et français. [*Anon.*] 116 p. 12°. Bruxelles, A. Decq, 1851.

HENLEY (Robert Henley, 2d baron Henley). A treatise on the law of injunctions. 8°. London, for J. Butterworth & son, 1821.
Contains: Injunctions to restrain the infringement of copyright, p. 264-289. *Also in the same :* 1st Am. ed. 8°. Albany, W. Gould & co., 1822, p. 190-208. *Also in the same :* With notes by T: W. Waterman. 3d ed. 2 v. 8°. New York, Banks, Gould & co., 1852. 113 p. in v. 2.

HERCULANO DE CARVALHO E ARAUJO (Alexandre). Da propiedade litteraria da recente convençao com Franca. Carta ao sr. visconde de Almeida Garrett. About 34 p. 8°. Lisboa, na imp. nacional, 1851.

HÉREAU (Edme Joachim). Propriété littéraire. Droits d'auteurs en Russie. *In* "Revue encyclopédique." v. 34. 12°. Paris, mai 1827, p. 533-537.

HÉROLD (Ferdinand). Sur la perpétuité de la propriété littéraire. Extrait de la Revue pratique de droit privé du 1er mai 1862. 46 p. 8°. Paris, A. Marescq, 1862.

HERTSLET (Lewis) *and* HERTSLET (E:) A complete collection of the treaties and conventions subsisting between Great Britain & foreign powers. v. 1-12. 8°. London, H. Butterworth, 1827-71.
Note.—Contains copyright conventions, acts of parliament and orders in council relating to cop. The index to the series, in v. 12, contains 150 references under "Copyright."

HETZEL (Pierre Jules). Deux lettres publiées en mai 1862 [?], dans le Journal des débats, contre l'assimilation de la propriété littéraire avec la propriété du droit commun, et pour la création du domaine public payant. About 36 p. 12°. Paris, Hetzel, 1878.

HETZEL (Pierre Jules). La propriété littéraire et le domaine public payant. 8°. Bruxelles, Van Buggenhout, 1860.

—— *Same.* About 32 p. 8°. Paris, E. Dentu, 1862 [?].

—— *See also* Paillottet (Prosper). Examen du système de m. Hetzel sur la propriété littéraire.

HEYDEMANN (Ludwig Eduard). Sammlung der gutachten des Königlich-preussischen literarischen sachverständigen-Vereins herausgegeben von L. E. Heydemann. Nebst einem vorworte über die praxis des vereins und einem anhange von gesetzen und rescripten. About xlvi, 310 p. 8°. Berlin, T. C. F. Enslin, 1848.

—— *and* DAMBACH (Otto). Die preussische nachdrucks-gesetzgebung erläutert durch die praxis des königlichen litterarischen Sachverständigen-vereins. About xxviii, 632 p. 8°. Berlin, T. C. F. Enslin, 1863. [*i.e.*, 1862.]

HIGGINSON (T: Wentworth). *See* The Publishers' weekly.

HIGH (James Lambert). A treatise on the law of injunctions. 8°. Chicago, Callaghan & co., 1873.
Contains: Injunctions against the infringement of copyrights, p. 361-385.
Also in the same: 2d ed. 2 v. 8°. Chicago, Callaghan & co., 1880, v. 2, p. 622-687.

—— *See also* Drone (Eaton Sylvester).

HILLERN (Hermann von). Streitfragen aus dem autorrecht mit bezug auf zwei entscheidungen des reichsoberhandelsgerichts. 81 p. 8°. Freiburg i. Br., F. Wagner, 1876.

HILLIARD (Francis). The law of injunctions. 8°. Philadelphia, Kay & Brother, 1865.
Contains: Copyrights, p. 390-398.
Also in the same: 2d ed. 8°. Philadelphia, Kay & Brother, 1869, p. 469-480.
Also in the same: 3d ed. 8°. Philadelphia, Kay & Brother, 1874, p. 524-539.

HINTON (J:) *vs* DONALDSON (Alexander). *et al. See* Boswell (James).

HISTORY (The) of international copyright in Congress, 1866. *See* Spofford (Ainsworth Rand).

HITZIG (Julius Eduard). Das königl. preussische gesetz vom 11. Juni 1837 zum schutze des eigenthums an werken der wissenschaft und kunst gegen nachdruck und nachbildung. Dargestellt und erläutert durch J. E. Hitzig. viii, 122 p. 1 l. 8°. Berlin, F. Dümmler, 1838.

HOFFMANN (—). De la propriété littéraire sous le point de vue international. *In* "Revue de législation et de jurisprudence." v. 14. 8° Paris, 1841, p. 235-*seq.*

—— Ueber das urheberrecht an briefen. Inaugural dissertation. 12°. St. Gallen, 1874.

HOFFMANNS (— de). De la propriété littéraire, sous le point de vue international. *In* "Revue de bibliographie analytique." v. 2. 8°. Paris, 1841, mai, p. 467-480.

—— *Same.* About 16 p. 8°. Paris, Mme. Dondey-Dupré, 1841.

HOLLAND (Josiah Gilbert). *See* The Publishers' weekly. *See also* Scribner's monthly.

HOLMES (Oliver Wendell). *See* The Publishers' weekly.

HÖLZL (Joseph). Abhandlung über den büchernachdruck und die sicherung schriftstellerischer rechte. 2 p. l. 48 p. 8°. Wien, L. Grund, 1840.

HOOD (T:) Copyright and copywrong. Letters I.-III. *In* "The Athenæum." 1837. 4°. London, no. 494, April 15, p. 263-265. no. 495, April 22, p. 285-287. no. 496, April 29, p 304-306.

—— *Same :* Letters IV.-V. *In* "The Athenæum." 1842. 4°. London, no. 763, June 11, p. 524-526. no. 764, June 18, p. 544, 545.

—— *Same :* Letters I.-V. *In* Prose and verse by T: Hood. Part 2. 12°. New York, Wiley & Putnam, 1845, p. 73-122.

—— *Same :* Letters I.-V. *In* The Works of T: Hood. Edited by his son. 12°. London, E. Moxon & co., 1862, v. 4, p. 185-221. v. 6, p. 91-114.

—— Petition. *In* The Works of T: Hood. v. 5. 12°. London, E. Moxon & co., 1862, p. 365-367.

—— *Same. In* "The Monthly magazine : edited by J: A. Heraud." v. 3. 8°. London, no. 15, March 1840, p. 326, 327.

—— *Same. In* "The Publishers' weekly." v. 19, 8°. New York, no. 468, Jan. 1, 1881, p. 18, 19.

—— *See also* Lowndes (J: James).—Talfourd (Sir T: Noon).

HOOPER (H:) *See* Fisher (Robert Alexander). A digest of cases relating to patents and copyrights.

HÖPFNER (Ludwig). Der nachdruck ist nicht rechtswidrig. Eine wissenschaftliche erörterung, begleitet von einigen bemerkungen zu dem beigefügten, den versammelten ständen des königreichs Sachsen am 21. Novbr. 1842 vorgelegten gesetzentwurfe, den schutz der rechte an literarischen erzeugnissen und werken der kunst betreffend. 2 p. l. 94 p. 8°. Grimma, verlags-comptoir, 1843.

HOTTEN (J: Camden). Literary copyright. Seven letters addressed by permission to the right hon. the earl Stanhope. 2 p. l. vii-155 p. 12°. London, J. C. Hotten, 1871.
Anon. review in "The Athenæum." 4°. London, no. 2299, Nov. 18, 1871, p. 649.

HOWE (U. Tracy). International copyright. *In* "Western law journal." v. 2. 8°. Cincinnati, no. 8, May 1845, p. 347-352.
Note.—"I shall endeavor to maintain that we ought to establish an international copyright for three reasons: 1. In justice to authors ; 2. Because it would afford some

protection against the indiscriminate introduction of foreign literature ; 3. Because it would aid us to build up a sound, healthy national literature," p. 347.

HOWELLS (W: Dean). *See* The Publishers' weekly.

HUARD (Adrien). Dialogue des morts sur la propriété littéraire. 1862. *See* Beaume (Alexandre) *and* Huard.

—— Étude comparative des législations française et étrangères en matière de propriété industrielle, artistique et littéraire. 242 p. 12°. Paris, Cosse & Marchal, 1863.

—— *See also* Pelletier (Michel) *and* Defert (Henry).

HUGO (Victor Marie, comte). Discours d'ouverture du Congrès littéraire international. [Séance publique du 17 juin.] Le domaine public payant. [Séance du 21 juin et séance du 25 juin.] 30 p. 1 l. 8°. Paris, C. Lévy, 1878.

HUGUET (Auguste). *See* Annales de la propriété industrielle, artistique et littéraire.

—— *See also* Collet (Emile) *and* Le Senne (C.)

HUISH (Marcus B.) The year's art. A concise epitome of all matters relating to the arts of painting, sculpture, and architecture. 1880. 12°. London, Macmillan & co., 1880.
Contains : The copyright commission, p. 135-153.

—— *Same :* 1881. 12°. London, Macmillan & co., 1881.
Contains : Copyright, p. 177-182.

HUNT (W: HOLMAN). Artistic copyright. *In* "The Nineteenth century." v. 5. 8°. London, no. 25, March 1879, p. 418-424.

HUNTINGTON (Jedediah Vincent). Dr. Huntington on copyright. [Letter to "The Morning chronicle," New York, July 26, 1851.] *In* "The International magazine." v. 4. 8°. New York, no. 3, Oct. 1, 1851, p. 303-306.

HUXLEY (T: H:) Professor Huxley before the English copyright commission. [Questions and answers.] *In* "The Popular science monthly." v. 14. 8°. New York, no. 80, Dec. 1878, p. 166-182.

INQUIRY into the copyright act. 1819. *See* Southey (Robert).

INTERNATIONAL copy-right. [*Anon.*] *In* "The American law journal." v. 8, n. s. v. 1. 8°, Philadelphia, Aug. 1848, p. 49-62.

INTERNATIONAL copyright. [*Anon.*] *In* "The American law register." v. 2. 8°. Philadelphia, No. 3, Jan. 1854, p. 129-144.

INTERNATIONAL copyright. [*Anon.*] *In* "The Knickerbocker." v. 22. 8 . New York, no. 4, Oct. 1843, p. 360-364.

INTERNATIONAL copyright. [*Anon.*] *In* "The New-Yorker." v. 8. 4°. New York, H. Greeley & co., no. 4. Oct. 1839, p. 49, 50.

INTERNATIONAL copyright. [*Anon.*] *In* "Putnam's magazine." v. 9. 8°. New York, no. 49, Jan. 1857, p. 85-91.

INTERNATIONAL copyright association. *See* Copyright (The) association for the protection and advancement of literature and art.

INTERNATIONAL copyright between Great Britain and America. 1869. *See* Helps (Sir Arthur).

INTERNATIONAL copy-right.—Injustice to authors. [*Anon.*] *In* "The Democratic age." v. 1. 8°. New York, 1859, p. 34-39.

INTERNATIONAL (The) copyright question. [*Anon.*] *In* "The United States magazine and democratic review." N. s. v. 12. 8°. New York, no. 56, Feb. 1843, p. 115-122.

INTERNATIONAL copyright.—The claims of literature. [*Anon.*] *In* "United States democratic review." N. s. v. 42. 8°. New York, no. 6, Dec. 1858, p. 454-464.

INTERNATIONAL copyright with Great Britain. *See* Carter (Timothy Harrington).

Is an abridgment an infringement of the copyright of the original work? [*Anon.*] *In* "The American law register." v. 3. 8°. Philadelphia, Jan. 1855, p. 129-136.

Is copyright perpetual? 1875. *See* Drone (Eaton Sylvester).

IST der nachdruck schon nach gemeinen deutschen positiven rechten für unerlaubt zu halten? [*Anon.*] 8°. Halle, Curt, 1796.

ITALY. *Ministero di agricoltura, industria e commercio. (Direzione dell' industria e del commercio).* Annali dell' industria e del commercio 1881. Num. 33. Legislazione sulla proprietà letteraria ed artistica. Convenzione tra l'Italia e la Spagna : legge e regolamenti vigenti in Spagna sulla proprietà intellettuale. 52 p. 8°. Roma, E. Botta, 1881.

—— *See also* Annuaire de législation étrangère, 1875.

JACOB (Ephraim A.) An analytical digest of the law and practice of the courts of England, comprising the reported cases from 1756 to 1878, founded on the digests of Harrison and Fisher. v. 2. 8°. New-York, G: S. Diossy, 1879.
Contains : Copyright, col. 2376-2432.

JACOB (Giles). The law-dictionary. Enlarged by T: E. Tomlins. 1st Am. from 2d London ed. 6 v. 8°. New-York, I. Riley, 1811.
Contains : Literary property, v. 4, p. 183-189.
Note.—The same article with additions *in* The law-dictionary. By sir T : Edlyne Tomlins, 4th ed. by T : C. Granger, 4th. Londou, for J. & W. T. Clarke etc., 1835, 7 cols. in v. 2.

JEFFERYS *vs.* BOOSEY. House of lords. Aug. 1, 1854. Reported by James Paterson. *In* "The Law times :" Reports. v. 23. fol. London, 1854, p. 275-282.

—— *Same. In* Leverson (Montague R:) Copyright. 8°. London, Wildy & sons, 1854. Appendix, p. i-lxii.

—— *Same.* Editorial remarks. *In* "The Jurist." v. 18, part 2, 1854. 8°. London, no. 919, p. 285, 286, no. 920, p. 293, 294.

JERROLD (Sidney). A handbook of English and foreign copyright in literary and dramatic works, being a concise digest of the laws regulating copyright in some of the chief countries of the world, together with an analysis of the chief copyright conventions existing between Great Britain and foreign countries. xiv p. 1 l. 112 p. 12°. London, Chatto & Windus, 1881.

Anon. notice in "The Athenæom." 4°. London, no. 2818, Oct. 29, 1881, p. 558, 559.

JOBARD (Jean Baptiste Ambroise Marcellin). Nouvelle économie sociale, ou monautopole industriel, artistique, commercial et littéraire. xii, 5-475+4 duplicate p. 8°. Paris, Mathias : Bruxelles, chez l'auteur, 1844.

Contains: Propriété littéraire, p. 172-175. Question des limites de la propriété intellectuelle. [With letter from J. Meeus Vandermaelen], p. 268-277. Un pas vers la propriété intellectuelle en Angleterre, p. 333-341.

—— Organon de la propriété intellectuelle. 353 p. 12°. Paris, Mathias, 1851.

Review by Gustave de Molinari in "Journal des économistes." v. 30. 1851. 8°. Paris, p. 176, 177.

JOLLY (Julius). Die lehre vom nachdruck. Nach den beschlüssen des deutschen bundes dargestellt. vi, 314 p. 8°. Heidelberg, J. C. B. Mohr, 1852. [Archiv für die civilistische praxis. Beilageheft. 35. band].

JONA (Giovanni). Alcune parole sulla proprietà letteraria. About 46 p. 8°. Padova, coi tipi della Minerva, 1841.

—— *Same.* Della proprietà letteraria, discorso pronunciato nel giorno della sua promozione alla laurea legale da Giovanni Jona di Gorizia. About 48 p. 8°. Padova, coi tipi della Minerva, 1841.

JONES (T. E.) *See* Britton (J:) The rights of literature.

JORDAO PAIVA MANSO (Levy Maria). A propriedade litteraria nao existia entre os romanos. 15 p. *In* Academia real das sciencias de Lisboa. Historia e memorias. Nova serie, v. 2, part 2. 4°. Lisboa, 1863.

—— *Same.* De la propriété littéraire chez les Romains. Traduit du portugais par L. Bonneville de Marsangy. *In* "Revue critique de législation et de jurisprudence." v. 20. 8°. Paris, 1862, p. 441-457.

—— *Same.* 8°. Paris, Cotillon, 1862.

JOURNAL (The) of the Society of arts. v. 1-29. 1852-1881. Sm. 4°. London, 1853-81.

Contains; v. 6. Cop. in fine arts. [Committee appointed], p. 91. [Circular signed by the secretary of the committee, P. Le Neve Foster], p. 103. Art cop. [Notice of report by D. R. Blaine], p. 167. Report of the art. cop. com., p. 293-296. Mr. Blaine's report to the com. on art. cop., p. 296-301. [Circulars], p. 302. Art. cop. [Petition to the House of Lords], p. 455. 456. Literary and art. cop. [Congress at Brussels], p. 578, 579. [Resolutions of the congress], p. 707, 708.—v. 10. Art. cp. [Address by sir T: Phillips], p. 12, 13. Literary and art. cop. in France, p. 164. Art. cop. [Efforts to amend the law], p. 511. Art. cop. An act for amending the law relating to cop. in works of the fine arts, 29th July, 1862, p. 592-594.—v. 12. [Art. cop. com. and Mr. Black's bill], p. 364. Cop. in engravings ; cop. bill in House of Commons, p. 577. Cop. act of engravings : case of infringement, p. 631.—v. 14. On copyright and trade marks. By G: W. Hastings, p. 135-137. Cop. in works of art ; [Report of the council], p. 544. Law of cop. in France, p. 560. A case of cop. [Lithograph from engraving of a picture by Pils], p. 619. Law of cop. [with America], p. 695.—v. 17. Case of art. property. [Photograph], p. 147. Cop. convention between France and Belgium, p. 399. Cop. in works of fine art : [A bill for consolidating and amending the law of cop. in

works of fine art. Speeches in the House of Lords, 30th April 1869 by lord Westbury, earl Stanhope, and the earl of Kimberley], p. 469-472.—v. 18. Cop. in newspaper articles, p. 124.—v. 19. Int. cop., p. 28.—v. 20. Cop. association, p. 358, 359.—v. 27. Cop. [Lord J: Manner's bill], p. 879, 880.—v. 29. Cop. [Com. of the Social Science association] p. 418, 419. Cop. [Law amendment society bill], p. 654.

JOYCE (W:) The doctrines and principles of the law of injunctions. 8°. London, Stevens & Haynes, 1877.

Contains: Copyright, p. 153-163.

—— The law and practice of injunctions in equity and at common law. 2 v. 8°. London, Stevens & Haynes, 1872.

Contains: Copyright, v. 1, p. 270-311.

Also in the same. v. 1, 8°. Cincinnati, R. Clarke & co., 1872, p. 270-308.

JUDEICH (Edm.) Vortrag über das recht der schriftsteller und künstler an ihren werken. Gehalten am 13. März 1867 zu Dresden. About 29 p. 8°. Dresden, [Burdach], 1867.

KAISER (Hermann). Die preussische gesetzgebung in bezug auf urheberrecht, buchhandel und presse. Zusammenstellung aller auf diesen gebieten zur zeit gültigen gesetze und verordnungen nebst gerichtlichen entscheidungen, anmerkungen und erläuterungen herausgegeben von H. Kaiser. xliv, 304 p. 8°. Berlin, E. H. Schroeder, 1862.

—— *Same:* Ergänzungsheft. xxii p. 1 l. 168 p. 8°. Berlin, E. H. Schroeder, 1865.

KANT (Immanuel). Von der unrechtmässigkeit des büchernachdrucks. 1785. *In his* Sämmtliche werke. Herausgegeben von Karl Rosenkranz und Friedr. Wilh. Schubert, 7ten theils 1ste abtheilung. 8°. Leipzig, L. Voss, 1838, p. 155-167.

Note.—Originally published in "Berliner monatsschrift," May 1785.

—— *Same.* Analysis of Kant's doctrine of the rights of authors. [By Luther Stearns Cushing.] *In* "The American jurist." v. 22. 12°. Boston, 1840, p. 84-92.

—— *Same.* Over het onregtmatige van het nadruk. *In* "Tijdschrift voor staathuishoudkunde en statistiek." (2de serie. 5de deel). 8°. Zwolle, 1859, p. 92-101.

KAPP (Friedrich). Der deutsch-amerikanische buchhandel. *In* "Deutsche rundschau." 4ter jahrgang. 8°. Berlin, heft 4, Jan. 1878, p. 42-70.

KAYSER (Albert Cristopher). Die abstellung des büchernachdrucks, als ein in der neuesten kaiserlichen wahlkapitulation der reichsoberhauptlichen abhülfe ebenso nöthig als unbedenklich zu übertragender gegenstand betrachtet. 8°. Regensburg, 1790.

KENRICK (W:) An address to the artists and manufacturers of Great Britain [etc.] To which is added, an appendix, containing strictures on some singular consequences attending the late decision on literary property. 4°. London, Domville, 1774.

Anon. review in "The Monthly review." v. 51. 8°. London, Oct. 1774, p. 276-281.

KENT (James). Commentaries on American law. v. 2. 8°. New York, O. Halsted, 1827.
Contains: Personal property. III. Of original acquisition by intellectual labour, p. 298-313.
Also in the same: 12th ed., edited by O. W. Holmes, jr. v. 2. 8°. Boston, Little, Brown, & co., 1873, p. [474-511].

KERN (J. Conrad). La convention entre la Suisse et la France sur la propriété littéraire, artistique et industrielle, du 30 juin 1864, et son application en Suisse, avec le texte du traité et d'autres documents officiels. 8°. Paris, J. Cherbuliez, 1867

KERR (W. Williamson). Injunctions against the infringement of copyright. *In* A treatise on the law of injunctions. By W. W. Kerr. 8°. London, W. Maxwell & son, 1867, p. 439-473.
Also in the same: Edited by W: A. Herrick. 8°. Boston, Little, Brown, & co., 1871, p. 456-492.
Also in the same: 2d ed. 8°. London, W. Maxwell & son, 1878, p. 317-356.
Also in the same: 2d Am., from the 2d Eng. ed. edited by W: A. Herrick. 8°. Boston, Little, Brown, & co., 1880, p. 256-291, or p. *317-*356.

KLETKE (G. M.) Gesetzgebung des königreichs Bayern über den schutz des eigenthums an erzeugnissen der literatur und kunst gegen veröffentlichung, nachbildung und nachdruck, sowie musikalischer und dramatischer werke gegen unbefugte aufführung; ferner über die freiheit der presse und des buchhandels, und bestrafung des missbrauchs der presse. About 103 p. 8°. Regensburg, Pustel, 1860.

KLOSTERMANN (Rudolf). Das geistige eigenthum an schriften, kunstwerken und erfindungen, nach preussischem und internationalem rechte dargestellt. 1. Bd. Allgemeiner theil.—Verlagsrecht und nachdruck, xii, 452 p. 8°. Berlin, I. Guttentag, 1867.
Note. Volume 2 treats of patents.

—— *Same:* 1. Band. Das urheberrecht und das verlagsrecht nach Deutschen und ausländischen gesetzen systematisch und vergleichend dargestellt. Nebst einem anhange: Das urheberrecht an schriftwerken etc. nach dem reichsgesetze vom 11. Juni 1870. 2 p. l. xii, 452 p. 2 l. 74 p. 8°. Berlin, I. Guttentag, 1871.

—— Das urheberrecht an schrift- und kunstwerken, abbildungen, compositionen, photographien, mustern und modellen, nach deutschem und internationalem rechte systematisch dargestellt. viii, 282 p. 8°. Berlin, F. Vahlen, 1876.

—— Das urheberrecht an schriftwerken, abbildungen, musikalischen compositionen und dramatischen werken nach dem reichsgesetze vom 11. Juni 1870 systematisch dargestellt. 2 p. l. 74 p. 8°. Berlin, I. Guttentag, 1871.

KNIGGE (Adolph Franz Friedrich Ludwig, freiherr von). Ueber den büchernachdruck, an Joh. Gottwerth Müller. 8°. Hamburg, A. Campe, 1791.

KOHLER (J.) Das autorrecht, eine zivilistische abhandlung. *In* "Jahrbücher für die dogmatik d. heutigen römischen und deutschen

privatrechts. Herausgegeben von R. Jhering." v. 18. 8°. Jena, 1880, p. 129-478.

KOHLER (J.) *Same:* Zugleich ein beitrag zur lehre vom eigenthum, vom miteigenthum, vom rechtsgeschäft und vom individualrecht. (Separatabdruck mit register versehn). 1 p. l, 352 p. 8°. Jena, G. Fischer, 1880.

KORB (Ferdinand). Was heisst und ist das geistige eigenthum an literarischen erzeugnissen. Ein beitrag zur theorie des nachdrucks und verlagsrechts. 1 p. l. 96 p. 1 l. 8°. Breslau, A. Gosohorsky, 1869.

KOWALZIG (F.) Das reichsgesetzliche urheberrecht an schriftwerken, das reichshaftpflichtgesetz, das reichs- und territorialgesetzliche versicherungsrecht, die altpreussischen und gemeinrechtlichen bestimmungen über schiedsgerichte erläutert. About iv, 163 p. 8°. Berlin, Springer, 1877 [*i. e.* 1876.]

KRAMER (Wilhelm August). Die rechte der schriftsteller und verleger. Ein versuch. 2 p. l. 164 p. 8°. Heidelberg, C. F. Winter, 1827.

KRAUSE (Chr. Sigismund). Ueber büchernachdruck. [Motto] That's wormwood.—Hamlet. 4 p. l. 52 p. 12°. Stuttgart, A. F. Macklot, 1823.

KRUG (Wilhelm Traugott). Schriftstellerei, buchhandel und nachdruck rechtlich, sittlich und klüglich betrachtet. Eine wissenschaftliche prüfung des Wangenheim'schen vortrags darüber beim bundestage. viii, 123 p. 8°. Leipzig, F. A. Brockhaus, 1823.

KÜHNS (Friedrich Julius). Gesetzentwurf der deutschen kunstgenossenschaft betreffend das recht des urhebers an werken der bildenden künste nebst einer rechtfertigenden denkschrift. About 54 p. 8°. Berlin, E. H. Schröder, 1864.

—— Der rechtsschutz an werken der bildenden künste. Eine denkschrift im namen der deutschen kunstgenossenschaft. About 53 p. 8°. Berlin, I. Guttentag, 1864.

LABOULAYE (Édouard René Lefebvre). De la propriété littéraire en Angleterre. *In* " Revue de législation et de jurisprudence." Nouv. coll. v. 1. 8°. Paris, 1852, p. 129-187.

—— *Same:* (2ème article). Législation de la propriété littéraire (copyright) en Angleterre [et aux États-Unis.] *In* "Revue de législation et de jurisprudence." Nouv. coll. v. 2. 8°. Paris, 1852, p. 289-321.

—— Études sur la propriété littéraire en France et en Angleterre, suivies des trois discours prononcés au parlement d'Angleterre par sir T. Noon Talfourd, traduits de l'anglais par Paul Laboulaye. 3 p. l. liv p. 1 l. 200 p. 8°. Paris, A. Durand, 1858.
Contents: I. De la propriété littéraire en France, 1 l. p. i-liv. II. De la propriété littéraire en Angleterre : Histoire du droit de propriété littéraire (copyright) en Angleterre, p. 1-82 : Discours par M. Talfourd [18 May 1837, 25 April 1838 and 28 Feb. 1839], p. 83-151 : Lois anglaises sur la propriété littéraire et convention avec la France. [Edited by Paul Laboulaye], p. 153-199.

—— *See also* Association pour la défense de la propriété littéraire.

LABOULAYE (Paul). Étude sur le droit de propriété littéraire en Allemagne. *In* " Revue historique de droit français et étranger." 1ère année. 8°. Paris, 1855.

—— *Same.* About 36 p. 8'. Paris, A. Durand, 1855.

—— *See also* Talfourd (Sir T: Noon). Three speeches in favour of copyright. Trois discours [etc.] 1858.

LACAN (Adolphe Jean Baptiste) *and* PAULMIER (Charles Pierre Paul). Traité de la législation et de la jurisprudence des théâtres, avec un appendice sur la propriété des ouvrages dramatiques, etc. 2 v. 8°. Paris, A. Durand, 1853.
Review by Charles Vergé in "Journal des écouomistes." 2e série v. 2. 8°. Paris, 1854, p. 279-281.

LAFERRIÈRE (Louis Firmin Julien). Histoire du droit français (époque révolutionnaire): propriété littéraire. Principe fondamental. *In* " Revue de législation et de jurisprudence." v. 5. 8°. Paris, 1837, p. 80–*seq.*

LA GUÉRONNIÈRE (Arthur, vicomte de). *See* Champagnac (Gustave de).

LAIDLEY (Theodore T. S.) Colonel Laidley's reply to the charge of infringement of colonel Wingate's copyright. 36 p. 8°. Boston, Mills, Knight & co., 1879.

LALLY TOLENDAL (Trophime Gérard, marquis de). Observations sur la nature de la propriété littéraire. About 12 p. 4°. Paris, Pillet ainé, 1826.

—— *Same :* [2e éd.] About 8 p. 4". Paris, Pillet ainé, 1826.
Note.—Originally published *in* FRANCE. *Commission de la propriété littéraire.* Collection des procès-verbaux. 4°. Paris, Pillet ainé, 1826, p. 113-122.

LAMARTINE (Alphonse Marie Louis Prat de). De la propriété littéraire. Rapport fait à la chambre des députés [mars 1841]. About 32 p. 8°. Paris, C. Gosselin, 1841.

—— *Same. In* Œuvres de m. A. de Lamartine. [v. 14, or] Tribune v. 2. 8°. Paris, F. Didot frères, 1849, p. 3–50.

—— Discours sur la propriété littéraire et artistique, prononcé à la chambre des députés le 13 mars 1841. 16 p. 8°. [Macon, imprimerie de Dejussieu, 1841.]

LANGE (Max). Kritik der grundbegriffe vom geistigen eigenthum. Auf grundlage der einleitung zum gesetze vom 11. Juni 1837 und mit besonderer rücksicht auf die preussische gesetzgebung überhaupt. vi, 116 p. sq. 12°. Schoenebeck, E. Berger, 1858.

LARNAUDE (—). De la protection de la propriété littéraire dans ses rapports internationaux. Rapport présenté au Congrès littéraire international. About 11 p. 8°. Paris, Chaix & ce, 1878.

LATHROP (G: Parsons). *See* The Publishers' weekly.

LAURENT (Émile). La liberté de l'imprimerie et de la librairie. *In* " Journal des économistes." 3e série. v. 16. 8°. Paris, 1869, p. 392-413.

LA VECCHIA (Gioacchino). Sull' indole del diritto degli autori di opere dell' ingegno : dissertazione. About 100 p. 4°. Palermo, B. Virzì, 1878.

LAW (Édmund, bishop of Carlisle). Observations occasioned by the contest about literary property. [*Anon.*] 8°. Cambridge, Archdeacon, 1770.

LAW (Stephen D.) Copyright and patent laws of the United States, 1790 to 1866. With notes of judicial decisions thereunder and forms and indexes. 12°. New York, by the author, and Baker, Voorhis & co., 1866. [Copyright, p. 14–73.]

—— *Same :* 2d ed. 12°. New York, by the author, and Baker, Voorhis & co., 1867.

—— Digest of American cases relating to patents for inventions and copyrights from 1789 to 1862. Arranged in chronological order with the year in which and the name of the judge by whom decided. 697 p. 8°. New York, by the author, 1862.
Anon. review by James T. Mitchell in " The American law register." v. 11, n. s. v. 2. 8°. Philadelphia, March 1863, p. 319, 320.

—— *Same :* Revised ed. References conformed to reports published since 1862. 697 p. 8°. New York, by the author, and Baker, Voorhis & co., 1870.

—— *Same :* 5th and revised ed., with a supplement containing the existing patent and copyright laws of the United States and Canada. 697 + [235] p. 1 l. 8°. New York, by the author, and F: D. Linn, Jersey City, 1877.
Anon. notice in " The American law review." v. 1. 8°. Boston, no. 2, Jan. 1867, p. 369, 370.

—— Statute laws of the United States of America relating to copyright and patents for inventions from 1790 to 1862 with notes. 128 p. 8°. New York, by the author, 1862. [Copyrights, p. 5-29. Index, p. 113-116.]

—— *Same :* 1790 to [1869]. 128 p.+112 a-c p. 8°. New York, 1870. [Copyrights, p. 8-29. Index, p. 113-116.]

LAW concerning property in literary productions, etc. [*Anon.*] 8°. London, 1794.

LAW of copyright. [*Anon.*] *In* "The British and foreign review." v. 8. 8°. London, no. 16, April, 1839, p. 333-359.

LAW of copyright. [*Anon.*] *In* " The United States law intelligencer." v. 1. 8°. Providence, no. 3, March 1829, p. 66-73.

LAW (The) of copyright as applied to oral lectures. [*Anon.*] *In* " The Medical news and abstract." v. 39. 8°. Philadelphia, no. 6, June 1881, p. 371, 372.

LAW of copyright, regarding authors, dramatic writers, and musical composers ; as altered by the recent statute of the 5 & 6 Victoria, analysed and simplified. By a barrister. [*Anon.*] 8°. London, 1842.

LAW (The) of copyright with respect to abridgments. 1847. *See* Walker (Timothy).

LAW (The) of literature and art. 1874. *See* Drone (Eaton Sylvester).

LAWRENCE (W: Beach) *vs.* DANA (R: H:, *jr.*) *et al.* Circuit court of the United States. Massachusetts district. [1866-1867]. In equity. Counsel for complainants B. R. Curtis. J. J. Storrow. Counsel for respondents. For Miss Wheaton, Sidney Bartlett, T. K. Lothrop. For Little, Brown & co., Causten Browne. For R. H. Dana, jr., W. G. Russell. [Bill.— Answers. — Complainant's evidence. — Respondents' evidence.—Exhibits. Also brief for complainant. 673 p. 1 l. 3 slips.] 8°. Boston, A. Mudge & son, 1867.

—— —— Brief for complainant. Counsel for complainant. B. R. Curtis. J. J. Storrow. 1 p. l. iii, 98, vii p. 3 slips. 8°. Boston, A. Mudge & son, 1867.

—— —— Complainant's affidavits. [And supplemental affidavit of E. R. Potter.] 1 p. l. 5-98, 5 p. 8°. Boston, A Mudge & son, 1866.

—— —— Arguments of B. R. Curtis and J. J. Storrow, esqs., for the complainant, on the question of title. Reported by J. M. W. Yerrinton. 2 p. l. 105 p. 8°. Boston, A. Mudge & son, 1868.

—— —— Closing argument for the complainant on the question of piracy. B. R. Curtis, J. J. Storrow, for the complainant. viii, 3-255 p. 1 slip. 8°. Boston, A. Mudge & son, 1868.

—— —— Clifford and Lowell, jj. Opinion of the court, delivered Sept. 20, 1869. [Also, Decree, Oct. term, 1869.] 47, 3 p. 8°. Boston, A. Mudge & son, 1869.

—— —— *Same.* Reported in "The American law times reports." N. s. v. 2. 8°. New York, Hurd & Houghton, no. 9, Sept. 1875, p. 402-432.

—— —— Synopsis, taken from the record of testimony of Dana, as to originality. The findings and decree of the court, and evidence as to notes copied and original. [*Anon.*] 11 p. 12°. [*n.p. n.d.*]

LE BARROIS D'ORGEVAL (Robert). La propriété littéraire en France et à l'étranger. Son histoire—sa législation suivie des conventions internationales conclues jusqu'à ce jour avec les principaux états de l'Europe. 199 p. 8°. Paris, E. Dentu, 1868.

LEBRET (Georges Adolphe). Faculté de droit de Paris. Droit romain : De l'acquisition de la propriété et de ses démembrements par actes entre vifs. Droit français : Du droit des auteurs et des artistes sur leurs œuvres. Thèse pour le doctorat. 2 p. l. 228 p. 8°. Paris, Lahure, 1878.

—— La propriété littéraire et artistique. Du droit des auteurs et des artistes sur leurs œuvres. 153, vi p. 8°. Paris, A. Lahure, 1878.

LEGGETT (W:) A collection of the political writings of W: Leggett, selected by Theodore Sedgwick, jr. 2 v. 12°. New York, Taylor & Dodd, 1840.

Contains : v. 2. Copy right law no monopoly. (From

the Evening post, Sept. 27, 1836.) p. 88-90. Rights of authors. (From the Plaindealer, Jan. 21, 1837) p. 174-180. The rights of authors. (From the Plaindealer, Feb. 11, 1837.) p. 207-214. Right of property in the fruits of intellectual labour. (From the Plaindealer, Feb. 25, 1837.) p. 225-227.

LEGISLACION de la propiedad literaria en España. Precedida de las discusiones habidas en las cortes con motivo de la ley de 10 de junio de 1847, y seguida de notas y comentarios por un abogado de esta corte. [*Anon.*] 268 p. 1 l. 8°. Madrid, Libreria de Moya y Plaza, 1863 [1864.]

LE HARDY DE BEAULIEU (Charles). *See* Vermeire (P.)

LEHR (Ernest). Éléments de droit civil germanique considérés en eux-mêmes et dans leurs rapports avec la législation française. xx, 464 p. 8°. Paris, E. Plon & cie, 1875. *Contains :* Du droit d'auteur, p. 26-35.

LEIGHTON (F:) *and* WELLS (H: T.) Government and the artists. [Letters to the editor on artistic copyright.] *In* "The Nineteenth century." v. 6. 8°. London, no. 34. Dec. 1879, p. 968-984.

—— *Same. In* "The Nineteenth century." [Am. reprint] v. 1. fol. New York, no. 5, Dec. 1879, p. 7-12.]

LELIUS (—). Le dernier traité littéraire conclu entre la France et la Saxe. *In* " Journal des économistes." 2e série. v. 11. 8°. Paris, 1856, p. 115-118.

LEMERCIER (Népomucène Louis). Principes et développemens sur la nature de la propriété littéraire. About 12 p. 4°. Paris, Pillet aîné, 1826. *Note.*—Originally published *in* FRANCE. *Commission de la propriété littéraire.* Collection des procès-verbaux 4°. Paris, Pillet aîné, 1826, p. 91-99.

LERMINA (Jules). Rapport supplémentaire au nom de la 3e commission du Congrès littéraire international. Communication de mm. Mendès Léal (Portugal) et Blanchard Jerrold (Angleterre). Résolutions et vœux du congrès. About 10 p. 8°. Paris, Chaix & ce, 1878.

LESAGE (Victor). *See* Calmels (Antoine Édouard).

LESENNE (Charles). A propos d'André Chénier. 1879. *See* Collet (Émile) *and* Lesenne.

LE SENNE (Napoléon Madeleine). Le livre des nations, ou traité philosophique, théorique et pratique des droits d'auteur et d'inventeur en matière de littérature, de sciences, d'arts et d'industrie. 2 p. l. iii, 327 p. 8°. Paris, A. Durand, 1846.

—— *Same :* Brevets d'invention. Traité des droits d'auteur et d'inventeur en matière de littérature, de sciences, d'arts et d'industrie. 2e éd. 8°. Paris, Comon, 1849.

LETTER (A) from a gentleman in Edinburgh, to his friend in London ; concerning literary property. [*Anon.*] 20 p. 8°. [Edinburgh], 1769.

LETTER (A) from an author to a member of parliament, 1747. *See* Warburton (W:, bishop of Gloucester).

LEVASSEUR (Pierre Émile). *See* Association pour la défense de la propriété littéraire et artistique. La propriété littéraire au 18e siècle. 1860.

LEVERSON (Montague R:) Copyright and patents ; or, property in thought : being an investigation of the principles of legal science, applicable to property in thought ; with their bearing on the case of Jefferys *v.* Boosey, recently decided by the house of lords. To which is appended a corrected report of the judgments delivered by the lord chancellor, lord Brougham, and lord St. Leonards. [Reported by James Paterson.] vii, 56, lxii p. fol'd chart. 12°. London, Wildy & sons, 1854.

LEVI (Leone). Copyrights and patents. *In* "The Princeton review." 54th year. 8°. New York, Nov. 1878, p. 743-775.

—— International commercial law. 2d ed. 2 v. 8°. London, V. & R. Stevens, sons & Haynes, 1863.
Contains: Copyright. v. 2. p. 567-597.

—— International copyright in relation to the United States of America and other foreign states. 13 p. 8°. London, W: Clowes & sons, 1879.
Note.—Published by the Association for the reform and codification of the law of nations.

—— Manual of the mercantile law of Great Britain and Ireland. xxiv, 286 p. 1 slip errata. 8°. London, Smith, Elder & co., 1854.
Contains: The law of copyright, p. 64-80.

—— *Same.* 8°. Philadelphia, T. & J. W. Johnson, 1854. [Law library. v. 84.]
Contains: The law of copyright, p. 63-74.

LEYPOLDT (F:) *See* The Publishers' weekly.

LIEBER (Francis). On international copyright ; in a letter to the hon. W: C. Preston, senator. 67 p. 8°. New York, Wiley & Putnam, 1840.

—— *Same. In* Contributions to political science. By F. Lieber. Being v. 2. of his miscellaneous writings. 8°. Philadelphia, J. B. Lippincott & co., 1881. [*i.e.* 1880], p. 329-367.
Anon. notice by Luther Stearns Cushing? in "The American jurist." v. 24. 8°. Boston, no. 47, Oct. 1840, p. 246-248.
Anon. notice in "The North American review." v. 51. 8°. Boston, no. 109, Oct. 1840, p. 513-515.
Anon. review by G: Mifflin Wharton in "The North American review." v. 52. 8°. Boston, no. 111, April 1841, p. 385-404.
Review by Silvestre Pinheiro-Ferreira in "Revue étrangère de législation et d'économie politique." v. 8. 8°. Paris, 1841, p. 170, seq.
Anon. review in "The Southern quarterly review." v. 1. 8°. Charleston, no. 1, Jan. 1842, p. 252-258.
—— *See also* Copyright (The) association.—Prussia.

LIMOUSIN (Charles M.) De la propriété intellectuelle industrielle. About 42 p. 8°. Amiens, imp. Jeunet ; Paris, Guillaumin & ce, 1873.

—— La propriété intellectuelle - industrielle. Réponse à l'article de m. Michel Chevalier. *In* "Journal des économistes." 4e série. v. 2. 8°. Paris, 1878, p. 425-432.

LINGUET (Simon Nicolas Henri). Betrachtungen über die rechte des schriftstellers und seines verlegers. Aus dem französischen. [By Ph. Erasmus Reich.] 8°. Bremen, Cramer, 1778.

LIPPINCOTT (Sarah Jane Clarke). Copyright, authors, and authorship. *In* Greenwood leaves. By Grace Greenwood. [*Pseud.*] 12°. Boston, Ticknor, Reed & Fields, 1850, p. 283-308.
Contains: Poems and sketches.—A call for a convention of authors, at Faneuil Hall, to discuss the question of international copyright. By J. G. W. (J: Greenleaf Whittier?), p. 283-285.—A touching incident. By J. R. C. (Joseph R. Chandler?), p. 285-287.—To a young poet. By W. C. B. (W: Cullen Bryant?), p. 287, 288.—A tale of horror. By E. A. P. (Edgar Allan Poe?), p. 288-291.—A song. By G. P. M. (G: P. Morris?), p. 291, 292.—Poet-dreams. By F. G. H. (Fitz-Greene Halleck?), p. 292, 293.—Letter from the author of "Typee." (Herman Melville), p. 294-296.—A sketch. By N. P. W. (Nathaniel Parker Willis?), p. 296-298.—Night's revealings. From the ancient Sclavonian of Hans Hammergafferstein. By H. W. L. (H: Wadsworth Longfellow?), p. 298-300.—Apollo in America. By O. W. H. (Oliver Wendell Holmes?), p. 300-302.—Letter from New York. By L. M. C. (Lydia Maria Francis Child), p. 303, 304.—Warblings. By F. S. O. (Frances Sargent Osgood), p. 304, 305.—A fragment. By L. H. S. (Lydia Huntly Sigourney), p. 305, 306.—A fable from the Burmese. By F. F. (Fanny Fern?--Sarah Parker Willis Parton), p. 306-308.
Note.—"Originally appeared anonymously, in the Saturday evening post of Philadelphia."

LITERARISCHE (Das) eigenthum. Eine rechtsfrage. [*Anon.*] *In* "Deutsche vierteljahrsschrift." 23ster jahrg. 1860. 8°. Stuttgart, J. G. Cotta, 1stes heft. p. 97-105.

LITERARY property. [*Anon.*] *In* "The American jurist and law magazine." v. 1. 8°. Boston, Jan. 1829, p. 157-177.

LITERARY property. [*Anon.*] *In* "The New York review." v. 4. 8°. New York, no. 8, April 1839, p. 273-307.
Note.—Reviews: Remarks on literary property. By P. H. Nicklin, 1838. A plea for authors. [*Anon.*] 1838.

—— *Same :* An article on literary property. From The New York review, no. viii. April 1839. [*Anon.*] 2 p. l. 35 p. 8°. New York, G: Adlard, 1839.

LITERARY property. [*Anon.*] *In* "The United States magazine and democratic review." v. 2. 8°. Washington, no. 7, June 1838, p. 289-311.

LITERARY property. Late judgments of the chancellor. [*Anon.*] *In* "The Edinburgh review." v. 38. 8°. Edinburgh, no. 76, May 1823, p. 281-314.

LOCRÉ DE BOISSY (Jean Guillaume, baron de). Discussions sur la liberté de la presse, la censure, la propriété littéraire, l'imprimerie et la librairie, qui ont eu lieu dans le conseil d'état, pendant les années 1808, 1809, 1810 et 1811. Rédigées et publiées par m. le baron Locré. 3 p. l. 300 p. 8°. Paris, Garnery, 1819.

LONGFELLOW (H: Wadsworth). *See* The Publishers' weekly.

LONGMAN (C: James). A publisher's view of
international copyright. *In* " Fraser's magazine." v. 103. 8°. London, no. 615, March
1881, p. 372-378.

—— *Same. In* " The Publishers' weekly." v.
19. 8°. New York, no. 482, April 9, 1881,
p. 408-411.

LOSANA (Cesare). Del diritto d'autore: dissertazione libera. About 80 p. 8°. Torino,
G. Derossi, 1872.

LOWE (Joseph). Copyright. Reprinted from
Napier's supplement to the Encyclopædia
Britannica. *In* Nicklin (Philip Houlbrooke).
Remarks on literary property. 16°. Phila-
pelphia, P. H. Nicklin & T. Johnson, 1838,
p. 97-144.

LOWNDES (J: James). An historical sketch of
the law of copyright; with remarks on serjeant Talfourd's bill ; and an appendix of the
copyright laws of foreign countries. 139 p.
8°. London, Saunders & Benning, 1840.

—— *Same:* 2d ed. 2 p. l. vii-xiii, 131 p. 8°.
London, Saunders & Benning, 1842.
Anon. notice in "The Athenæum." 4°. London, no.
641, Feb. 8. 1840, p. 114.
Review by T; Hood, in The works of T: Hood. v. 5. 12°.
London, E. Moxon & co., 1862, p. 363-365.
Anon. review signed S. in " The Jurist." v. 4. 8°. Lon-
don, no. 166, March 14, 1840, p. 162-164.

LOZZI (Carlo). Della proprietà letteraria e
delle edizioni privilegiate. *In* " Il Bibliofilo.
Giornale dell' arte antica in istampe e scrit-
ture e ne' loro accessorii e ornati colla rela-
tiva giurisprudenza." Anno I. 8°. Firenze,
nr. 11, Nov. 1880.

LYON-CAEN (Charles). *See* Fliniaux (Charles).

M. (E.) Copyright. 1879. *See* Marston (E:)

MACAULAY (Mrs. Catherine Sawbridge). *Afterwards Mrs. Graham.* A modest plea for the
property of copy-right. By Catherine Macaulay. 4°. London, Dilly, 1774.
Anon. review in " The Monthly review." v. 51. 8°.
London, Oct. 1774, p. 272-276.
Anon. notice in "The United States law intelligencer."
v. 3. 8°. Philadelphia, no. 8, Aug. 1831, p. 276-280.

MACAULAY (T: Babington, baron Macaulay).
A speech delivered in the house of commons
on the 5th of Feb. 1841. A speech delivered
on the 6th of April, 1842. [Both on copyright.] *In* The Works of Macaulay. Edited
by his sister, lady Trevelyan. v. 8. 8°. London, Longmans, 1866, p. 195-208 ; and p. 209
-216.

MACFIE (Robert Andrew). Copyright and patents for inventions. Pleas and plans for
cheaper books and greater industrial freedom,
with due regard to international relations,
the claims of talent, the demands of trade,
and the wants of the people. v. 1. xx, 406 p.
8°. Edinburgh, T. & T. Clark, 1879.
Anon. notice in " The Athenæum." 4°. London, no.
2694, June 14, 1879, p. 751.
Anon. review in " The Journal of jurisprudence." v.
23. 8°. Edinburgh, no. 272, August 1879, p. 436, 437.
Editorial notice in "The Publishers' weekly." v. 16. 8°.
New York, no. 390, July 5, 1879, p. 12.

MACFIE (Robert Andrew). Copyright in its relation to the supply of books to libraries and
the public. *In* Transactions and proceedings
of the third annual meeting of the Library
association of the United Kingdom held at
Edinburgh, Oct. 5, 6 and 7, 1880. Edited by
Ernest C. Thomas and C: Welch. 4°. London, C. Whittingham & co., 1881, p. 107-113.

—— Literary copyright : how to practically deal
with it. *In* National association for the promotion of social science. Transactions. 1880.
8°. London, Longmans, 1881, p. 164-171.

—— On patent and copyright monopolies. *In*
National association for the promotion of
social science. Transactions. 1874. 8°.
London, Longmans, 1875, p. 256-261.

—— The patent question under free trade :
a solution of difficulties by abolishing or
shortening the inventor's monopoly, and in-
stituting national recompenses. 8°. London,
Longmans, 1864.
Contains : On the distinction between copyright and
patent-right.

—— Recent discussions on the abolition of
patents for inventions in the United Kingdom, France, Germany, and the Netherlands.
Evidence, speeches, and papers in its favour.
With suggestions as to international arrangements regarding inventions and copyright,
viii, 342 p. 8°. London, Longmans, 1869.
Contains : Notes and extracts on royalty in copyright,
with especial reference to international negotiations affecting North America, p. 291-332.

MACLAURIN (J:, lord Dreghorn). Considerations
on the nature and origin of literary property :
wherein that species of property is clearly
proved to subsist no longer than for the terms
fixed by the statute 8vo Annæ. [*Anon.*] 1 p. l.
34 p. 8°. Edinburgh, A. Donaldson, 1767.

—— On the origin and progress of literary property. *In* The works of the late J: MacLaurin. v. 2. 8°. Edinburgh, J. Ruthven & sons,
1798, p. 73-136.

—— *Same. In* Macfie (Robert Andrew). Copyright and patents. v. 1. 8°. Edinburgh, T.
& T. Clark, 1879, p. 1-32.

MACLEOD (H: Dunning). Copyright. *In* Cyclopædia of political science. Edited by
J: J. Lalor. v. 1. 8°. Chicago, Rand, McNally
& co., 1881, p. 642-648.

—— A dictionary of political economy. v. 1.
2 p. l. 683 p. 8°. London, Longmans, 1863.
Contains : Copyright, p. 552-557.

MALAPERT (Pierre Antoine Frédéric). Histoire abrégée de la législation sur la propriété
littéraire avant 1789. *In* " Journal des économistes." 4e série. 8°. Paris, v. 12, no. 35,
nov. 1880, p. 252-291 ; v. 13, no. 37, mars
1881, p. 437-476.

—— *Same.* About 83 p. 8°. Paris, Guillaumin
& cie, 1881.

MANCINI (Pasquale Stanislao). Intorno alla proprietà letteraria italiana e ad un opuscolo di Raffaele Carbone [entitled La voce de' tipografi e degli studiosi del regno delle Due Sicilie]. Ragionamento dell' avvocato P. S. Mancini. 8°. Napoli, tipografia di R. Trombetta, 1841.

—— *Same:* 2a ed. 39 p. 8°. Napoli, tipografia di R. Trombetta, 1841.

MANDRY (Gustav). Das gesetz vom 28. Juni 1865 zum schutze der urheberrechte an literarischen erzeugnissen und werken der kunst erläutert. About x, 53–453 p. 8°. Erlangen, Palm & Enke, 1867. [Die Gesetzgebund des königreichs Bayern seit Maximilian II. mit erläuterungen herausgegeben von F. von Dollmann. 1ster theil, 5. Bd. 2. heft.]

—— *Same:* Das urheberrecht an literarischen erzeugnissen und werken der kunst. Ein kommentar zu dem königl. bayer. gesetze vom 28. Juni 1865. Separatabdruck aus der "Gesetzgebung des königreichs Bayern." About viii, 401 p. 8°. Erlangen, Palm & Enke, 1867.
Anon. review signed F. D. in "Literarisches centralblatt für Deutschland." 4°. Leipzig, nr. 52, Dec. 1869, col. 1542–1544.

MANSFIELD (Earl of). *See* Murray (W:)

MANZONI (Alessandro). Considerazioni intorno ad un parere legale sopra una questione di proprietà letteraria. Insorta tra il cav. A. Manzoni e l'ed. F. Lemonnier. 36 p. 8°. Genova, tipografia del r. i. de' Sordo-Muti, 1861.
Review by Jules Pautet in "Journal des économistes." 2e série. v. 34. 8°. Paris, 1862, p. 318–320.

MARCHI (F. de). La propriété littéraire, artistique et industrielle, en Turquie et en Egypte. 8°. Paris, Maisonneuve, 1881.

MARESCHAL (Jules). Du droit héréditaire des auteurs, et des erreurs du congrès de Bruxelles, suivi d'un discours sur les beaux-arts. 4 p. l. 174 p. 8°. Paris, L. Hachette & cie, 1859.

——· Les droits de l'auteur et le droit du public, relativement aux œuvres de l'esprit. About 40 p. 8°. Paris, Hachette & cie., 1866.

—— Mémoire à consulter sur la question juridique de la propriété perpétuelle et héréditaire des œuvres de l'esprit. About 116 p. 8°. Paris, Librairie nouvelle, 1861.

—— Observations lues en la séance du 9 janvier, 1826. *In* France. *Commission de la propriété littéraire.* Collection des procès-verbaux. 4°. Paris, Pillet aîné, 1826, p. 123–135. Note additionnelle, p. 159–162.

MARIE (—). De la propriété intellectuelle. *In* "Revue de législation et de jurisprudence." 8°. Paris. v. 1, 1835, p. 81, *seq.* p. 262, *seq.* v. 2, 1835, p. 161, *seq.*
Note.—This is perhaps Pierre Thomas Alexandre de St. Georges Marie.

MARSH (G: Perkins). *See* The Publishers' weekly.

MARSHALL (Walker). Copyright in the fine arts. (Read on the 20th April, 1863.) *In* The Juridical society. Papers read before the society. v. 2. 8°. London, W. Maxwell, 1863, no. 34, p. 722–734.

MARSTON (E:) Copyright, national and international, from the point of view of a publisher. [By E. M., *Anon.*] 48 p. 8°. London, S. Low, Marston, Searle & Rivington, 1879.
Anon. notice in "The Academy." v. 15. 4°. London, no. 359, n. s. March 22, 1879, p. 258.
Anon. notice in "The Athenæum." 4°. London, no. 2690, May 17, 1879, p. 631.

—— International copyright with America. *In* "The Academy." v. 11. 4°. London, no. 249, n. s. Feb. 10, 1877, p. 117, 118.

—— [Letter on international copyright. By E. M. London, March 15, 1881.] *In* "The Publishers' circular." v. 44. 8°. London, no. 1044, March 15, 1881, p. 201–203.

—— *Same. In* "The Publishers' weekly." v. 19. 8°. New York, no. 482, April 9, 1881, p. 407, 408.

MARTINEAU (Harriet). *See* Scribner's monthly.

MATHEWS (Albert). *See* Murray (W:, earl of Mansfield)

MATHEWS (C: James). Lettre de m. Charles Mathews aux auteurs dramatiques de la France : with a translation. 8°. London, J. Mitchell, 1852.
Anon. review in "The Athenæum." 4°. London, no. 1293, Aug. 7, 1852, p. 838, 839.
Anon. review in "The Literary gazette." 4°. London, no. 1853, July 24, 1852, p. 581, 582.
Review by C: Reade in The eighth commandment. By C: Reade. 8°. London, Trübner & co., 1860. p. 42–64.

MATHEWS (Cornelius). An appeal to American authors and the American press in behalf of an international copyright. *In* "Graham's lady's and gentleman's magazine." v. 21, 8°. Philadelphia, no. 3, Sept. 1842, p. 121–124.

—— *Same.* 16 p. 16°. New-York and London, Wiley & Putnam, 1842.

—— *Same. In* The various writings of C. Mathews. 8°. New York, Harper & brothers, 1843, p. 358–362.

—— The better interests of the country, in connexion with international copy-right : (a lecture delivered at the lecture-room of the Society library, Feb. 2, 1843.) 30 p. 16°. New-York and London, Wiley & Putnam, 1843.

—— *Same. In* The various writings of C. Mathews. 8°. New York, Harper & brothers, 1843, p. 362–370.
Anon. review by W: Gilmore Simms in "The Southern quarterly review." v. 4. 8°. Charleston, no. 7, July, 1843, p. 1–46.

—— A speech on international copyright, delivered at the dinner to C: Dickens, at the City Hotel, New York, Feb. 19, 1842. (Revised by the speaker.) 16 p. 12°. New York, published at the office of "Arcturus," by G: L. Curry & co., 1842.

—— *Same. In* The various writings of C. Mathews. 8°. New York, Harper & brothers, 1843, p. 355–358.

—— *See also* American copyright club.

MATTHEWS (J. Brander). *See* Scribner's monthly.

MAUGHAM (Robert). A treatise on the laws of literary property, comprising the statutes and cases ; with a historical view, and disquisitions on the principles and effects of the laws. xxii p. 1 l. 262 p. 8°. London, Longmans, 1828.
Anon. review in "The American jurist." v. 2. 8°. Boston, July-Oct. 1829, p. 248-267. *Anon. review in* "The Westminster review." v. 10. 8°. London, no. 20, April 1829, p. 444-465.

MEEUS VANDERMAELEN (J.) *See* Jobard (Jean Baptiste Ambroise Marcellin). Nouvelle économie sociale. 1844.

MÉGRET (Léon). *See* Cappellemans (Victor).

MEINERT (F. W.) Drei abhandlungen. vi., 38, 20 & 14 p. 8°. Leipzig, B. G. Teubner, 1844.
I. Ueber die rechte der autoren und ihrer erben bei neuen auflagen eines werkes, (unter hinweisung auf mehrere deutsche gesetzgebungen und vornehmlicher bezugnahme auf die bestimmungen in §§. 4 und 5 des bevorstehenden neuen königlich Sächsischen "Gesetzes zum schutz der rechte an literarischen erzeugnissen und werken der kunst."), p. 1-38.
— Das Königlich Sächsische gesetz vom 22. Febr. 1844, zum schutz der rechte an litterarischen erzeugnissen und werken der kunst, mit kritisch-exegetischen erläuterungen versehen. iv, 81 p. 1 l. 8°. Leipzig, B. G. Teubner, 1844.

MELE (Carlo). Sulla proprietà letteraria, ragionamento di C. Mele. About 28 p. 8°. Napoli, dalla tipografia Flautina, 1837.

MEMORIAL of the printers and booksellers of Glasgow, most humbly addressed to the honorable the house of commons, assembled in parliament ; occasioned by a petition given in by booksellers of London, for a new act to lengthen out the monopoly further than the act of Queen Anne ; and thereby put Scotland in a worse situation than hitherto with respect to this matter. About 23 p. 4°. Glasgow, 1774.

MERGER (C. B.) Dictionnaire de droit commercial. 1852. *See* Goujet (Charles) *and* Merger.

MERLIN (Philippe Antoine). Recueil alphabétique de questions de droit. 4ème éd. v. 12. 8°. Bruxelles, H. Tarlier, 1829.
Contains: Propriété littéraire, p. 174-196.

METZ (Friederich). Geschichte des buchhandels und der buchdruckerkunst. 8°. Darmstadt, J. W. Heyer, 1835.
Contains: Bücher-nachdruck, p. 37-51 : Bücher-privilegien, p. 52-57.

METZ-NOBLAT (Alexandre de). Des brevets d'invention et des droits d'auteur. *In* Mémoires de l'Académie de Stanislas. 1857. 8°. Nancy, Grimblot, veuve Raybois & comp., 1858, p. 48-76.
— *Same.* About 31 p. 8°. Nancy, Grimblot, ve Raybois & cie, 1858.

MILLAR (Andrew) *vs.* TAYLOR (Rob.) [Easter term, 1769. Literary property.] *In* Burrow (Sir James). Reports of cases in the court of king's bench. 2d ed. v. 4. 8°. London, A. Strahan & W. Woodfall, 1790, p. 2303-2417.

MILLAR (Andrew) *vs.* TAYLOR (Rob.) The question concerning literary property, determined by the court of king's bench on 20th April, 1769, in the cause between Millar and Taylor : with the separate opinions of the four judges. iv, 127 p. 4°. London, W. Strahan & M. Woodfall, for B. Tovey, 1773.
Note. Edited by Sir James Burrow.
Anon. review in "The Monthly review." v. 51. 8°. London, Aug. 1774, p. 81-90.
— Speeches or arguments of the judges of the court of king's bench, viz. mr. justice Willes, mr. justice Aston, sir Joseph Yates, and lord c. justice Mansfield in April 1769 ; in the cause Millar against Taylor. To which are added notes, and an appendix, containing a short state of literary property, by the editor. [*Anon.*] viii, 128 p. 12°. Leith, W. Coke, 1771.
Note. The anonymous editor is strongly opposed to Lord Mansfield's opinion.
— *See also,* Evans (W: D:)

MITCHELL (Donald Grant). *See* The Publishers' weekly.

MODESTE (Victor). *See* De la propriété intellectuelle. 1859.

MOLINARI (Gustave de). De la propriété littéraire et de la contrefaçon belge. *In* "Journal des économistes." v. 31. 8°. Paris, 1852, p. 252-270.
— Propriété littéraire et artistique. *In* Coquelin (Charles) *and* Guillaumin (Urbain Gilbert). Dictionnaire de l'économie politique. 3e éd. v. 2. 8°. Paris, Guillaumin & cie., 1864, p. 473-478.
— *See also* Muquardt (Charles).—Nion (Alfred).

MONTAGU (Basil). Enquiries and observations respecting the university library. 1 p. l. 30 p. 8°. Cambridge, F. Hodson, 1805.
— Enquiries respecting the proposed alteration of the law of copyright, as it affects authors and the universities. 1 p. l. lvii p. 8°. London, for J Butterworth, 1813.

MONTALEMBERT (Comte de) *contre* LOYSON (Charles). Propriété littéraire et mandat testamentaire. La famille et les exécuteurs testamentaires du comte de Montalembert contre m. Charles Loyson (ex Père Hyacinthe) et la Revue suisse. About 108 p. 8°. Paris, Plon & ce, 1877.

MONTEFIORI (Joshua). The law of copy-right ; being a compendium of acts of parliament and adjudged cases. 8°. London, 1802.

MORGAN (James Appleton). Anglo-American international copyright, being an open letter to hon. W: M. Evarts, secretary of state. 1 p. l. 55 p. 12°. New York, Brentano's literary emporium, 1879.
Anon. notice in "The Academy." v. 15. 4°. London, no. 367, n. s. May 17, 1879, p. 433.
— International copyright. *In* "The Athenæum." 4°. London, no. 2449, Oct. 3, 1874, p. 447, 448.
— International copyright. An address, delivered before the Manhattan liberal club,

(New York, Aug. 23, 1878). 2 p. l. 27 p. 8°.
New York, Cockcroft & co., 1878.
Notice with extract in " The Publishers' weekly." v.
14, 8°. New York, no. 349, Sept. 14, 1878, p. 299.

MORGAN (James Appleton). The law of literature reviewing the laws of literary property in manuscripts, books, lectures, dramatic and musical compositions; works of art, newspapers, periodicals, &c. ; copyright transfers, and copyright and piracy, etc. With an appendix of the American, English, French, and German statutes of copyright. 2 v. xviii, 513 p. xvii, 817 p. 8°. New York, J. Cockcroft & co., 1875.

— *Same.* 2 v. 8°. London, 1876.
Notice in " The Forum." v. 3. 8°. New York, no. 7, July 1875, p. 595.
Anon. review by Eaton Sylvester Drone in " New York daily Tribune," Nov. 5, 1875, p. 6.
Review by James O. Pierce in "The Southern law review." N. s. v. 1. 8°. St. Louis, no. 4, Jan. 1876, p. 763-774.
Anon. notice in " The Spectator." v. 50. fol. London, no. 2538, Feb. 17, 1877, p. 223.

— Piracy by memorization. *In* " The American law register." v. 23, n. s. v. 14. 8°. Philadelphia, April 1875, p. 207-214.

— *See also.* The Publishers' weekly.—Shortt (J:)

MORILLOT (André). De la nature du droit d'auteur, considéré à un point de vue général. *In* " Revue critique de législation et jurisprudence." Nouv. série. v. 7. 8°. Paris, no. 2, fév. 1878, p. 111-136.

— De la protection accordée aux œuvres d'art, aux photographies, aux dessins et modèles industriels et aux brevets d'invention dans l'empire d'Allemagne. About xi, 264 p. 8°. Paris, Cotillon, 1878.

— *See also* Germany. Loi du 9 jan.—11 jan. 1876 concernant le droit d'auteur.

MORISON (B:) An embodiment of the patent laws in force, to which are added a brief synopsis of the copy-right laws in force. 3d ed. 1 p. l. 16 p. 8°. Philadelphia, 1869.

MORISON (W: Maxwell). The decisions of the court of session, digested under proper heads, in the form of a dictionary. v. 20. 4°. Edinburgh, printed for Bell & Bradfute, 1804.
Contains: Literary property [14 cases, 1748-1804], p. 8295-8320 and Appendix 19 p.

MORSTADT (Carl Eduard). C. E. Morstadt's kritisch-pragmatischer commentar über Mittermaier's grundsätze des deutschen privatrechts is (arretirt gewesenes) heft, als probe. Commentar über Mittermaier's theorie von verlagscontract, schrifteigenthum, nachdruck und collegienheften. xvi, 102 p. 1 l. 8°. Heidelberg, Im selbstverlage des verfassers, 1831.

MOURLON (Frédéric). Examen du projet de loi sur la propriété littéraire et artistique, précédé d'une dissertation sur l'imperfection de notre droit privé et la méthode à suivre pour éviter à l'avenir les défauts qui le déparent. Extrait de la Revue pratique de droit français (tomes 17, 18.) 2 p. l. 116 p. 8°. Paris, Marescq aîné, 1864.

MOVENS pratiques de garantir la propriété littéraire. [By Un libraire éditeur. *Anon.*] 4 p. 12°. [Paris, Crapelet 1850.]

MUDIE (Robert). The copyright question, and mr. serjeant Talfourd's bill. About 54 p. 8°. London, 1838.

MUNSELL (Joel). Catalogue of books on printing and the kindred arts : embracing also works on copyright, liberty of the press, libel, literary property, bibliography, etc. 2 p. l. 47 p. 8°. Albany, J. Munsell, 1868.
Contains: Copyright, titles no. 37-80. Literary property, titles no. 210-216.

MUQUARDT (Charles). De la propriété littéraire internationale, de la contrefaçon et de la liberté de la presse. 62 p. 12°. Bruxelles ; Leipzig ; Gand, C. Muquardt, 1851.

— *Same :* Das literarische eigenthumsrecht, der nachdruck und das wesen der presse in beziehung auf journal- und bücher-literatur. Eine analyse. 80 p. 12°. Brüssel ; Leipzig ; Gent, C. Muquardt, 1851.

— Le droit d'auteur et le brevet d'invention. 8°. Bruxelles, C. Muquardt, 1853.
Review by Gustave de Molinari in " Journal des économistes." v. 35. 8°. Paris, 1853, p. 302-304.

MURRAY (W:, earl of Mansfield). The arguments of lord Mansfield, in favour of the author's perpetual copyright, and of those judges whose arguments he read, approved and adopted. *In* Duppa (R:) An address to the parliament. of Great Britain. 2d ed. 8°. London, Longmans, 1813, p. 47-58.

— *Same.* Lord Mansfield's opinion. Letter from Albert Mathews. *In* Copyright (The) association for the protection and advancement of literature and art. International copyright. 8°. New York, 1868, p. 33-35.

— *See also* Evans (W: D:)

NATION (The). v. 1-34, 4°. New York, 1865-1882.
Contains : v. 1, 1865. Editorial notice of G: Ticknor Curtis's opinion in copyright case of Ticknor & Fields *vs.* Bunce & Huntington ; " Home ballads by our home poets," p. 437. One branch of native industry that needs protection. *Anon.* by W. Dean Howells, p. 774, 775.
—v. 2, 1866. Ed. notice of the decision in the case of " Haunted Hearts " by Maria S. Cummins ; Residence in Canada at the time of publication in England, p. 19. Ed. review of the case of the proprietorship of an opera by Nicolai ; Foreigners can hold and transfer a cop. in England, p. 213. Notice of the case of the Christmas illustration of the Illustrated London news ; Protection to prints from paintings, p. 611. Ed. notice of the case of Pierre Hubert Nysten's Dictionnaire de médecine, p. 659.—v. 3, 1866. International cop. in Congress, the duty on books ; Cop. in songs, the right of an author of a song to control the public singing of it, Editorial, p. 24.—v. 4, 1867. Who owns an author's ideas? *Anon.* reply by Edwin Lawrence Godkin, to Mr. Merriam's letter in The Springfield republican arguing against int. cop., p. 520-522.—v. 6, 1868. Authors versus readers. *Anon.* review by E. L. Godkin of H: C: Carey's Letters on international copyright, p. 147, 148. Copyright and patent right. By Alfred Eastman Walker, p. 168, 169. Ed. note on J: Denison Baldwin's int. cop. bill, p. 169. Simple justice. *Anon.* art. in favor of int. cop., p. 265-267. Ed. notice of " International copyright " by the Copyright association, p. 452, 453. Notice of S. Low, Son & Marston *vs.* G: Routledge & sons, case of Haunted hearts by M. S. Cummins, p. 511.—v. 7, 1868. Abstract right of copyright. Letter signed A. Aaron Mich. Rejoinder by ed. Nation, p. 248, 249.—v. 10, 1870. Ed. notice of " Copy before publication " ; an *anon.* review of the case of Crowe *vs.* Aiken, p. 320, 321. Notice of case of " Frou-Frou," p. 338.—v.

Index to Nation.

NATIONAL association for the promotion of social science. Transactions 1859–1880. 8°. London, 1860–81.

Contains: 1859. On the protection of property in intellectual labour as embodied in inventions, books, designs, and pictures. By T: Webster, p. 237–244: On international copyright property in works of literature and the fine arts. [Summary of paper by Delabere Roberton Blaine], p. 272, 273.—1862. On international copyright in works of literature, music, and the fine arts. By D. R. Blaine, p. 866–869.—1866. On the best means of extending and securing an international law of copyright. By Anthony Trollope, p. 119–125, and discussion, p. 243, 244.—1874. On patent and copyright monopolies. By Robert Andrew Macfie, p. 256–261.—1879. What action should be taken on the report of the Royal commission on copyright? By C: H: E: Carmichael, p. 195–204; [Review of the evidence of the copyright commission on the royalty system. By J. N. Porter], p. 446, 447.—1880. Trade marks and copyright. How can the international difficulty with regard to trade marks and copyright, caused by recent judgments of the supreme court of the United States, best be met? By C: H: E: Carmichael, p. 154–164; Literary copyright: how to practically deal with it. By R. A. Macfie, p. 164–171; Copyright. Report of a sub-committee appointed Dec. 3, 1880, and adopted by the council, Feb. 17, 1881. [Signed by J: Westlake, J: Leybourn Goddard, and W: Fooks], p. 862–865.

NEFF (Paul). Ueber die eigenthumsrechte der schriftsteller und künstler und ihrer rechtsnachfolger. 16 p., 8°. Stuttgart, P. Neff, 1838.

NEUMANN (Max). Beiträge zum deutschen verlags- und nachdrucksrechte bei werken der bildenden künste, im anschluss an die frage vom rechtsschutze der photographie gegen nachdruck. xii, 142 p. 8°. Berlin, I Guttentag, 1866.

—— Der rechtschutz der photographie gegen nachdruck nach den deutschen nachdrucksgesetzen. Eine denkschrift. About 50 p. 8°. Leipzig, R. Hoffmann in comm., 1866.

NEUSTETEL (Leopold Joseph). Der büchernachdruck, nach römischem recht betrachtet. 1 p. l. 84 p. 12°. Heidelberg, C. Groos, 1824.

NEW (The) copyright bill. [*Anon.*] *In* "The Eclectic review." N. s. v. 3. 8°. London, June 1838, p. 693–704.

NEW (The) copyright law. [*Anon.*] *In* "The American monthly magazine," v. 11, or v. 5, n. s. 8°. New York, no. 2. Feb. 1838, p. 105–112.

NEWCOMB (Simon). See Andrews (E: L.)

NEVRON (Pierre Joseph, translator). *See* Pütter (Johann Stephan). La propriété littéraire défendue, 1774.

NICKLIN (Philip Houlbrooke). Remarks on literary property. 144 p. 16°. Philadelphia, P. H. Nicklin & T. Johnson, 1838.

Contains also: Copyright by Joseph Lowe, p. 97–144. *Anon. review* signed C. [Luther Stearns Cushing?] in "The American jurist." v. 19. 8°. Boston, p. 476–479.
Anon. review [By Willard Phillips] in "The North American review." v. 48. 8°. Boston, no. 102, Jan. 1839, p. 257–270.

—— *See also* Literary property.

NICOLSON (James Badenach). [Law of copyright.] *In* Erskin (J:) An institute of the

law of Scotland, v. 1. 4°. Edinburgh, Bell & Bradfute, 1871, p. 264–269.

NIGON DE BERTY (Louis). *See* Gastambide (Joseph Adrien).

NIMROD. *Pseud.* Common-law rights to literary property. *In* "The Albany law journal." v. 15. 4°. Albany, June 9, 1877, p. 445–447 ; June 16, 1877, p. 465–468.

NION (Alfred). Droits civils des auteurs, artistes et inventeurs, ou application des dispositions des codes civil, de commerce et de procédure, aux droits attribués par les lois existantes aux auteurs et inventeurs en matière d'art, de science, de littérature et d'industrie. 2 p. l. iii, 488 p. 8°. Paris, Joubert, 1846.

Anon. Review by G. M. [Gustave de Molinari ?] in "Journal des économistes." v. 16. 8°. Paris, 1847, p. 88, 89.
Review by Raymond de Fresquet in "Revue de droit français et étranger." v. 13, part 2. 8°. Paris, 1846, p. 18 *seq.*

No international copyright law. [*Anon.*] *In* "The American athenæum." v. 1. fol. New York, no. 1, Jan. 4, 1868, p. —, no. 7, Feb. 15, 1868, p. 105, 106.

NOCH einige worte über den büchernachdruck und zugleich über den buchhandel. [*Anon.*] 8°. Pappenheim, 1823.

NORMAN (J: Paxton). The law and practice of the copyright, registration and provisional registration of designs ; and the copyright and registration of sculpture ; with practical directions: the remedies, pleadings & evidence in cases of piracy: with an appendix of statutes [etc.]. xii, 185 p. 16°. London, S. Sweet, 1851.

NORTON (C: Eliot). *See* The Publishers' weekly.

NORWAY. *See* Annuaire de législation étrangère. 1875, 1876 & 1877.

NOTE sur la propriété littéraire, 1836. *See* Baudouin (Alexandre).

NOVELLO (Joseph Alford.) The true theory of literary copyright. *In* "The Athenæum." 1862, part 2. 4°. London, no. 1821, Sept. 20, 1862, p. 371, 372.

—— *Same.* Abstract in "The Jurist." N. s. v. 8, part 2. 8°. London, no. 404, Oct. 4, 1862, p. 447, 448.

OBSERVATIONS occasioned by the contest about literary property. 1770. *See* Law (Edmund).

OBSERVATIONS on the law of copyright. 1838. *See* Webster (G:).

OBSERVATIONS sur l'article 18 du projet de loi contenant la propriété littéraire. [*Anon.*] 8°. Paris, Crapelet, 1839.

OF the copy-right and good will of newspapers. [*Anon.*] *In* "The United States law intelligencer and review." Ed. by Joseph K. Angell. v. 3. 8°. Philadelphia, no. 12, Dec. 1831, p. 443–450.

ON international copyright. [*Anon.*] *In* "Tinsley's magazine." v. 9. 8°. London, Dec. 1871, p. 528–533.

On the justice and expediency of establishing an international copyright law. [*Anon.*] *In* "The Metropolitan magazine." American ed. v 2. 8°. New York, Aug. 1836, p. 63–68.

—— *Same.* De la propriété littéraire en Europe, et de la nécessité d'en régler l'action par une loi internationale. [*Anon.* A free translation with additions.] *In* "Revue britannique." 4e série. v. 4. 8°. Paris, août 1836, p. 255–274.

[*Note.* This, together with an article from "Revue de Pari ," 9 Oct. 1836, was published without title, about iv–16 p. 8°. Paris, Éverat, 1836.

OPPEN (Otto Heinrich Alexander von). Beiträge zur revision der gesetze · 1. Büchernachdruck. 2. Duell. 3. Ehe und scheidung. 4. Gesinderecht. vi, 161 p. 8°. Köln am Rhein, J. P. Bachem, 1833.

Contains: Ueber büchernachdruck, p. 1–44.

ORTLOFF (Hermann Friedrich). Das autor- und verlagsrecht als strafrechtlich zu schützendes recht. *In* "Jahrbücher für die dogmatik d. heutigen römischen und deutschen privatrechts. Herausgegeben von Rud. Ihering. v. 5. 8°. Jena.

OSGOOD (S:) *See* Copyright (The) association.

PAILLOTTET (Prosper). Examen du système de M. [Pierre Jules] Hetzel sur la propriété littéraire. *In* "Journal des économistes." 2e série. v. 34. 8°. Paris, 1862, p. 430–444.

—— *See also* De la propriété intellectuelle. 1859.—Vermeire (P.)

PALFREY (J: Gorham). International copyright. *In* "The North American review." v. 55. 8°. Boston, no. 116, July 1842, p. 245–264.

PARSONS (Theophilus). Laws of business. Revised ed. 8°. Hartford, S. S. Scranton & co., 1875.

Contains: The law of copyright. [With forms.] p. 591–598.

Also in the same: 1876, p. 591–598; 1879, p. 695–702 ; 1880, p. 695–702.

PARTON (James). International copyright. *In* "The Atlantic monthly." v. 20. 8°. Boston, Oct. 1867, p. 430–451.

—— *Same.* *In* Topics of the times. By J. Parton. 12°. Boston, J. R. Osgood & co., 1871, p. 95–131.

—— *Same.* Abridged. *In* Duyckinck (Evert A:) *and* Duyckinck (G: Long). Cyclopædia of American literature. Ed. by M. Laird Simons. v. 2. 4°. Philadelphia, T. E. Zell, 1875, p. 805–808.

—— *See also* The Publishers' weekly.

PASSY (Frédéric). De la propriété intellectuelle au point de vue du droit. *In* "Journal des économistes." 2e série. v. 22. 8°. Paris, 1859, p. 397–404.

—— *See also* De la propriété intellectuelle, 1859.

PATAILLE (Henri Jules Simon). Appendice au Code international de la propriété industrielle [etc.] 1865. *See* Pataille (H. J. S.) *and* Huguet (Auguste), Code international.

—— Commentaire de la loi du 14 juillet 1866, combinée avec les lois et décrets antérieurs sur la propriété littéraire et artistique. *In* "Annales de la propriété industrielle, artistique et littéraire." v. 13. 8°. Paris, 1867, p. 177–236.

PATAILLE (Henri Jules Simon). Propriété littéraire. Droit de traduction. Ouvrages étrangers. Traités internationaux. Décret du 28 mars 1852. Jurisprudence. 8°. Paris, 1856.

—— Propriété littéraire et artistique.—Droit international.—État de situation de nos rapports avec les nations étrangères.—Conventions diplomatiques et législations. *In* "Annales de la propriété industrielle, artistique et littéraire." v. 5. 8°. Paris, 1859, p. 289–313.

—— Propriété littéraire.—Œuvres dramatiques. *In* "Annales de la propriété industrielle, artistique et littéraire." v. 1-2. 8°. Paris, 1856, p. 207–220.

—— *See also* Annales de la propriété industrielle, artistique et littéraire.—Collet (Émile) *and* Le Senne (Charles).

PATAILLE (Henry Jules Simon) *and* HUGUET (Auguste). Code international de la propriété industrielle artistique et littéraire. Guide pratique des inventeurs, auteurs, compositeurs, artistes et fabricants français et étrangers. Devisé en deux parties, contenant 1°, Des précis de la législation et de la jurisprudence française, suivis des textes des lois, ordonnances, décrets et arrêtés ; 2°, Des résumés pratiques des législations étrangères, et le texte de tous les traités internationaux conclus entre la France et les gouvernements étrangers, en matière de brevets d'invention, littérature, [etc.] viii, 364 p. 8°. Paris, Marescq & Dujardin, 1855.

Review by Charles Vergé in "Journal des économistes." 2e série. v. 10. 8°. Paris, 1856, p. 444–446.

—— —— *Same.* Appendice au Code international de la propriété industrielle, artistique et littéraire, contenant les traités internationaux et les lois françaises et étrangères depuis 1855 jusqu' à ce jour, avec des précis et des notes ; par J. Pataille. About 240 p. 8°. Paris, au bureau des Annales de la propriété industrielle, 1865.

PATERSON (James). The liberty of the press, speech, and public worship. Being commentaries on the liberty of the subject and the laws of England. 12°. London, Macmillan & co., 1880.

Contains: Copyright, p. 241–317.

Anon. review in "The Journal of jurisprudence and Scottish law magazine." v. 25. 8°. Edinburgh, no. 289, Jan. 1881, p. 43, 44.

PATERSON (S:) Literary property. *In* Joineriana : or the book of scraps. [*Anon.* by S: Paterson.] v. 1. 16°. London, for J. Johnson, 1772, p. 170–177.

PAULMIER (Charles Pierre Paul). Traité de la législation et de la jurisprudence des théâtres, 1853. *See* Lacan (Adolphe Jean Baptiste) *and* Paulmier.

PAUTET (Jules). *See* Manzoni (Alessandro).

PELLETIER (Michel) *and* DEFERT (Henry). Procédure en matière de contrefaçon industrielle, littéraire et artistique, avec formules ; ouvrage précédé d'une préface par m. Adrien Huard. About iii, 272 p. 12°. Paris, A. Rousseau, 1879.

PERROT DE CHAUMEUX (L.) *See* Annales de la propriété industrielle artistique et littéraire.

PETITIONS and prayers relating to the bill of the booksellers now before the House of Commons. [*Anon.*] About 24 & 12 p. 4°. London, 1774.

PHELPS (Elizabeth Stuart). *See* The Publishers' weekly.

PHILLIMORE (Robert). Commentaries upon international law. v. 4. 8°. London, W. Benning & son, 1861.
Contains : Copyright, p. 400-406.
Also in the same : 2d ed. v. 4. 8°. London, Butterworths, 1874, p. 438-444.

PHILLIPS (C: Palmer). The law of copyright in works of literature and art and in the application of designs. With the statutes relating thereto. xvi, 261 p. 1 l. cxiii p. 8°. London, V. & R. Stevens, sons, & Haynes, 1863.
Anon. review in "The Jurist." N. s. v. 10, part 2. 8°. London, no. 470, Jan. 9, 1864, p. 6, 7.

PHILLIPS (Willard). *See* Nicklin (Philip Houlbrooke).

PHILOMATHIC (The) institution, *London.* Discussion : are the laws regarding literary property founded in justice ? *In* "The Philomathic journal." v. 3. 8°. London, 1825, p. 390-403.

PIC (François Antoine). Dissertation sur la propriété littéraire et la librairie chez les anciens, lue le 27 novembre 1827 à la Société d'émulation du département de l'Ain. About 16 p. 8°. Lyon, imp. de Barret, 1828.
Note. Another ed. was issued same year, about 20 p.
Notice by Augustin Charles Renouard in "Revue encyclopédique." v. 38. 12°. Paris, juin 1828, p. 752, 753.

PIERCE (James O.) Anomalies in the law of copyright. *In* "The Southern law review." N. s. v. 5. 8°. St. Louis, no. 3, Aug. 1879, p. 420-436.

—— Morgan on the history, curiosities and law of literary property. *In* "The Southern law review." N. s. v. 1. 8°. St. Louis, no. 4, Jan. 1876, p. 763-774.

PINHEIRO FERREIRA (Silvestre). Observaçoes sobre os direitos da propriedade litteraria e artistica. *In* "Diario do Governo," no. 225, de 23de septembro de 1842.

PLEA (A) for authors, and the rights of literary property. By an American. [*Anon.*] 32 p. 8°. New York, Adlard & Saunders, 1838.
Note.—Has been ascribed to Grenville A. Sackett.
Anon. review see Literary property.

PLEADINGS (The) of the counsel before the house of lords, in the great cause concerning literary property ; together with the opinions of the learned judges on the common law right of authors and booksellers. To which are added, the speeches of the noble lords who

spoke for and against reversing the decree of the court of chancery. [*Anon.*] 4°. London, Wilkin, 1774.
Anon. notice in "The Monthly review." v. 51. 8°. London, Sept. 1774, p. 202-209.

POOLE (W: F:) *See* The Publishers' weekly.

PORTALIS (Le comte Joseph Marie). Commission de la propriété littéraire : Projet rédigé par m. le comte Portalis. About 8 p. 4°. Paris, Pillet âiné, 1826.

PORTER (J. Neville). International copyright in books between Great Britain and the United States of America. *In* "Modern thought." v. 2. 4°. London, no. 10, oct. 1, 1880, p. ——: no. 11, nov. 1, 1880, p. 534-537.

—— *See also* National association for the promotion of social science. Transactions, 1879.

POTTER (Agathon de). De la propriété intellectuelle et de la distinction entre les choses vénales et non vénales. Examen des Majorats littéraires de P. J. Proudhon. 12°, Bruxelles, chez l'auteur, 1863.

POUILLET (Eugène). Traité théorique et pratique de la propriété littéraire et artistique et du droit de représentation. x, 741 p. 8°. Paris, Marchal, Billard & ce, 1879.
Anon. notice in "Journal du droit international privé et de la jurisprudence comparée." 7me année. 1880. tome 7. 8°. Paris, p. 531, 532.
Review by Fernand Worms in "Le Livre." 1ère année : Bibliographie moderne. v. 1. 8°. Paris, no. 1. 10. jan. 1880, p. 33-35.
— See also Worms (Fernand).

PRIME (S: Irenæus). The right of copyright. A concise statement of the question. *In* "Putnam's magazine." N. s. v. 1. 8°. New York, no. 5, May 1868, p. 635-637.

—— *Same. In* Copyright (The) association for the protection and advance of literature and art. International copyright. 8°. New York, 1868, p. 29-33.

—— *Same. In* The American view of the copyright question. By R: Grant White. 12°. London & New York, G: Routledge & sons, 1880, p. 63-68.

—— *See also* The Publishers' weekly.

PROCESSO verbale del secondo congresso per la proprietà letteraria tenuto in Milano il 12 settembre 1881 nella sala della Camera di commercio. *In* "Bibliografia italiana. Giornale dell' Associazione ;ipografico-libraria italiana." Anno 15. 8°. Milano, 1882, Parte 2a : Cronaca, no. 19, 15 ottobre 1881, p. 73-84.

—— *Same.* About 16 p. 8°. Milano, tip. Bernardoni di C. Rebeschini e c. 1881.

PROPOSED (A) new law of copyright ; of the highest importance to authors ; in a letter to T: Noon Talfourd. [*Anon.*] 8°. London, [1838.]

PROPRIÉTÉ (La) industrielle, littéraire et artistique. Journal bimensuel. 1re année. no. 1, jan. 1880. 8°. Paris, Marescq aîné, 1880.

PROPRIÉTÉ (La) intellectuelle est un droit, 1858. *See* Curmer (Henri Léon).

PROPRIÉTÉ (De la) littéraire.   *See* De la propriété littéraire.

PROPRIÉTÉ (La) littéraire et les traités internationaux.   Lettre de m. le ministre des affaires
étrangères, au délégué du comité de la Société
des gens de lettres, Paris, le 28 juin 1879.   M.
le ministre des affaires étrangères à m. le ministre de l'intérieur, Paris, le 25 juin 1879.   Réponse du comité de la Société des gens de
lettres à m. le ministre des affaires étrangèrs,
Paris, le 21 juillet 1879.   Note annexée à la
lettre en date du 21 juillet 1879.   *In* " Journal
du droit international privé et de la jurisprudence comparée."   1879.   8°.   Paris, nos.
9-10, p. 465-476.

PROPRIÉTÉ (La) littéraire n'est pas une propriété.   Production intellectuelle.   Exchange.
Perpétuité.   [*Anon.*]   About 63 p. 8°.   Riom,
imp. Leboyer ; Paris, E. Dentu, 1866.

PROUDHON (Pierre Joseph).   Les Majorats littéraires, examen d'un projet de loi ayant pour
but de créer, au profit des auteurs, inventeurs
et artistes un monopole perpétuel.   About
276 p. 12°.   Paris, E. Dentu, 1863.

—— *Same :* 2e éd.   About 266 p. 12.°   Paris,
E. Dentu, 1863.

—— *Same.   In* Œuvres complètes de P.-J.
Proudhon.   v. 16.   12°.   Paris, A. Lacroix,
Verboeckhoven & ce, 1868.   2 p. l.   p. 1-124.

—— *Same :* Die literarischen Majorate.   Prüfung des plans zu einem gesetze, welches die
schöpfung eines ewigen monopols zum besten
der erfinder, schriftsteller und künstler be-
zweckt.   Aus dem französischen.   8°.   Leipzig, Weber, 1863.

—— *See also* Potter (Agathon de).

PRUSSIA.   Das preussische gesetz gegen nachdruck und nachbildung, zum schutz des eigenthums an den werken der wissenschaft und
kunst, gegeben am 11. Juni 1837.   8°.   Berlin,
Eichler, 1840.

—— *Same :* Dargestellt in seinem entstehen
und erläutert in seinen einzelnen bestimmungen aus den amtlichen quellen durch Julius
E. Hitzig.   8°.   Berlin, F. Dümmler, 1838.

—— *Same :* Prussian law of copyright of [June
11] 1837.   [Translated by Francis Lieber.]   *In*
" The Law reporter.   Edited by P. W. Chandler."   v. 2.   8°.   Boston, no. 5, Sept. 1839, p.
129-133.

—— *See also* Kaiser (Hermann).—Lange (Max).

PUBLICATIONS on the subject of literary property.
[*Anon.* reviews of eight works.]   *In* " The
Monthly review."   v. 51.   8°.   London, 1874,
Aug. p. 81-94 ; Sept. p. 202-213 ; Oct. p. 272-
281 ; Nov. p. 357-360.

PUBLISHERS' (The) weekly.   v. 1-22, Jan. 1872-
Dec. 1882.   8°.   New York, F: Leypoldt,
editor and publisher, 1872-82.

INDEX TO COPYRIGHT ARTICLES, ETC.

v. 1, Jan.-June, 1872.

Int. cop. ; A bill for securing to authors, in certain
cases, the benefit of int. cop.   In the House of Representa-

tives, Dec. 6, 1871, p. 36-40.—Relating to cop.; Report of
the Librarian of Congress for 1871, on cop. deposits, p. 42.
—Editorial notice of H: C: Carey's " The international
copyright question," p. 42.—Int. cop. in Germany ; Int.
cop. in Russia, p. 42.—Int. cop., letter by G: Tawse, New
York, p. 68-69.—The Int. cop. treaty ; Meeting of publishers and others in Philadelphia, p. 69-70.—Int. cop.,
various, p. 71.—Int. cop. ; Official minutes and documents
of the meeting of publishers, Feb. 6, 1872: *a* An act to
grant cop. to foreign authors ; *b* Minority report ; *c* Mr.
Appleton's argument for the bill ; *d* Memorial of British
authors on cop. in the United States, p. 91-95.—Int. cop.,
letter signed Justice, New York, Feb. 1, p. 95-96.—The
cop. question ; Cop. association bill to be presented to the
joint committee of Congress, p. 96.—The int. cop. movement in England, p. 96.—Article first of the international
treaty proposed by the German " Börsenverein," p. 96.—
Int. cop., Philadelphia, Feb. 9, Letter signed W: B.
Evans, p. 121.—Cop. developments, various, p. 134.—The
international treaty proposed by the German " Börsenverein," p. 135-136.—Letter from Boston, Feb. 12, 1872,
signed B., p. 138.—Int. cop. treaty, letter from Philadelphia, Feb. 24, 1872, signed J. V. W., p. 182.—Int. cop.
treaty, letter from Philadelphia, Feb. 26, signed H. C. S.,
p. 184.—Letter by Willis P. Hazard, Philadelphia, March
2, 1872, p. 199.—Letter on Mr. Sherman's bill, New York,
March 5, 1872, signed H. H., p. 199.—Int. cop. movement ;
Report of Mr. W. P. Hazard, chairman of the Philadelphia
committee, p. 208-209.—Mr. Sherman's bill, p. 209.—Copyright national and international, letter from H: Carey
Baird, Philadelphia, March 4, 1872, p. 223.—The int. cop.
hearing before the joint committee of Congress ; communication from " One of the committee," p. 231-233.—A
dream about cop. *Not* by a millionaire publisher, signed
L., p. 247.—Letter by Willis P. Hazard, Philadelphia,
March 23, 1872, p. 263.—The Elderkin or Sherman bill to
secure int. cop. ; communication from O. C., p. 295-296.—
The London *Bookseller* on int. cop., p. 393.—Letter signed
R. T., Philadelphia, April 27, p. 393.—The cop. question,
letter signed E. C. B., London, April 29, p. 441.

v. 2, July-Dec. 1872.

Canadian cop., p. 91 and 134.—Int. cop.; Cambridge,
Eng., Nov. 5, 1872, E. H. Palmer, p. 653.

v. 3, Jan.-June, 1873.

Int. cop. bill in the Senate of the United States ; Report
of the library committee, p. 191-195.—International copyright. (From *Appletons' Journal*, March 1), p. 243.

v. 5, Jan.-June, 1874.

Notes on copyright, editorial, p. 30.

v. 6, July-Dec. 1874.

The copyright amendment, editorial, p. 43.

v. 8, July-Dec. 1875.

Editorial notice of Eaton Sylvester Drone's article " Is
copyright perpetual ?" p. 642.—Cop. in notes, [By Rowland Cox], p. 685-686.

v. 9, Jan.-June, 1876.

Protecting reprints by cop. claim, editorial, p. 229.—Int.
cop., letter by James Appleton Morgan, New York, Feb.
21, 1876, p. 254-255.—Cop. notes. (By Rowland Cox), p.
327.—Cop. notes, editorial : Italian cop. case ; Case of
Frances E. Tilton *v.* W: F. Gill, p. 476.—Cop. notes :
British cop. commission ; Letter from A. R. Spofford, p.
529.

v. 10, July-Dec. 1876.

A cop. question. J: H. Tomlinson and U. D. Ward, regarding " collection envelopes," p. 472-473. — The cop.
laws ; Letter from " Howard" to the *Christian Weekly*
quoted, p. 474.—Dr. J. G. Holland on cop., p. 537-538.—
The facts as to cop., letter from " Howard," New York,
Sept. 25, 1876, p. 569-570.—Cop. notes ; Case of S: Smiles
vs. Belford Brothers, p. 706.

v. 11, Jan.-July, 1877.

Dr. [C: E: C. B.] Appleton on int. cop., editorial, p. 190-
191.—British cop. commission, editorial, p. 323.

v. 12, July-Dec. 1877.

Theories and practice of cop. Notice of Daniel de Folleville's " De la propriété littéraire," from the *Nation* of Oct.
11, 1877, p. 466.—Pending legislation ; Cop. and trade-
marks, editorial, p. 579.—British cop. commission ; The
Athenæum quoted, p. 784-785.

v. 13, Jan.-June, 1878.

English publishers and American authors, p. 246.—Paris literary congress, p. 405; 442.—The British cop. commission, p. 509.—The international commercial relations of books, p. 526-527.—The British cop. commission report, p. 527.—English comments on the American trade, p. 527-529.—Int. cop.; The British commission report, p. 554-555.—The proposed alterations in the British cop. act, p. 558a.—Letter by J: C. Nimmo, Boston, June 7, 1878, p. 631.

v. 14, July-Dec. 1878.

The Paris literary congress, editorial, p. 13.—American publishers and foreign authors; editorial comments upon G. W. Smalley's letter to the *New York Tribune*, p. 114-115.—American publishers and foreign authors; from H: Holt & Co., a letter to the *New York Tribune* in answer to G. W. Smalley, p. 115.—The literary congress, Paris, from G. W. Smalley's letter to the *New York Tribune*, July 17, 1878, p. 119.—On perpetual cop. [Edmond About], p. 173.—Moy Thomas on the British cop. commission report, p. 214-215.—Rights in MS., a French decision, p. 237.—Henry Holt & Co.'s exhibit of translations at the Paris exposition, p. 261.—An address on international cop. by James Appleton Morgan; editorial notice with quotation, p. 299.—Stanley's new book [pirated], p. 357.—Imported cop. books, editorial on the Stanley book, p. 534.—C: Reade and Mrs. Frances Hodgson Burnett, editorial, p. 534.—English playwright *vs.* American author; C: Reade's letter to Dr. Swan M. Burnett; Mrs. Burnett's letter to C: Reade, p. 535-536.—The Stanley book, circular from Harper & Brothers, p. 536.—The Stanley book, letter from Robert Clarke & Co., p. 596.—The Canadian invasion; from the *New York Sun*, Nov. 22, 1878, p. 780-781.—Int. cop, a case in point, Mrs. Brassey's "Cruise of the Sunbeam," reprinted by Henry Holt & Co., p. 844.

v. 15, Jan.-June, 1879.

Cop., home and international, editorial, p. 72-73.—Int. cop. by judicial decision. [By Arthur G: Sedgwick], abridged from the *Atlantic Monthly*, p. 77-78.—Mr. Farrer on cop., summarized by the *Academy*, p. 79.—The last attempt at int. cop., letter by J: Denison Baldwin, Worcester, Mass., Jan. 18, 1879, p. 79.—Mr. [W. I.] Prime on domestic cop., letter, New York, Jan. 20, 1879, p. 79-80.—The protection of American publishers on foreign books, letter, Boston, Jan. 1, 1879, p. 80.—New light on the cop. question, from the *Evening Post*, p. 147.—A discussion on int. cop.; G: H. Putnam's paper, p. 151.—Drone on cop. [By G: Ripley], from the *New York Tribune*, p. 167-169. —G: H. Putnam's paper, editorial, p. 193.—International copyright. By G: Haven Putnam, p. 194-196, 236-238, 260-261, 282-285, 305-306, 350-352.—"American publishers and English authors," editorial notice, p. 196-197.—The cop. question. Opinions of publishers and authors; I. J. B. Lippincott & Co., Roberts Brothers, G. W. Carleton, Theo. L. De Vinne, p. 197.—Int. cop. in Spain, p. 198.—The cop. question. Opinions of publishers and authors; II. J: Habberton, Lindsay & Blakiston, W: A. Hammond, Sower, Potts & Co., Joseph Cook, J: Wiley, p. 239.—The cop. question. Opinions of publishers and authors; III. H: W. Longfellow, G. W. Green, E: E. Hale, W: D. Howells, W: Wood & Co., p. 262.—A proposed int. cop. basis, editorial, p. 304.—The cop. question. Opinions of publishers and authors; IV. S. C. Griggs, Van Antwerp, Bragg & Co., Dana Estes, p. 306-307.—Memorandums in regard to int. cop. treaty between Great Britain and the United States: Convention proposed (1870) by Lord Clarendon, with amendments proposed in America. A suggestion from Messrs. Harper & Brothers to the Department of State [1878.]—Bill proposed by Mr. W: H. Appleton, 1873.—Extracts from Mr. W. H. Appleton's letter to the London *Times*, [1871], p. 317-324.—The new outlook on cop., editorial, p. 339.—Notice of E: Marston's "Copyright, national and international," p. 341.—The cop. question. Opinions of publishers and authors; V. Theo. D. Woolsey, D: A Wells, J: Elderkin, J. G. Holland, E. C. Stedman, C: E. Norton, James Parton, "Marion Harland," p. 352-353.—Property in subscription orders. The rights of publishers of subscription-books; J. M. Stoddart & Co. *vs.* Moses Warren, by J. R. Sypher, p. 355-357.—The cop. question. Opinions of publishers and authors; VI. E: P. Roe, S: Iræneus Prime, Miss Warner, E: Eggleston, J. M. Hart, Elizabeth Stuart Phelps, J: T. Headley, p. 396-398.—Foreign editions of cop. books; S: Mullen quoted, p. 398.—The Canadian incursion, editorial, p. 439.—Elderkin-Sherman bill, editorial, p 440.—The cop. question. Opinions of publishers and authors; VII. Donald G. Mitchell, G: P. Marsh, O.

J. Victor, p. 468-469.—The "Easy Chair" on cop. (G: W: Curtis in May *Harper's*), p. 466-470.—The London *Times* on the Harper plan, p. 470.—The Stanley cop. suits, editorial, p. 490.—The "monopoly" of cop., editorial, p. 508-509.—Baird (H: Carey). Copyright national and international ; a bill of exceptions, p. 510-511.—Editorial notice of James Appleton Morgan's "Anglo-American international copyright," p. 511.—Int. cop., letter from W: Black, London, April 28, p. 562.—Letter from T: Hill, p. 562.—Present status of the cop. movement, p. 579-580.—Lovell (J: W.) The royalty *vs.* the monopoly scheme of cop., p. 580-582.—Int. cop. letters to Messrs. Harper from G: T. Curtis, B: J. Lossing, J. R. Osgood, Hamilton Fish, E. P. Whipple, C: E. Norton, p. 582-583.—"Untrammelled copyright," from a letter by E: Marston, to the London *Times*, p. 601. —The English attitude on cop., editoral, p. 644.—Int. cop., letter of Harper & Bros. to the London *Times*, May 30, 1879, p. 645.—A debate on int. cop.; Quotations from S. S. Conant's article, and the rejoinder by "C", Leonard H: Courtney, in *Macmillan's magazine* for June, 1879, p. 645-646.—London *Bookseller* on Messrs. Harper & Brothers, p. 695.—Cop. notes, p. 699.—The int. literary congress, editorial, p. 712-713.

v. 16, July-Dec. 1879.

A cop. *omnium gatherum*; notice of R. A. Macfie's "Copyright and patents for inventions," p. 12. — Cop. notes, p. 176.—Int. cop., letters to Messrs. Harper, from H: C. Lea, F: R: Daldy, J. A. Morgan and James Parton, p. 220-221.—British cop. bill, p. 258-259.—The proposed British cop. bill, p. 277-281.—Mrs. [Frances Hodgson] Burnett on int. cop., p. 358.—International copyright and "Macmillan's magazine," (from the *Academy*), letter by S. S. Conant, New York, June 25, 1879, p. 387-388.—Cop. in titles of books, p. 474-475.—Int. cop. and American periodical literature, p. 562-563.—Editorial comment on the reprint of Irving's works, p. 805.—The "Works" of Washington Irving, letter from G. P. Putnam's Sons, Nov. 26, 1879, p. 807.—Free mailing of cop. copies, p. 807.—The cop. question. Opinions of authors and others, Oliver Wendell Holmes, C: W. Eliot, J: Hay, Justin Winsor and W: F: Poole, p. 881.

v. 17, Jan.-June, 1880.

Cop. in the courts; editorial on the suit regarding Irving's works, and the Scribner-Stoddart case—" Encyclopædia Britannica," p. 23-24.—The " Encyclopædia Britannica" suits, p. 25-27.—The cop. question. Opinions of authors and others; C: Dudley Warner, T: W. Higginson, Mrs. A. D. T. Whitney, J. W. De Forest, (New Haven), M. D. Conway, p. 82-83.—Cop. cases—Cop. in systems of teaching—Cop. in adaptations—The Wingate-Laidley case, p. 212-213.—The losses in literature (from the *Boston Daily Advertiser*, March 4, 1881), p. 238-239.—The condition of the cop. movement, editorial, p. 287.—Matthew Arnold on int. cop., extracts, p. 296-297.—A new cop. suggestion, [by Eduard Quaas], p. 297-298.—Int. and "national" cop. (The *New York Times*, March 20th, on Matthew Arnold), p. 335.—Cop. cases, Lucas *vs.* Cooke and Hoby *vs.* The Grosvenor library (limited), p. 335-336.—Canon Farrar's royalties ; a case in point, with editorial remarks, p. 355-356.—Int. cop. between France and America, p. 356.—Cop. cases—The Irving suit—The "Essentials of anatomy" case—" Unpublished" librettos, p. 384-385.—Dr. Holland and Mr. Didier on int. cop., editorial, p. 426-427.—English authors and American publishers; letters from Edwin Arnold and F: W: Farrar to I. K. Funk & Co., p. 457.—Cop. notes, p. 457.—Property in subscription orders; J. M. Stoddart & Co., *vs.* Key, Hall; & Scribner, Armstrong & Co., p. 516-517.—Editorial remarks on Wilkie Collins's " Considerations on the copyright question," p. 536.—Wilkie Collins and int. cop., from the *Boston Traveller*, June 5, 1880, p. 605.—Mr. Stedman on int. cop., letter to the *New York Tribune*, p. 605.

v. 18, July-Dec. 1880.

Cop. matters ; G: P. Lathrop on Wilkie Collins, p. 12.—Cop. matters ; Cooper *vs.* Whittingham, p. 30-31.—" Mentioned" once more; Int. cop. in Parliament, editorial, p. 233.—Int. cop., from the London *Publishers' Circular*, Aug. 2, 1880, p. 236.—A new phase of literary piracy, [Jean Ingelow's Poems], from the *New York Evening Post*, p. 236.—Cop. in the Bible [by E. S. Drone], from the *New York Herald*, Aug. 29, 1880, p. 264.—The Chicago pirates, from the London *Times*, Aug. 13, 1880, p. 265.—Roberts Brothers and J: W. Lovell, editorial, p. 302-303. —Int. cop. treaty with Great Britain, p. 323.—Int. cop. The Berne conference on international law, p. 382.—Int. cop., from the *New York Herald*, Oct. 4, 1880 ; *New York*

Times, Sept. 22, 1880 ; Philadelphia *Telegraph* ; Philadelphia *North American*, Oct. 7, 1880, p. 486–489.—The cop. question; important stand taken by the Philadelphia publishers, from the *New York Herald* with editorial remarks, p. 518.—Law and morals in cop., from the *New York Evening Post*, Oct. 1, 1880, p. 518.—Int. cop., action of the Book Trade Association of Philadelphia, compiled from the *Ledger* and *North American*, p. 547.—Int. cop., letter from Walter Lippincott, Philadelphia, Oct. 25, 1880, p. 550.—Int. cop. again; "The Harper treaty," from the *New York Tribune*, Nov. 7, 1880, p. 610–611.—The present status of int. cop.; Harper treaty ; List of signers in favor of int. cop., etc., editorial, p. 835–837.—The objections, I.; Editorial and quotations from G: Haven Putnam, Edmund C. Stedman, the *New York Herald*, Oct. 4, 1880; the *New York Tribune*, Nov. 7, 1880 ; the *Nation*, Dec. 16, 1880, p. 856–858.—Int. cop., its history in the United States, from G: H. Putnam's paper on int. cop., p. 858–859.—C: Reade on the Harper treaty, from the *New York Tribune*, Dec. 15, 1880, p. 859–861.—Another proposition. Justice to foreign authors, from the *New York Herald*, Dec. 13, 1880, p. 861.

v. 19, Jan.-June, 1881.

The objections, II.; Editorial, p. 16–17.—Int. cop. treaty or act? from *Harper's Weekly*, Jan. 1, 1881, p. 17–18.—From the *Literary World*, Dec. 4, 1880, p. 18.—T: Hood on cop.; his petition reprinted, p. 18–19.—Int. cop., letter from Robert Clarke Co., Jan. 3, 1881, p. 30–31.—Editorial notice of the Int. literary association, p. 160.—Editorial notice of Cop. association of London, p. 185.—Editorial notice of meeting of London publishers, p. 203.—Mr. Chamberlain on int. cop. treaty, p. 232.—Editorial remarks and quotation from London *Publishers' Circular* on int. cop. movements in England, p. 266–267.—Editorial notice of review in the *Athenæum* of R: G. White's "American view of the copyright question," p. 304.—Editorial remarks on London *Bookseller's* attitude towards int. cop., p. 304.—Int. cop., quotations from London *Publishers' Circular*, March 1, 1881, *Boston Traveller*, Feb. 12, 1861, London *Daily Telegraph* ; *Bookseller*, March 3. 1881, and Dec. 1, 1880 ; *New York Times*, March 17, 1881, p. 305–307.—Notice of the abandonment of 3d modification by British board of trade of the cop. treaty, p. 307.—Editorial remarks on R: G. White's views, p. 333.—Int. literary association on cop., and letter from "Ouida" [Louise De la Ramé] to the London *Times*, p. 333–334.—Editorial remarks and quotations from the *New York Herald* for March 28, 1881, and from Moncure Daniel Conway, p. 406–407.—Article by E. M. [E: Marston] in London *Publishers' Circular*, March 15, 1881, p. 407–408.—C: J. Longman, in *Fraser's Magazine*, p. 408–411.—From the *Boston Traveller*, March 29. and *Boston Advertiser*, April 5, 1881, p. 411–412.—English and American authors, *Harper's Weekly*, April 16, 1881, p. 432—Int. literary association, p. 432.—Treaties and laws, *Harper's Weekly*, p. 432.—British cop. law, from the *Athenæum*, March 19, 1881, p. 433.—America on the offensive ; American publishers—British publishers, editorial, p. 457.—Int. cop., G: W: Curtis in *Harper's* for May, 1881, p. 457–458.—Copyright at home and abroad, J. G. Holland in *Scribner's* for May, 1871, p. 458–459.—British cop., from London *Publishers' Circular*, April 1, 1881, [Bill from Law amendment society], p. 459–461.—Postal matters ; infringement of cop., p. 461.—Herbert Spencer on the cop. bill, from London *Publishers' Circular*, April 16, 1881, p. 512–513.—Int. literary association, p. 532.—Contraband editions, from the *Athenæum* ; Order of Postmaster-General to prevent the illegal transmission through the post of pirated copies of the works of American authors, p. 619.—Int. cop. Chinese compared with American sense of justice, from the *New York Times*, and *Trübner's Literary Record*, p. 694.

v. 20, July-Dec. 1881.

Int. cop., extract from the *Athenæum*, London, July 16, 1881, p. 126.—President Garfield and the cop. negotiations, p. 126.—Int. cop., editorial announcement of the bibl. of literary property, p. 147.—Extract, from the *Critic*, New York, on Mr. Sackville West and the cop. negotiations, p. 147.—Int. cop.; E. C. Stedman in *Scribner's Monthly*, p. 163.—G. W. Smalley in the *New York Tribune*, p. 163–164.—Int. literary congress at Vienna, p. 164.—Prof. Payne's explanation, p. 164.—Literary property. Index to articles on cop., etc., published in the *Publishers' Weekly*, v. 1–19, by T. Solberg, p. 205–208.—Editorial note, p. 209.—Int. cop. question in Vienna, Milan and Madrid congresses, editorial, p. 405.—The new cop. treaty with America ; Letter by E: Marston, London, Sept. 9, 1881, from the London *Times*, p. 467–468.—Author's rights [as discussed at the Vienna congress], extract from a letter by E; King, foreign correspondent of the *Evening Post*, New York, p. 491.—Int. cop., a reply to E: Marston's article "The new copyright treaty with America," from the *Boston Advertiser*, Sept. 29, 1881, p. 492.—Int. cop., quotation from article by G. W. Smalley in the *New York Tribune*, Oct. 14, 1881, relating to Mr. E: Marston's last letter to the *Times* (London), with editorial comments, p. 519–520.—Letter from E. P. Roe, Cornwall-on-Hudson, Oct. 18, 1881, to the *New York Tribune*, disowning the authorship of "Give me thine heart," which was published as having been written by him, by I. Ross Robertson of Toronto, p. 547.—Int. cop., from the *New York Tribune*, Oct. 22, 1881, editorial notice of contribution by Simon Newcomb on the English view of the proposed int. cop. treaty, p. 577.—The Int literary congress, from the London *Athenæum*, Oct. 8, 1881, p. 608–609.—Int. cop. [By Simon Newcomb, Washington, D. C., Oct. 15, 1881.], p. 609–610.—Int. cop., views of G. P. Putnam's sons, from the *New York Tribune*, Oct. 31, 1881, in regard to the three months stipulation and favoring a longer or unlimited time, p. 798.—Int. cop. negotiations and Mr. Daldy, p. 801.—Int. cop., S. S. Conant in reply to G. W. Smalley, New York, Nov. 25, 1881, from the *New York Tribune*, explaining how the Harper's draft was first submitted to the Secretary of State, etc., and reviewing W. F. Rae's article on cop. in the *Nineteenth Century*, p. 825–827.—Int. cop.; The international association; The cause in Canada, p. 851–852.—Int. cop. treaty between France and Belgium, from the London *Academy*, p. 868.—The rule that did not work both ways; Refusal of the application of S: L. Clemens (Mark Twain) for a Canadian cop.—Two weeks' residence in Montreal not a legal domicile, p. 868.—Int. cop. Mark Twain's cop., from the *New York Times*, p. 884. Mark Twain explains: To the editor of the *Springfield* (Mass.) *Republican*, Hartford, Conn., Dec. 18, 1881, p. 884–885.

v. 21, Jan.-June, 1882.

Int. cop., officers of the "Syndicat pour la protection de la propriété littéraire et artistique à l'étranger," p. 9.—Extract from Mark Twain's speech at Montreal, p. 9–10.—Int. cop. Mr. Marston's reply to Mr. Conant [the three months clause etc.], to the editor of the *New York Tribune*, London, Dec. 19, 1881, p. 56.—The true cop., *i.e.* the granting by Congress and Parliament of an authors' cop.—putting every author, native or foreign, on a par with his brother, the inventor, and giving him absolute control of the works of his brain ; from the *Boston Traveller*, Jan. 12, 1882, p. 56–57.—The three months clause, p. 57.—English publishers and the int. cop. negotiations, from the *Athenæum*, p. 57.—Int. cop., its bearing on medical literature, from the *Medical News*, Jan. 28, 1882, p. 138.—Injustice to authors, from *Appletons' Literary Bulletin* ; Letter by Hamilton W. Pierson, author of "In the Brush;" Geneva, N. Y., Jan. 16, 1882, complaining of the constant printing of extracts from his book without due acknowledgment, p 139–140.—Int. cop., the cop. negotiations. Extract from the *Century Magazine*, March 1882, p. 193–194.—The question forty years ago ; letter from Harriet Martineau to R. Shelton Mackenzie, Tynemouth, Dec. 24, 1843, from the *Century Magazine*, March 1882, p. 194.—Notes from the London *Athenæum* ; Canadian cop. ; Negotiations with England, etc., p. 258.—Announcement of cop. bibliography, p. 275.—Int. cop., telegram from Mr. G W. Smalley to the *New York Tribune*, March 12, 1882, giving the *Athenæum* announcement of the suspension of negotiations, and reply to the contrary from the Department of State, March 13, 1882, p. 275.—Quotation from London *Publishers' Circular*, March 1, 1882, giving a question in the House of Commons as to the status of the cop. negotiations, p. 275.—The int. cop. negotiations, from *Harper's Weekly*, March 25, 1882, p. 302–303.—Mr. G. W. Smalley's telegram reaffirming the failure of the cop. negotiations, from the *New York Tribune*, March 19, 1882 ; and comment upon Mr. Smalley's dispatch, from the *New York Evening Post*, p. 303.—Editorial announcement of Judge Tourgee's article on cop., p. 303.—Int. cop., from *The American*, March 18, 1882, [an anon. article in favor of "protection"], p. 357–358.—The law of copyright, by Albion W. Tourgee, favoring cop. as perpetual protection to *authors*, from *Our Continent*, March 29, 1882, p. 358–359.—Literary property. A catalogue of books and articles relating to literary property, by Thorvald Solberg (A., J. K.–Carey), p. 381–384.—Jean Ingelow and American reprinters, p. 406.—J: W. Lovell Co. and Longfellow's "Hyperion" and "Outremer," p. 406.—The truth, the whole truth, and nothing but the truth," a communication in favor of unrestricted int. cop. from a publisher and signed Silver Gray, p. 408.—Int. cop., note from the London *Athenæum* of April 1, 1882, as to Mr. Daldy and the cop. negotiations, p. 408.—

The J: W. Lovell Company's statement, concerning cop. upon Longfellow's "Hyperion" and "Outre-mer," New York, April 13, 1882, p. 429-430.—Reply to "Silver Gray," by "B." who also favors int. cop., New York, April 19, 1882, p. 430.—Int. cop., article from the *Bookseller*, London, April 4, 1882, on cop. in Longfellow's works ; with editorial comments, p. 453-454.—Robinson's cop. bill, from the *New York Evening Post*, p. 454.—Literary property : catalogue by T. Solberg (Carlyle-Congrès), p. 473-475.—Int. cop., terms of proposed int. cop. treaty, from *Appletons' Literary Bulletin*, p. 475.—E: Eggleston in April *Century ;* American authors and int. cop., p. 475-476.—Young's Concordance, letters from Funk & Wagnalls, and Dodd Mead & Co., p. 476-477.—Literary property : catalogue by T. Solberg (Congrès-Drone), p. 504-506.—English cop. bill, works of fine art and photographs, from the London *Athenæum*, April 22, 1882, p. 508-509.—Cop. matters ; The international literary congress, from the London *Academy*, April 29, 1882, p. 509—Literary property : catalogue by T. Solberg (Drone-Fischer), p. 529-530.—Int. cop., quotation from Matthew Arnold's "Word to America" in the *Nineteenth Century*, p. 531.—Literary property : catalogue by T. Solberg (Fisher-Goujon), p. 548-549.—Cop. "All rights reserved" by Albion W. Tourgee, in *Our Continent*, May 24, 1882, p. 550-552.—Int. cop., notice of Matthew Arnold on cop., by G: W: Curtis, from *Harper's Weekly*, p. 599.— International literary congress at Rome and cop. negotiations between Great Britain and United States, p. 602.— Int. cop., musical cop., from the London *Literary World* [Mr. Gorst's bill], p. 644.—International literary congress, p. 644.—Editorial article on some publisher's proposal to mail cheap reprints of English cop. books to England, p. 661

v. 22, July-Dec. 1882.

Literary property : catalogue by T. Solberg (Gournot-Great Britain), p. 30-32.—Cop., Canadian reprints, editorial ; Importation of books copyrighted in America, sec. 4964 of the Revised Statutes, p. 33.—Cop. ; Prices of books abroad, from the *Pall Mall Gazette*, p. 33-34.—The moral of piracy, editorial, p. 230.—The *New York Evening Post* on the failure of the int. cop. negotiations, p. 230.—Circular from G: W. Carleton & Co., regarding the reprinting of many of their cop. publications by a Canadian publishinghouse, p. 230.—Ruling of the Treasury Department, Washington, Aug. 11, 1882, upon sec. 4964 Revised Statutes, regarding the seizing of imported cop. books, with editorial remarks, p. 230-231.—Cop. in the Liverpool congress, extract from the *New York Herald's* report of the proceedings relative to int. cop., p. 254-255.—Int. cop. ; the cop. negotiations, from the *Critic*, Sept. 9, 1882, p. 430.— The author's best friend, from the *New York Evening Post*, Sept. 1, 1882, p. 430-431.—The new pirate, from the *New York Evening Post*, Sept. 4, 1882, p. 431-432.—The books of foreign authors, from the *New York Sun*, Sept. 11, 1882, p. 432.—The Tauchnitz editions, from the *Boston Advertiser*, p. 432-433.—Tariff on books, E. Steiger's

papers on behalf of the "Removal of the duty on books" ; Proceedings of the Book Trade Association of Philadelphia, p. 517-518.—Tariff on books, statement of Phila. Book Trade Association, p. 546.—The duty on books, from the *New York Evening Post*, p. 547.—Int. cop. ; The int. cop. treaty, from *Harper's Weekly*, Sept 16, 1882, p. 547-548.— Negotiations for int. cop. between France and Germany, from the *Athenæum*, London, p. 548.—Musical cop., from the *Publishers' Circular*, London, p. 548.—Literary property : catalogue by T. Solberg (Griesinger-LeSenne), p. 578-581 and p. 609-611.—Cop., Clark Russell's statement explained, p. 612.—G. W. Smalley's telegram to the *New York Tribune*, Oct. 29, 1882, p. 612.—Harper & Brothers' card, from the *New York Tribune*, Oct. 31, 1882, p. 612.— Cop. administration [by W: McCrillis Griswold], from the *New York Evening Post*, p. 651-652.—Int. cop., the cop. controversy ; "Misstatements corrected," from *Harper's Weekly*, Nov. 25, (a reply to letters from English authors in the London *Athenæum*), p. 837-838.—Extract from the London letter to the *New York Times*, p. 838.—Extract from the *New York Tribune* of Nov. 18, 1882, giving summary of Sampson Low's letter to the *Athenæum*, of Nov. 4, a *verbatim* report of F. W. Robinson's letter to the *Athenæum*, of Nov. 4, Mr. Smalley's dispatches of Nov. 12, Nov. 19, and Nov. 25, and Harper & Brothers' letter to the *Tribune* of Nov. 13, p. 838.—Importation of books copyrighted in the United States, Treasury Department circular, no. 119, Oct. 19, 1882, p. 839.—Tariff on books, extract from James Morgan Hart's paper "Custom-house abuses," p. 839.— Int. cop. ; The cop. controversy, from the *Athenæum*, Oct. 28, 1882, from the *New York Tribune*, Nov. 11, 1882, from the *Critic*, Dec. 2, 1882, (including letters and statements from Harper & Brothers, D. Appleton & Co., G. P. Putnam's Sons, J. B. Lippincott & Co., Houghton, Mifflin & Co., C: Scribner's Sons, Dodd, Mead & Co., and J. Wiley's Sons as to sums paid by them to English authors, p. 866-867.—Letters from the *Athenæum* of Nov. 18, (W. Clark Russell and Sampson Low), p. 867-868.—Letters from the *Athenæum* of Nov. 25, (Horace N. Pym, E: Marston, "A," F. W. Robinson and Katharine S. Macquoid), p. 868-869.—The tariff on books, letter from H: Carey Baird, Philadelphia, Dec. 6, 1882, p. 869.—Int. cop. ; The cop. controversy, from the London correspondent of the *New York Times*, Dec. 10, 1882, p. 886.—Making free. [*Anon.* article charging W. Clark Russell with plagiarism] from the *New York Times*, Dec. 9, 1882, p. 886-887.— Letter from J: Wiley & Sons denying the statement quoted from the *Critic* that they had paid Mr. Ruskin $5000, p. 889.—Literary property : catalogue by T. Solberg (Letter-Macleod), p. 904-905.—The tariff on books ; the book trade protests, from the *New York Times*, Dec. 15, 1882 ; uncorrected tariff abuses, extract from the *New York Times*, Dec. 17, 1882, p. 906.—Int. cop. ; The cop. controversy, letters from H: Holt & Co., and J. B. Stevenson, Pittsburg, to the *Critic*, in regard to paying British authors, p. 907.

PURDAY (C: H:) Copyright. A sketch of its rise and progress : the acts of parliament and conventions with foreign nations now in force, with suggestions on the statutory requirements for the disposal and security of a copyright, literary, musical and artistic. 2 p. l. 132 p. 8°. London, Reeves & Turner, 1877.

PUTNAM (G: Haven). International copyright considered in some of its relations to ethics and political economy. An address delivered Jan. 29, 1878, before the New York free-trade club. 2 p. l. 54 p. 8°. New York, G. P. Putnam's sons, 1879. [Economic monographs, no. 15.]

—— *Same.* About 54 p. 8°. London, 1879.

—— *Same. In* "The Publishers' weekly." v. 15. 8°. New York, 1879, no. 370, Feb. 15, p. 194–196 ; no. 371, Feb. 22, p. 236–238 ; no. 372, March 1, p. 260–261 ; no. 373, March

8, p. 283–285 ; no. 374, March 15, p. 305–306 ; no. 375, March 22, p. 350–352. v. 18, no. 467, Dec. 25, 1880, p. 858–859.

—— *Same :* Internationaler schutz gegen den nachdruck. In einiger seiner beziehungen auf ethik und politische oekonomie betrachtet. Ein vortrag, gehalten am 29. Januar 1879 im New-Yorker free-trade club. Deutsch von Eduard Wiebe. 59 p. 8°. Berlin, F. Vahlen, 1880.

Anon. notice in "The Academy." v. 15. 4°. London, no. 364 new series, April 26, 1879, p. 365.
Anon. notice in "Trübner's American and Oriental literary record." v. 12. 4°. London, nos. 9, 10, p. 112.

—— Messrs. Putnam and international copyright. [Letter from G: H. Putnam, New York, April 29, 1879. *In* "The Academy." v. 15. 4°. London, no. 367, May 17, 1879, p. 437.

—— *and* PUTNAM (J: R.) Authors and publishers. A manual of suggestions for beginners in literature, comprising a description of publishing methods and arrangements. [*Anon.*] 2 p. l. 96 p. 8°. New York, G. P. Putnam's sons, 1883.

Contains : Securing copyright, p. 27-43.

—— *vs.* POLLARD (Walter F.) *See* Alexander & Green.

PUTNAM (G: Palmer). The copyright question. *In* "The Literary world." v. 1. 4°. New York, no. 26, July 31, 1847, p. 611-612.

PUTNAM'S monthly magazine. v. 1-10 and new series, v. 1-6, 1853-1857 & 1868-1870. 8°. New York, G: P. Putnam & co., 1853-70.

Contains : v. 1, 1853. International copyright, editorial notes, p. 335.—v. 2, 1853. Notes from H: C: Carey, p. 229-231 : Letter from H: C: Carey [International copyright], p. 342-344.—v. 3, 1854. Literary piracy. [*Anon.* review by C: F: Briggs of " Letters on international copyright." By H: C: Carey. Philadelphia, A. Hart, 1853], p. 96-103 : Letter to the editor [regarding H: C: Carey's views on international copyright ; signed by G. W. E., Phillips, Me., Jan. 21, 1854], p. 332-333.—v. 9, 1857. International copyright. [*Anon.*], p. 85-91.— New series, v. 1, 1868. Int. cop., editorial, p. 517 : The right of copyright. A concise statement of the question. [*Anon.*], p. 635-637 : Brief editorial notice of the organization of the Copyright Association, p. 776.—v. 2, 1868. Int. cop., [editorial notice of the proceedings of the International copyright association], p. 120.—v. 3, 1869. [Int. cop. Auerbach's " The Villa on the Rhine," editorial], p. 754-755.—v 4, 1869. [Two letters from Sir T: Noon Talfourd to Mr. G: P. Putnam on int. cop., dated Feb. 23 & 28, 1844], p. 559-560 : " Copyright" courtesies. [Remarks on the authorized translation of " The countess Gisela" b y E. Marlitt, *i.e.* Eugenie John], p. 639-640.— v. 6, 1870 [Ed. notice of J: C. Hotten's " Literary copyright," p. 240.

PÜTTER (Johann Stephan). Der büchernachdruck nach ächten grundsätzen des rechts geprüft. 7 p. l. 206 p. 4°. Göttingen, im verlage der wittwe Vandenhoeck, 1774.

Anon. review in "Göttingische anzeigen von gelehrten sachen." v. 1. 16°. Göttingen, 78. stück, den 30. Junii 1774, p. 565-669.

—— La propriété littéraire défendue, ou mémoire abrégé dans le qvel on examine jusqu'à quel point la contrefaçon peut être légitime. Traduit de l'allemand [par Pierre Joseph Neyron.] 3 p. l. 48 p. 8°. à Goettingue, chez la veuve d'A. Vandenhoeck, 1774.

QUELQUES observations sur le projet de loi relatif à la propriété littéraire. [*Anon.*] 4°. *Paris, J. Renouard*, 1839.

QUESTION (The) concerning literary property, determined by the court of king's bench on 20th April, 1769, in the cause between Andrew Millar and Robert Taylor : with the separate opinions of the four judges [E: Willes, R: Aston, Joseph Yates and W: Murray, earl of Mansfield] ; and the reasons given by each, in support of his opinion. iv., 127 p. 4°. London, W. Strahan & M. Woodfall, for B. Tovey, 1773.

Note.—Edited by Sir James Burrow. Willes's opinion occurs, p. 9-40; Aston's, p. 40-62; Yates's, p. 62-111 ; Mansfield's, p. 112-127.

RAE (W: Fraser). English views of international copyright. [*Anon.* letter], London, March 18, 1881. *In* "The Nation." v. 32. 4°. New York, no. 823, April 7, 1881, p. 236.

—— International copyright. *In* " The Nineteenth century." v. 10. 8°. London, no. 57, Nov. 1881, p. 723-734.

RALPH (James). The case of authors by profession or trade, stated ; with regard to booksellers, the stage, and the public. No matter by whom. [*Anon.*] About 68 p. 8°. London, Griffiths, 1758.

RAVELET (Armand). Code manuel de la presse, comprenant toutes les lois sur l'imprimerie la librairie—la presse périodique—l'affichage le colportage—les délits de presse et la propriété littéraire mises en ordre et annotées d'après la jurisprudence. About vii, 208 p. 16°. Paris, imp. Balitout, Questroy & cie, 1868.

—— *Same ;* 2ème éd. 2 p. l. viii, 225 p. 16°. Paris, F. Didot frères, fils & cie, 1872.

Contains : De la propriété littéraire, p. 185-202.

READE (C:) The eighth commandment. 2 p. l. 162 p. 5 l. 181-379 p. 1 port. 1 facs. 8°. London, Trübner & co., 1860.

Note.—Deals entirely with the production of translations from French dramas upon the English stage.

Notice by James Fraser, in A handy-book of patent and copyright law. By James Fraser. 12°. London, S. Low, son & co., 1860, p. 223-228.

—— [Letter on literary property.] *In* FRANCE. *Ministère d'état. (Commission de la propriété littéraire et artistique).* Rapports à l'empereur. 4°. Paris, 1863, p. 83-88.

—— *See also* Mathews (C: James).—The Publishers' weekly.

REASONS for a modification of the act of Anne [etc.] 1813. *See* Turner (Sharon).

RECHT (Das) der briefe und photographien. 1863. *See* Wächter (Oscar).

RECHT (Das) des künstlers. 1859. *See* Wächter (Oscar).

RECHTE (Die) der autoren auf dem congress zu Brüssel und in dem Entwurfe des Börsenvereins der deutschen buchhändler. [*Anon.*] *In* " Deutsche vierteljahrs-schrift." 22ster jahrgang. 1859 : 1stes heft. 8°. Stuttgart und Augsburg, p. 185-217.

RECHTLICHES und vernunftmässiges bedenken eines unpartheyischen rechtsgelehrten über den schändlichen nachdruck andern gehöriger bücher. [*Anon.*] 8°. Frankfurt und Leipzig, 1774.

REFLEXIONEN über den büchernachdruck, besonders zu gewinnung eines neuen gesichtspunktes in betreff seiner widerrechtlichkeit. Aus veranlassung des vortrags der königlichen Würtembergischen gesandtschaft bei der hohen deutschen bundesversammlung. [*Anon.*] About 48 p. 8°. Heidelberg, Groos, 1823.

REGNAULT (Théodore). *See* Godson (R:) De la propriété littéraire. 1826.

REICH (Ph. Erasmus). *See* Linguet (Simon Nicolas Henri). Betrachtungen über die rechte des schriftstellers. 1778.

REIMARUS (Johann Albert Heinrich). Der bücherverlag, in betrachtung der schriftsteller, der verleger und des publikums nochmals erwogen. [*Anon.*] 8°. Hamburg, 1773.

—— Erwägung des verlagsrechts in ansehung

des nachdrucks. About 35 p. 8°. Hamburg, Hoffman, 1792.

REIMPRESSION (La). 1851. *See* Hen (Charles).

RENAUDIN (Edmond). Le congrès international de la propriété artistique tenu à Paris en Septembre 1878. *In* "Journal des écono- mistes." 4e série,˙v. 4. 8°. Paris, no, 10, Oct. 1878, p. 104-109.

— Le congrès international littéraire tenu à Paris en 1878. *In* "Journal des écono- mistes." 4e série. v. 3. 8°. Paris, no. 9, Septembre 1878, p. 395-398.

RENAULT (Louis). De la propriété littéraire et artistique au point de vue international. *In* "Journal du droit international privé." 5me année. 8°. Paris, 1878, nos. 3-4, p. 117- 138 ; nos. 9-10, p. 454-477.

— *Same:* Extrait du Journal du droit inter- national privé. About 47 p. 8°. Paris, Marchal, Billard & cie, 1879.

RENDU (Ambroise). Le congrès littéraire de Rome. *In* "Le Génie civil." v. 2. 4°. Paris, no. 16, 15 juin 1882, p. 383.

— Traité pratique du droit industriel ou ex- posé de la législation et de la jurisprudence sur les établissements industriels, les brevets d'invention, la propriété industrielle, artis- tique et littéraire [etc.], par. A. Rendu, avec la collaboration de m. Charles Delorme. 8°. Paris, Cosse, 1855.
   Review by Charles Vergé in "Journal des écono- mistes." 2e série. v. 9. 8°. Paris, 1856, p. 287-289.

RENOUARD (Augustin Charles). Des droits des auteurs sur les produits de leur intelli- gence. *In* "Revue de législation et de ju- risprudence." v. 5. 8°. Paris, 1837, p. 241- 274.

— *Same :* [With changes and additions : Théorie du droit des auteurs.] *In* Traité des droits d'auteurs, par A. C. Renouard. v. 1. 8°. Paris, J. Renouard & cie, 1838, p. 433-475.

— *Same :* Theory of the rights of authors. [Translated by L. S. C., *i.e.* Luther Stearns Cushing, who has added : — Analysis of Kant's doctrine of the rights of authors.] *In* "American jurist and law magazine." v. 22. 12°. Boston, C: C. Little & J. Brown, Oct. 1839, pp. 39-92.

— *Same :* Theory of the rights of authors in literature, sciences, and the fine arts. (Trans- lated for and republished from the American jurist and law magazine for October, 1839.) [Signed L. S. C., *i.e.* Luther Stearns Cush- ing.] 56 p. 8°. Boston, C: C. Little & J. Brown, 1839.

— Théorie des droits des auteurs sur les pro- ductions de leur intelligence. *In* "Archives de droit et de législation." v. 1. 8°. Brux- elles, 1837, p. 27-49 of 1st pagination.

— Propriété littéraire, artistique, industrielle. *In* "Dictionnaire universel théorique et pra- tique du commerce et de la navigation." 2me éd. v. 2. 8°. Paris, Guillaumin & cie, 1863, p. 1255-1257.

RENOUARD (Augustin Charles). Traité des droits d'auteurs, dans la littérature, les sci- ences et les beaux-arts. 2 v. 3 p. l. 480 p. ; 2 p. l. 501 p. 8°. Paris, J. Renouard & cie., 1838-39.
   Anon. review in "Archives de droit et de législation." v. 3. 8°. Bruxelles, 1840, p. 220-224.

— *See also* Blanc (Étienne) *and* Beaume (Alex- andre).—Pic (François Antoine).

REPORT (A) of the proceedings of a meeting (consisting chiefly of authors), held May 4th [1852], at the house of Mr. John Chap- man, 142 Strand, for the purpose of hasten- ing the removal of the trade restrictions on the commerce of literature. 3d ed. 30 p. 8°. London, J. Chapman, 1852.
   Note.—Reported by Mr. J: Chapman.

RESTELLI (Francesco). Sulla proprietà let- teraria ed artistica. Memoria letta nelle tornate 15e 29 dicembre 1859. *In* "Atti del Reale istituto Lombardo di scienze, lettere ed arti." v. 2. fol. Milano, tipografia Ber- nardoni, 1860, p. 28-44.

RICHTER (Karl). Kunst und wissenschaft und ihre rechte im staate. 2 p. l. 220 p. 8°. Ber- lin, G. Jansen, 1863.

RIDDER (J. Herman de). Beschouwingen over kopierecht. 8°. Utrecht, 1875.

RIGHT (The) of copyright. A concise state- ment of the question. [*Anon.*] *In* "Put- nam's magazine." New series. v. 1. 8°. New York, no. 5, May 1868, p. 635-637.

RIGHT (The) to sue for infringement of literary copyright. [*Anon.*] *In* "The Jurist." v. 17, part 2. 8°. London, no. 883, Dec. 10, 1853, p. 486-490.

RIPLEY (G:) *See* Drone (Eaton Sylvester).

RITTER (— *Land und stadtgerichts-rath*). Ueber nachdruck nach preussischem recht. About 96 p. 8°. Berlin, Mittler & sohn, 1845.

ROBERTSON (Edmund) *and* Drone (Eaton Syl- vester). Copyright. *In* "The Encyclopædia Britannica." 9th ed. v. 6. 4°. Edinburgh, A. & C. Black, 1877, p. 356-363.
   Also in the same: "The Encyclopædia Britannica," 9th ed. v. 6. 4°. Boston, Little, Brown, & co., 1877, p. 356-367.
   Also in the same : (American reprint). v. 6. 8°. Phila- delphia, J. M. Stoddart & co., 1877, p. 316-325.

ROBIN (Eugène). De la contrefaçon Belge. La situation réelle. La librairie française. *In* "Revue des deux mondes." Tome 5ème 14ème année, nouvelle série. 8°. Paris, 15 janvier, 1844, p. 204-239.
   Contains : I. De la contrefaçon étrangère : II. His- torique de la contrefaçon des livres français : III. Situa- tion actuelle de la contrefaçon belge : IV. De l'abolition de la contrefaçon belge.

ROCCHIETTI (Joseph). Why a national litera- ture cannot flourish in the United States of North America. 84 p. 12°. New York, J. W. Kelley, 1845.
   Contains : International copyright, p. 61-69.

ROE (E: Payson). *See* The Publishers' weekly.

ROGERS (H; Wade). Literary property. *In*

"The Central law journal." v. 12. 8'. St. Louis, no. 14, April 15, 1881, p. 338-343.

—— *Same. In* "The Irish law times." v. 15. large 8°. Dublin, no. 749, June 4, 1881, p. 266-299.

—— *Same. In* " Pittsburgh legal journal." v. 11, old series, v. 28. 8°. Pittsburgh, no. 46, June 29, 1881, p. 417-419 ; no. 47, July 6, 1881, p. 427-429.

—— Literary property at common law, [etc.] *In* "The Federal reporter." v. 17. 8°· Saint Paul, West publishing co., 1883, no. 7, Sept. 18, 1883, p. 593-603.

ROMBÈRG (Édouard). Compte rendu des travaux du Congrès de la propriété littéraire et artistique, suivi d'un grand nombre de documents et d'un appendice contenant les lois de tous les pays sur les droits d'auteur, avec notices historiques. 2 v. 2 p. l. xvi., 350 p.; 2 p. l. ii., 324 p. 8°. Bruxelles et Leipzig, É. Flatau, 1859.

ROSCOE (E:) A few words about copyright. *In* "The Victoria magazine." v. 19. 8°. London, August 1872, p. 340-345.

RÖSSIG (Karl Glo.) Handbuch des buchhandelsrechts systematisch dargestellt für rechtsgelehrte, buchhändler und schriftsteller. About 476 p. 8°. Leipzig, Hinrichs, 1804.

ROTTECK (Carl Wenzeslas Rodecker von) *and* WELCKER (Carl Theodor). Das staats-lexikon. v. 9. 8°. Altona, J. F. Hammerich, 1847. *Contains:* Nachdruck. By P. Pfizer, with appendix by Carl Theodor Welcker, p. 326-333.

ROUTH (J: Martin). The law of artistic copyright : a handy book for the use of artists, publishers, and photographers. With explanatory dialogues. 2 p. l. iv., 147 p. 12°. London, Remington & co., 1881.

RÜDIGER (Johann Chr. Eph.) Juristisch-physiokratischer briefwechsel über verlagseigenthum und nachdruck, auch andere gegenstände der teutschen literaturpolizey. Erstes sendschreiben. [*Anon.*] 8°. Dessau & Leipzig, 1783.

—— Juristisch - physiokratischer briefwechsel über büchernachdruck und eigenthum an geisteswerken, mit herren von Sonnenfels, Ehlers, Becker und Krause. [*Anon.*] 8°. Halle, Dreissig, 1791.

S. *See* Lowndes (J: James).

S. The international copyright question. Protest against the doctrine of the Democratic review thereon. [*Anon.* With note by editor added.] *In* "The United States magazine and Democratic review." New series. v. 12. 8°. New York, no. 60, June 1843, p. 609-616.

S. (G.) British copyright in foreign works. [*Anon.*] *In* "The Jurist." v. 12, part 2. 8°. London, no. 605, Aug. 12, 1848, p. 322-324.

—— English copyright in foreign composition. [*Anon.*] *In* "The Jurist." v. 14, part 2. 8°. London, no. 684, Feb. 16, 1850, p. 46-49.

—— *Same. In* "The United States monthly

law magazine. Edited by J: Livingston." v. 2. 8°. New York, no. 6, Dec. 1850, p. 524-532.

—— *Same :* English copyright in foreign compositions. Reprinted from the Jurist. [*Anon.*] 8°. London, 1850.

—— The importation of reprints of English books into the United Kingdom and the colonies. [*Anon.*] *In* "The Jurist." New series, v. 6, part 2. 8°. London, no. 266, Feb. 11, 1860, p. 44-46.

—— Registration of literary copyright. [*Anon.*] *In* "The Jurist." New series, v. 6, part 2. 8°. London, no. 265, Feb. 4, 1860, p. 33-35.

S. (V.) Ein wort über die lage deutscher verleger von werken nicht deutscher urheber. [*Anon.*] *In* "Deutsche vierteljahrs schrift." 2tes heft, 1846. 8°. Stuttgart und Tübingen, nr. 34, p. 196-204.

SAINT GERMAIN (J. T. de) *pseud. See* Tardieu (Jules Romain).

SAINTE-BEUVE (Charles Augustin). Rapport sur la propriété littéraire. [6 juillet, 1866.] *In* Nouveaux lundis par C. A. Sainte-Beuve. v. 9. 12°. Paris, Lévy frères, 1867, p. 453-461.

SALVANDY (M. — de). Projet de loi sur les droits de propriété littéraire et artistique, présenté par m. de Salvandy, et voté par la chambre des pairs en 1839. *In* Législation de la propriété littéraire et artistique par Jules Delalain. 8°. Paris, 1862, p. 97-102.

SAUNDERS (Robert) *and* BENNING (W:) *vs.* SMITH (J: W:) *and* MAXWELL (Alexander). Copyright in law reports. The case of Saunders *v.* Smith. Before the vice-chancellor [June 8th and 9th, 1838] ; and on appeal before the lord chancellor [June 22d and 23d, 1838.] With a preface, table of cases cited, notes, and an appendix. By G: Morland Crawford. vii. p. 2 l., 60 p. 8°. London, A. Maxwell, 1839.

SAUVAGE (René Eugène). République des lettres, constitution de la propriété littéraire et de la librairie. About 20 p. 8°. Paris, E. Dentu, 1861.

SAXONY. Gesetz, den schutz der rechte an literarischen erzeugnissen und werken der kunst betreffend ; vom 22sten Feb. 1844. [*Also*] Verordnung zu ausführung des gesetzes über den schutz der rechte an literarischen erzeugnissen und werke der kunst ; vom 22sten Feb. 1844. *In* "Gesetz- und verordnungsblatt für das königreich Sachsen vom jahre 1844." 4°. Dresden, C. C. Reinhold & sohn, p. 27-31 end p. 32-36.

—— *Same :* Mit kritisch-exegetischen erläuterungen von dr. F. W. Meinert. 8°. Leipzig, Teubner, 1844.

SCHAFF (Philip). *See* Copyright (The) association.

SCHÄFFLE (Albert Eberhard Friedrich). Die nationalökonomische theorie der ausschliessenden absazverhältnisse insbesondere des litterarisch-artistischen urheberrechtes, des

References

Macfie, Robt A. Copyright & patents for inventions. Pleas for ... cheaper books. Edinburgh, 1879.

Cyclopedia of pol. sci. ed by J. J. Lalor v.1 p. 642-48 (1881)

Marston, E. Int. cop. with Amer. "the Academy v. 11 no. 249 n.s. '77 p. 117, '18

Mathews, Corn. "Better interests of the country." Various writings of C.M. N.Y. Harper, 1843 - p. 362·30

Morgan, James. Ipp. Law of literature 2 v. 1875 N.Y. Corkcroft Co.

Nicklin, Philip H. : Remarks agt. lit. copyr.
phil. P.H. Nicklin 1838

Dodd vs. Smith. Penn. Sup. ct. Per curiam
144 Pa St 340. Underselling by reprints of
paper-covered eds. not enjoinable.

Rocaficcii, Joseph. Why a national lit. cannot
fl. in U.S. n.y. 1845 Kelley

Ticknor, George. Int cop. in Life, letters
+ journals Boston Osgood 1876 p.278-80

References

Atlantic monthly
    Cheap reprints v. 43, 1879 p. 217 - 30
    Literary plunderers v. 42, 1878 p. 370, 371
Drone, Eaton Sylvester.
    A treatise on the law of property etc. 774 p.
    Boston, Little 1879
Eggleston, Edward
    Blessing of piracy (Century ("Scribners mo)
    v. 23 n.s. v.1 8° no. 6 apr 1882 p. 942 -45
Froude, James A. Copyright Commission. In
    Edinburgh Review v.148 no. 30, Oct '78 p. 295-343
Gerhard, Frederick   Will the pauper be
    benefited by it. 27 p. N. Y. 1868 [(no)]

Messrs Harpers & int copyright. Academy v. 15
no 364 n.s. apr 26 1879 p. 371
Harpers new mo. mag. v. 46 (73) p. 456-91
v. 58 '79 p. 929-31; v. 61 '80 p. 469-70; v. 62, 1881
p. 946-47.
Helps, Sir Arthur. Int. cop. between G.B. & U.S.
Macmillans mag v. 20 1869 p. 89-95 (June)
Hood, Thos. Copyright & copywrong. Letters I-V
In works ed by son. 1862 v. 4 p. 185-221 v. 6 p. 91-
Howe, M Tracy. Int. Copy. Western Law Journal
v. 2 no. 8 May 1845 p. 347-352
Lawrence, W. Beach. Closing argument... piracy
Boston. Mudge 1868

patent-, muster- und firmenschuzes nebst bei-
trägen zur grundrentenlehre. x., 286 p. 8°.
Tübingen, H. Laupp, 1867.

Contains: Das autorrecht als künstliche sicherung der
lohn- und der lohnrentenfunction, p. 102–220. Der schuz
von schriftwerken, musikalien und kunstwerken im positiven rechte und in der juristischen doctrin Deutschlands,
p. 221–238. Der artistische autorschuz insbesondere, p.
239–258.
Note.—Originally published in " Zeitschrift für die ge-
sammte staatswissenschaft."

SCHELLWITZ (Hartmann). Das recht des autors
an seinen werken nach den grundsätzen des
preussischen landrechts in einer kritischen
beleuchtung eines erkenntnisses des königlichen appellationsgerichts zu Köln, den
Becker'schen nachdruck von Theodor Kör-
ner's Sämmtlichen werken betreffend. Dargestellt von H. Schellwitz. iv. p. 1l., 41 p.
8°. Berlin, verlag der Nicolai'schen buchhandlung, 1855.

—— Ueber den grund, das wesen und die grenzen des rechtes der erzeuger an den schöpf-
ungen der kunst und wissenschaft. *In*
" Deutsche vierteljahrs schrift." 1stes heft,
1839. 8°. Stuttgart & Tübingen, nr. 5, p.
252–281.

SCHENK (Johann). Der französische gesetzentwurf zum schutze des literarischen und artistischen eigenthums. (Publicirt am 13. April
1863.) 38 p. 8°. Wien, F. Manz & comp.,
1863.

SCHLETTER (Hermann Theodor). Handbuch
der deutschen press-gesetzgebung. Sammlung der gesetzlichen bestimmungen über
das literarische eigenthum und die presse in
allen deutschen bundesstaaten, nebst ge-
schichtliche einleitung. xxxii., 352 p. 8°.
Leipzig, E. F. Steinacker, 1846.

Contents: Sammlung der gesetzlichen bestimmungen
über literarisches eigenthum, p. 1–141. Sammlung der
gesetzlichen bestimmungen über press-recht, p. 143–345.

SCHLICKEYSEN (C.) Die anerkennung des
geistigen eigenthums, eine soziale frage.
About 25 p. 8°. Berlin, Berggold, 1871.

SCHMID (Karl Ernst). Der büchernachdruck
aus dem gesichtspunkte des rechts, der moral
und politik : Gegen dr. Ludwig Friedrich
Griesinger. Der hohen deutschen bundesversammlung verehrungsvoll zugeeignet.
168 p. 12°. Jena, F. Frommann, 1823.

SCHNAASE (Karl ?) Ueber das künstlerische
eigenthum. Aus den Annalen für die rechtspflege und verwaltung. 8°. Trier, 1843.

SCHOLZ (Christian). Actenmässige darstellung
meiner gerichtlichen verfolgung durch die
literarische anstalt zu Frankfurt a. M. wegen
angeblichen nachdrucks des Struwelpeter
durch übersetzung desselben in das Schwe-
dische, Holländische und Englische. Meine
freisprechung in erster und meine verurtheil-
ung in zweiter instanz. Beitrag zur lehre
vom nachdruck. Nebst bemerkungen über
die deutschen verträge mit England und
Frankreich wegen gegenseitigen schutzes für
literarische und artistische erzeugnisse, sowie
über die ungültigkeit solcher durch Preussen
oder andere staaten des Zollvereins abge-

schlossenen verträge diesem gegenüber.
About vi., 105 p. 8°. Darmstadt, Leske,
1852.

SCHRECK (August Hermann). Die deutsche
reichsgesetzgebung über den schutz des
geistigen eigenthums. *In* " Unsere zeit.
Deutsche revue der gegenwart." Neue folge.
13ter jahrgang. 1ste hälfte. 8°. Leipzig, 7tes
heft, 1. April 1877, p. 511–527 ; 8tes heft, 15.
April 1877, p. 621–634.

SCHRÖTER (L.) Das eigenthum im allgemeinen
und das geistige eigenthum insbesondere für
gelehrte und laien natur- und rechtsgeschicht-
lich dargestellt. viii p., 1 l. 62 p. 8°. Breslau, G. P. Aderholz, 1840.

SCHÜRMANN (August). Der rechtsschutz gegen
übersetzungen in den internationalen' verträgen zum schutze des literarischen urheberrechts. Vom standpuncte des literarischen
verkehrs. v., 42 p. 8°. Leipzig, selbstverlag
des verfassers, [druck von C. P. Melzer],
1860.

SCHUTZ der autoren gegen übersetzung. 1855.
See WÄCHTER (Oscar).

SCOTT (Leonard). Piratical publishers. *In*
" The Popular science monthly." v. 22. 8°.
New York, no. 5, March, 1883, p. 656–659.

SCRIBNER'S monthly. (The Century magazine.)
25 v. 8°. New York, 1870–83.

Contains : v. 3, 1872. International copyright, editorial, p. 375–376.—v. 10, 1875. International copyright,
editorial, p. 378–379.—v. 11, 1875. Foreign dramatists
under American laws. By Eaton S. Drone, p. 90–97 ;
also Appendix, p. 136 : American authorship, editorial,
p. 280–281.—v. 14, 1877. Dr. Appleton on copyright, editorial, p. 108–109.—v. 16, 1878. Points in the copyright
discussion. By J. Brander Matthews, p. 897–899.—v. 17,
1879. Drone on copyright, p. 911.—v. 20, 1880. Congress
and international copyright. By Eugene L. Didier, p.
132–138 : International copyright, editorial, p. 146–147.—
v. 22, 1881. Copyright at home and abroad, editorial, p.
144–145.—v. 23 " The Century magazine," 1882. The
copyright negotiations. [By Arthur G: Sedgwick], p.
667–671 : Authors' rights, editorial, p. 779 : Two letters
on the international copyright question : i. Harriet Martineau, Tynemouth, Dec. 24, 1843, p. 781–782 : ii. P. A.
Towne, New York, Jan. 12, 1882, p. 782 : The blessings
of piracy. [By E: Eggleston], p. 942–945.

SCRUTTON (T: E:) The laws of copyright. An
examination of the principles which should
regulate literary and artistic property in England and other countries. Being the Yorke
prize essay of the University of Cambridge
for the year 1882, revised and enlarged.
About xix., 335 p. 8°: London, J: Murray,
1883.

SEDGWICK (Arthur G:) The copyright negotiations. *In* " The Century magazine."
[Scribner's monthly.] v. 23. 8°. New York,
no. 5, March 1882, p. 667–671.

—— [International copyright. *Anon.*] *In* " The
Atlantic monthly." v. 29. 8°. Boston, no.
173, March 1872, p. 387–388.

—— International copyright by judicial decision. *In* " The Atlantic monthly." v. 43.
8°. Boston, no. 256, Feb. 1879, p. 217–230.

—— *See also* Drone (Eaton Sylvester).

SEIDENSTÜKKER (Johann Heinrich Philipp). Ist
der staat, nach reinen grundsätzen des ge-

sellschaftlichen vertrags und nach den gemeinen grundsätzen des bürgerlichen rechts befugt, den büchernachdruck zu verbieten, oder nicht ? Gegen den freiherrn von Knigge. 8°. Helmstadt, Fleckeisen, 1792.

SELECT foreign cases. Copyright. *In* "The Law magazine and review." 4th series. v. 2. 8°. London, no. 244, May 1877, p. 381-387.

SEUFFERT (Lothar). Das Autorrecht an literarischen erzeugnissen. 44 p. 8°. Berlin, E. G. Lüderitz'sche verlagsbuchhandlung, 1873. [Sammlung gemeinverständlicher wissenschaftlicher vorträge, herausgegeben von Rud. Virchow und Fr. v. Holtzendorff. 8. serie, heft 186.]

SHALER (Nathaniel Southgate). Thoughts on the nature of intellectual property and its importance to the state. 1 p. l. 16 p. 8°. Cambridge, Welch, Bigelow & co., 1877.

Contents : Thoughts on the advantages of patent and copyright laws to the state. The nature of intellectual property.
—— *Same.* iv., 75 p. 8°. Boston, J. R. Osgood & co., 1878.

Contents : Considerations on the nature of intellectual property, p. 1-16. Effect of invention on national culture, p. 17-31. American communism, p. 33-44. Does the fostering of inventiveness profit a state?, p. 45-57. International property in patents and copyrights, p. 59-75.

SHEARD (H.) Brief statement on assumed foreign copyright. 8°. London, 1851.

SHEPHERD (H: J:) The law of copyright. A bill to amend the law relating to copyright. [Signed S., *Anon.*] *In* "The Law magazine." v. 19. 8°. London, May 1838, p. 365-378.
—— *See also* Wheaton (H:) *and* Donaldson (Robert) *vs.* Peters (R:) *and* Grigg (J:)

SHOARD (J:) A handy-book of the law of copyright. 1863. *See* Chappell (F: Patey) *and* Shoard.

SHORT (A) view of literary property. [*Anon.*] *In* Millar (Andrew) *vs.* Taylor (Robert). Speeches or arguments of the judges of the court of king's bench, April 1769. 8°. Leith, for W. Coke, 1771, p. 113-128.

SHORTT (J:) The law relating to works of literature and art: embracing the law of copyright, the law relating to newspapers, the law relating to contracts between authors, publishers, printers, &c., and the law of libel. With the statutes relating thereto, forms of agreements between authors, publishers, &c., and forms of pleadings. xxii., 780 p. 8°. London, H. Cox, 1871.

Review by James Appleton Morgan. *In* "The Forum." v. 3. 8°. New York, no. 5, Jan. 1875, p. 35-51.
Anon. notice in "The Journal of jurisprudence." 1871. v. 15. 8°. Edinburgh, no. 178, Oct. 1871, p. 517.
Anon. notice in "The Solicitors' journal and reporter." v. 15. 8°. London, no. 43, Aug. 26, 1871, p. 787.

SIMMS (W: Gilmore). International copyright. [*Anon.*] *In* "The Southern quarterly review." v. 4. 8°. Charleston, no. 7, July 1843, p. 1-46.
—— International copyright law. Views in regard to an extension of the privileges of copyright in the United States, to the citizens of other countries, in a letter to the hon. Isaac E. Holmes, of S. C., Member of Congress. *In* "The Southern literary messenger." v. 10. 8°. Richmond, 1844, no. 1, January, p. 7-17 ; no. 3, March, p. 137-151 ; no 6, June, p. 340-349 ; no. 8, August, p. 449-469.
—— *See also* Campbell (J:).—Dabney (J: Blair).—Mathews (Cornelius).

SIMON (Jules). *See* De la propriété intellectuelle. 1859.

SOCIÉTÉ d'économie politique de Paris. Compte rendu du Congrès de la propriété littéraire et artistique. Discussion sur la nature de cette propriété. *In* "Journal des économistes." 2e série. v. 20. 8°. Paris, 1858, p. 134-153, p. 284-313, p. 442-470.
—— *Same :* Discussion de la Société d'économie politique de Paris sur la question de la propriété littéraire et artistique. *In* "Compte rendu des travaux du Congrès de la propriété littéraire et artistique, par Édouard Romberg." v. 2. 8°. Bruxelles & Leipzig, É. Flatau, 1859, p. 261-311.

SOCIÉTÉ de législation comparée. *See* Annuaire de législation étrangère.

SOCIÉTÉ des gens de lettres. Proposition de loi sur la propriété intellectuelle, par le comité de la Société des gens de lettres. About 24 p. 8°. Paris, Brière, 1861.
—— La propriété littéraire et les traités internationaux. Lettre à m. le ministre des affaires étrangères au comité de la Société des gens de lettres et réponse du comité à m. le ministre des affaires étrangères. About 7 p. 8°. Paris, Société des gens de lettres, 1879.

SOCIÉTÉ pour la défense de la propriété littéraire et artistique. *See* Association pour la défense de la propriété littéraire.

SOCIETY for obtaining an adjustment of the law of copyright. [Prospectus.] About 4 p. 8°. London, 1851.

SOCIETY of arts. *London.* Artistic copyright. [A report prepared at the request of a committee of the society, by Delabere Roberton Blaine.] *In* "The Athenæum." 1858. Part 1. 4°. London, no. 1580, Feb. 6, 1858, p. 179-181.
—— *Same. In* "The Journal of the Society of arts." v. 6. sm. 4°. London, no. 279, March 26, 1858, p. 293-301.
—— *Same. In* "The Jurist." New series. v. 4, part 2. 8°. London, no. 163, Feb. 20, 1858, p. 86-90.
—— Artistic copyright. Reasons in favour of a bill to establish artistic copyright, prepared by the council of the Society of arts. fol. London, 1861.
—— Report of the artistic copyright committee. [With protest by D. R. Blaine upon the decision as to the registration of works of art.] *In* "The Athenæum." 1858, part 1. 4°. London, no. 1587, March 27, 1858, p. 401-403.

—— *Same. In* "The Jurist." New series, v.
4, part 2. 8°. London, no. 170, April 10,
1858, p. 168–170.

—— *See also* Journal (The) of the Society of
arts.

SOME remarks on the law of copyright. [*Anon.*]
About 15 p. 8°. [London, 1848?]

Anon. notice in "The Jurist." v. 12, part 2. 8°.
London, no. 597, June 17, 1848, p. 240–241.

SOME thoughts on the state of literary property,
humbly submitted to the consideration of the
public. [*Anon.*] 8°. London, Donaldson,
1764.

SOUTHERN (The) literary messenger. 8°. Richmond, 1837–44.

Contains: v. 3, 1837. Rights of authors. [*Anon.*],
p. 37–39.—v. 5, 1839. International law of copy-right.
[*Anon.*], p. 663–666.—v. 6, 1840. Rights of authors.
[Signed H. G.], p. 69–72.—v. 10, 1844. International
copyright law. By W: Gilmore Simms, p. 7–17, 137–151,
340–349, 449–469 : Cheap literature. [Signed E. D.], p.
33–39 : Reply to E. D. and Mr. Simms. [Signed J. B.
D., *i.e.* J: Blair Dabney], p. 193–199, 289–296 : E. D. to
J. B. D., [*i.e.* J: Blair Dabney], p. 415–422.

SOUTHEY (Robert). Inquiry into the copyright
act. [*Anon.*] *In* "The Quarterly review."
v. 21. 8°. *London*, no. 41, Jan., 1819, p.
196–213.

—— *Same :* Copyright. Extract from the cri-
tique on the copyright question. *In* BRYDGES
(Sir S: Egerton). The anti-critic. 8°. Geneva,
W. Fick, 1822, p. 132–133.

—— Southey, †††††, and Wordsworth on the
copyright question. [Two letters and a
poem.] *In* "The Athenæum." 4°. London,
no. 549, May 5, 1838, p. 323–324.

SPALDING (Hugh Mortimer). The law of copyright. With practical forms and notes.
Brevier ed. 2 p. l. 17–114 p. 24°. Philadelphia, P. W. Ziegler & co., [1878.] (Handy
law series.)

SPEECHES or arguments of the judges of the
court of king's bench, 1771. *See* Millar (Andrew) *vs.* Taylor (Robert).

SPENCER (Herbert). Herbert Spencer before
the English copyright commission. [Ques-
tions and answers.] *In* "The Popular science
monthly." v. 14. 8°. New York, no. 81,
Jan. 1879, p. 296–303 ; no. 82, Feb. 1879, p.
440–460.

—— [Letters on the Law amendment society's
copyright bill.] *In* "The Publishers' circular. v. 44. 8°. London, no. 1046, April 16,
1881, p. 301–303.

—— *Same. In* "The Publishers' weekly."
v. 19. 8°. New York, no. 486, May 7, 1881,
p. 512–513.

SPENNATI (*Cav.* —) Consultazione sulla proprietà letteraria dei Discorsi del sommo pontefice Pio IX., pronunziati in Vaticano, rac-
colti e pubblicati dal padre don Pasquale de
Franciscis. About 24 p. 16°. Napoli, tip.
di Luica di Tomaso, 1874.

SPOFFORD (Ainsworth Rand). Copyright in its
relations to libraries and literature. *In* "The

Library journal." v. 1. 4°. New York, nos.
2–3, Nov. 30, 1876, p. 84–89.

—— The history of international copyright in
congress. [*Anon.*] *In* "The Round table."
v. 3. fol. New York, no. 28, March 17,
1866, p. 161–162 ; no. 29, March 24, 1866, p.
178–179.

—— *See also* The Publishers' weekly.

SPÖNDLIN (R.) Ueber das wesen des verlagsrechts und dessen verletzung durch den
Nachdruck mit rücksicht auf das deutsche,
französische und schweizerische recht. Inaugural-dissertation zur erlangung der juristischen doctorwürde. Der hohen staatswissen-
schaftl. facultät der universität Zürich vorge-
legt. 2 p. l. 81 p. 1 l. 8°. Zürich, F. Schulthess,
1867.

STEDMAN (Edmund Clarence). *See* Copyright
(The) association.—The Publisher's weekly.

STEIGER (E.) Der nachdruck in Nord-Amerika.
Mein wirken als deutscher buchhändler.
Zwei aufsätze von E. Steiger. Als manu-
script gedruckt. About 119 p. 16°. New
York, 1867.

STEINITZ (Heinrich). Die neuen deutschen
reichsgesetze, betreffend das urheberrecht an
werken der bildenden kunste, den schutz der
photographieen gegen unbefugte nachbildung, und das urheberrecht an mustern und
modellen. About 112 p. 8°. Berlin, Hem-
pel, 1876.

STEPHEN (Sir James). Digest of the law of
copyright. *In* Great Britain. *Royal commission on copyright.* Report. fol. London, G.
E. Eyre & W. Spottiswoode, 1878, p. lxi–xc.

STEVENS (H:) The universal postal union and
international copy-right. [A paper read before the Library association at Oxford, Oct.
3d, 1878.] *In* Library (The) association of
the United Kingdom. The transactions of
the first annual meeting. 1878. 4°. Oxford,
p. 108–120.

STOUPE (J. G. Antoine). Réflexions sur les
contrefaçons en librairie, suivies d'un mémoire sur le rétablissement de la communauté
des imprimeurs de Paris. 8°. Paris, Stoupe,
[1804.]

—— *Same :* Mémoire sur le rétablissement de
la communauté des imprimeurs de Paris,
suivi de Réflexions sur les contrefaçons en
librairie, et sur le stéréotypage. About 39 p.
12°. Paris, les marchands de nouveautés,
1806.

STUBENRAUCH (Moritz, *edler* von). Entwurf
eines gesetzes zum schutze der autor-rechte
an werken der literatur und kunst. Projet
d'une loi garantissant les droits des auteurs
aux œuvres de littérature et d'art. *In* Compte
rendu des travaux du congrès artistique d'Anvers par Eugène Gressin Dumoulin. 8°.
Anvers & Leipzic, M. Kornicker, 1862, p.
339–364.

—— Die neuesten bestrebungen zum schutz des
urheberrechtes an erzeugnissen der kunst. 8°.
Wien, 1862.

STYLUS, *pseud.* American publishers and English authors. By Stylus. 23 p. 8°. Baltimore, E. L. Didier, 1879.
Notice in "The Publishers' weekly." v. 15. 8°. New York, no. 370, Feb. 15, 1879, p. 196-197.

SUMMARY of evidence on the copyright amendment bill. 8 p. 8°. [London, Barnard & Farley, 1818?]

SUMNER (C:) [International copyright. Letter on this subject, February 17, 1868.] *In* The Copyright association for the protection and advancement of literature and art. International copyright. 8°. New York, 1868, p. 15-16.

—— *Same. In his* Works. v. 12. 8°. Boston, Lee & Shepard, 1877, p. 270-271.

SWEDEN. *See* Annuaire de législation étrangère. 1877.

SYNOPSIS taken from the record of testimony of Dana. *See* Lawrence (W: Beach) *vs.* Dana (R: H:, *jr.*) *et als.*

TALFOURD (Sir T: Noon). A speech delivered in the house of commons, on Thursday the 18th of May 1837, on moving for leave to bring in a bill to consolidate the law relating to copyright, and to extend the term of its duration. 8°. London, E. Moxon, 1837.

—— *Same. In his* Critical and miscellaneous writings. 2d American ed. 8°. Philadelphia, Carey & Hart, 1846, p. 159-164.

—— *Same:* Amendment of the law of copyright. [An abridgement of his speech.] "The Legal observer." v. 14. 8°. London, Richards & co., 1837, p. 65-68.
Anon. notice in "The Athenæum." 4°. London, no. 501, June 3, 1837, p. 402.
Anon. review [by T: Watts?] *In* "The Mechanics' magazine." v. 27. 8°. London, no. 725, July 1, 1837, p. 196-199.
Anon. review: The copy-right law, in "The Monthly review." v. 1, new series. 8°. London, no. 1, Jan. 1838, p. 52-63.

—— A speech delivered in the house of commons on Wednesday, 25th April 1838, on moving the second reading of the bill to amend the law of copyright. About 22 p. 8°. London, E. Moxon, 1838.

—— *Same. In his* Critical and miscellaneous writings. 2d American ed. 8°. Philadelphia, Carey & Hart, 1846, p. 165-171.

—— Sergeant Talfourd's speech on the copyright question, delivered in the house of commons, February 28, 1839. To which is added Mr. Tegg's Letter to the 'Times,' on the copyright monopoly. 8°. London, Foster & Hextall, 1839.
Anon. notice in "The Eclectic review." New series, v. 5. 8°. London, April 1839, p. 434-437.

—— *Same. In his* Critical and miscellaneous writings. 2d American ed. 8°. Philadelphia, Carey & Hart, 1846, p. 171-176.

—— Three speeches delivered in the house of commons in favour of a measure for an extension of copyright. To which are added, the petitions in favour of the bill, and remarks on the present state of the copyright

question. xxxi., 148 p. 16°. London, E. Moxon, 1840.
Anon. notice in "The monthly magazine: edited by J: A. Heraud." v. 3. 8°. London, no. 15, March 1840, p. 325-327.
Review by T: Hood in "The works of T. Hood. Edited by his son." v. 5. 12°. London, E. Moxon & co., 1862, p. 363-365.

—— *Same:* Trois discours prononcés au parlement d'angleterre par Sir T. Noon Talfourd; traduits de l'anglais par Paul Laboulaye. *In* "Études sur la propriété littéraire en France et en Angleterre, par Édouard Laboulaye." 8°. Paris, A. Durand, 1858, p. 83-151.

—— Serjeant Talfourd's copyright bill. *In* "The Jurist." 8° London, no. 19, May 20, 1837, p. 321-323 : "The Legal observer." 8°. London, v. 14, 1837, p. 125-126; v. 15, 1838, p. 449-451 : "The Monthly magazine, edited by J: A. Heraud." v. 1. 8°. London, no. 5, May, 1839, p. 583-584.

—— Speech for the defendant in the prosecution of the Queen v. Moxon, for the publication of Shelley's works. 8°. London, 1841.

TALLICHET (Édouard). La propriété littéraire. Un congrès de gens de lettres à Paris. *In* "Bibliothèque universelle et revue suisse." v. 63. 8°. Lausanne, July 1878, p. 110-128.

TARANTINI (Leopoldo). In difesa della proprietà letteraria dei discorsi del sommo Pontefice pel rev. D. Pasquale de Franciscis, contro il sig. Girolamo Milone. About 34 p., 2 tab. 8°. [Napoli, 1876.]

TARDIEU (Jules Romain). De la perpétuité en matière de littérature et d'art. Lettre à l'Académie impériale des sciences, belles-lettres et arts de Rouen ; par J. T. de Saint Germain [*pseud.*] About 16 p. 8°. Paris, J. Tardieu, 1858.

—— *See also* Curmer (Henri Léon).

TEGG (T:) Remarks on the speech of sergeant Talfourd, on moving for leave to bring in a bill to consolidate the laws relating to copyright, and to extend the term of its duration. About 23 p. 8°. London, Tegg & son, 1837.
Anon. review: The copy-right law. *In* "The Monthly review." v. 1, new series. 8°. London, no. 1, Jan. 1838, p. 52-63.

—— *Same:* Produce of copy-right. Extract from letter of Mr. Tegg, in answer to sergeant Talfourd's copyright bill. *In* "The American almanac." 1840. 12°. Boston, D. H. Williams, p. 100-102.

TÉNINT (Wilhelm). De la propriété littéraire. *In* "La France littéraire." Nouv. série. v. 4. 8°. Paris, 7 mars 1841, p. 249-256.

TERHUNE (Mary Virginia). *See* The Publishers' weekly.

THOMAS (Émile). Contrefaçon. *In* Coquelin (Charles) *and* Guillaumin (Urbain Gilbert). Dictionnaire de l'économie politique. 3° éd. v. 1. 8°. Paris, Guillaumin & cie., 1864, p. 477-479.

THOMAS (J: Penford). A legal and constitutional argument against the alleged judicial right of restraining the publication of reports of judicial proceedings, as assumed in the King v. Thistlewood and others, enforced against the proprietor of the Observer by a fine of £500, and afterwards confirmed by the court of King's bench. 2 p. l. 148 p. 8°. London, I. L. Turner, for S. Sweet, 1822.

THOMAS (Moy). *See* Appleton (C: E: Cutts Birchall).— Great Britain. *Royal commission on copyright.* Report. 1878. — Harper & Brothers.

THOMPSON (G: Carslake). Remarks on the law of literary property in different countries, and the principles on which it is founded. 31 p. 8°. London, The National press agency, 1883.

THORNTON (W. W.) The universal cyclopædia of law. 8°. Northport, N. Y., E: Thompson, [1883.]
Contains: Copyright, p. 230-238.

THULLIEZ (Louis). Étude législative, historique et juridique sur la propriété littéraire. 306 p. 8°. Paris, E. Thorin, 1876.

TICKNOR (G:) International copyright. *In* "Life, letters, and journals of G: Ticknor." v. 2. 8°. Boston, J. R. Osgood & co., 1876, p. 278-280.

TITLES of newspapers and books. [*Anon.* From the Solicitors' journal.] *In* "The Central law journal." v. 10. 8°. St. Louis, 1880, no. 5, Jan. 30, p. 82-84; no. 6, Feb. 6, p. 104-106; no. 7, Feb. 13, p. 123-126.

TOMLINS (Sir T: Edlyne). Literary property. *See* Jacob (Giles).

TOMMASEO (Nicolò). Lettera di N. Tommaseo di Librai Italiani sulla proprietà letteraria. 8°. Venezia, 1839.

TOSCANI (Odoardo). Studio sulla proprietà letteraria ed artistica. About 147 p. 8°. Roma, 1881.

TOURGÉE (Albion Winegar). The law of copyright. *In* "Our Continent." v. 1. fol. Philadelphia, no. 7, March 29, 1882, p. 104.

TOURNACHON-NADAR (Félix) *contre* Tournachon (Adrien, jeune) & cie. 1857. *See* Tribune (La) judiciaire.

TOWNE (P. A.) *See* Scribner's monthly.

TRIBUNE (La) judiciaire. Recueil des plaidoyers et des réquisitoires les plus remarquables des tribunaux français et étrangers par J. Sabbatier. v. 5. 8°. Paris, C. Borrani, 1857.
Contains: Cour impériale de Paris. Présidence de m. le premier président Delangle. Audience du 12 déc. 1857. Revendication de la propriété exclusive du pseudonyme Nadar. Félix Tournachon-Nadar, contre A. Tournachon jeune et cie., p. 295-323 (Plaidoirie de me Henry Celliez, p. 295-311 : Plaidoirie de me Ernest Desmarest, p. 311-322 : Arrêt, p. 322-323).

TROLLOPE (Anthony). On the best means of extending and securing an international law of copyright. *In* National association for the promotion of social science. Transactions. 1866. 8°. London, Longmans, 1867, p. 119-125 : Discussion on this paper, p. 243-244.

TROMP (T. van Hettinga). De Koninklijke akademie van wetenschappen en de zoogenaamde letterkundige en kunsteigendom, 8°. Leeuwarden, 1863.

TUCKERMAN (H: Theodore). Violations of literary property. The Federalist.—Life and character of John Jay. *In* "The Continental monthly." v. 6. 8°. New York, no. 3, Sept. 1864, p. 336-355.

TURCHIARULO (A.) La proprietà letteraria. 8°. Napoli, 1857.

TURNER (Sharon). Reasons for a modification of the act of Anne respecting the delivery of books, and copyright. [*Anon.*] 1 p. l. 60 p. 8°. London, Nichols, son, & Bentley, 1813.

—— To the chairman of the committee upon the copyright laws. 16 p. 8°. [London, Barnard & Farley, 1818.]

TURNER (T:) On copyright in design in art and manufactures. With addenda [of statutes in force and rules of registrar of designs.] viii., 124 p. 8°. London, F. Elsworth, 1851.

TYLER (Moses Coit). *See* The Publishers' weekly.

TYNDALL (J:) Professor Tyndall before the English copyright commission. [Questions and answers.] *In* "The Popular science monthly." v. 14. 8°. New York, no. 79, Nov. 1878, p. 39-44.

UNDERDOWN (Emanuel Maguire). The law of art copyright. The engraving, sculpture and designs acts, the international copyright act, and the art copyright act, 1862. With an introduction and notes. Also an appendix, containing the evidence communicated to the Society of arts on piracy of works of art, and forms for the use of artists, etc. 2 p. l. 211 p. 12°. London, J. Crockford, 1863.
Anon. notice in "The Art journal." New series v. 2. 4°. London, April 1, 1863, p. 84.
Anon. review in "The Athenæum." 4°. London, no. 1852, April 25, 1863, p. 549-550 : Note from P. Le Neve Foster, no. 1853, May 2, 1863, p. 587.

UNDERHILL (Arthur). A summary of the law of torts, or wrongs independent of contract. 12°. London, Butterworths, 1873.
Contains: Infringement of copyright, p. 173-180.

—— *Same :* Principles of the law of torts. 1st American from the 2d English ed., by A. Underhill, assisted by Claude C: M. Plumptre. With American cases, by Nathaniel C. Moak. 8°. Albany, W: Gould & son, 1881.
Contains: Infringement of copyright. [Prepared by J: T. Cook], p. 666-689.

UNITED STATES. Acts passed by the United States Congress relating to copyright. *In* "The Statutes at large." v. 1-22. 8°. Boston & Washington, 1845-83.
Summary : An act for the encouragement of learning by securing the copies of maps, charts, and books, to the authors and proprietors of such copies, during the times therein mentioned. [1st congress, 2d session, chapter 15, May 31, 1790], v. 1, p. 124-126. An act supplementary to an act, intituled "An act for the encouragement of learning [1790], and extending the benefits thereof to the arts of designing, engraving, and etching historical and other prints. [7th cong., 1st sess., chap. 36, April 29, 1802], v. 2, p. 171-172. An act to continue a copyright to J: Rowlett. [20th cong., 1st sess., chap. 145, May 24, 1828], v. 6, p. 389. An act to amend the several acts respecting

copyrights. [21st cong., 2d sess., chap. 16, Feb. 3, 1831], v. 4, p. 436-439. An act to amend "An act to continue a copyright of J: Rowlett." [21st cong., 1st sess., chap. 13, Feb. 11, 1830], v. 6, p. 403. An act supplementary to the act [1831] to amend the several acts respecting copyrights. [23d cong., 1st sess., chap. 157, June 30, 1834], v. 4, p. 728. An act supplementary to the act of 24th May, 1828, to continue a copyright to J: Rowlett. [27th cong., 3d sess., chap. 140, March 3, 1843], v. 6, p. 897. [Enactment that of copyrighted books one copy shall be deposited with the Smithsonian Institution and one copy in the Library of Congress. 29th cong., 1st sess., chap. 179, sec. 10. Aug. 10, 1846¹, v. 9, p. 106. [Copyright deposits may be sent free by mail. 33d cong., 2d sess., chap. 201, sec. 5, March 3, 1855], v. 10, p. 685. An act supplemental to an act entitled "An act to amend the several acts respecting copyright," approved Feb. 3, 1831. [34th cong., 1st sess., chap. 169, Aug. 18, 1856], v. 11, p. 138-139. [Act removing copyright deposits from the Department of State to the Department of the Interior. 35th cong., 2d sess., chap. 22, sec. 8, Feb. 5, 1859, v. 11, p. 380-381. An act to extend the right of appeal from decisions of circuit courts to the Supreme court of the United States [in copyright cases. 36th cong., 2d sess., chap. 37, Feb. 18, 1861], v. 12, p. 130-131. An act supplemental to an act entitled "An act to amend the several acts respecting copyright," approved Feb. 3, 1831, and to the acts in addition thereto and amendment thereof. [38th cong., 2d sess., chap. 126, March 3, 1865], v. 13, p. 540-541. An act amendatory of the several acts respecting copyrights. [39th cong., 2d sess., chap. 43, Feb. 18, 1867], v. 14, p. 395. An act to revise, consolidate, and amend the statutes relating to patents and copyrights. [41st cong., 2d sess., chap. 230, (sec. 86 to 110 concerning copyrights), July 8, 1870, v. 16, p. 198-217. An act to amend the law relating to patents, trade-marks and copyrights. [43d cong., 1st sess., chap. 301, June 18, 1874], v. 18, p. 78-79. An act for the relief of W: Tod Helmuth, of New York. [Authorizing him to enter for copyright a corrected title of "A system of surgery, by William Tod Helmuth," and to deposit two copies of the book with the Librarian of Congress, in lieu of an imperfect title entered in 1872. 43d cong., 1st sess., chap. 534, June 23, 1874], v. 18, p. 618. [Act forbidding the transmission through the mails of any publication which violates any copyright granted by the United States. 45th cong., 3d sess., chap. 180, sec. 15, March 3, 1879], v. 20, p. 359. An act to amend the statutes in relation to copyright. [Relating to the position of claim of copyright upon designs. 47th cong., 1st sess., chap. 366, Aug. 1, 1882], v. 22, p. 181.

—— Acts in force as to the jurisdiction of copyright cases. *In* "The Revised Statutes of the United States." 2d ed. 8°. Washington, Government printing office, 1878.
Summary: Circuit courts, acts of 8 July, 1870 and 16 Feb., 1875, sec. 692, clause 9, p. 111. Supreme court, act 8 July, 1870, sec. 699, clause 1, p. 130. Jurisdiction of United States courts exclusive of the courts of the several states, act 8 July, 1870, sec. 711, clause 5, p. 135. Procedure, act 8 July, 1870, sec. 972, p. 183.

—— Copyrights. [The laws now in force]. *In* "The Revised Statutes of the United States." 2d ed. 8°. Washington, Government printing office, 1878, title lx., chap. 3, p. 957-960.

——— The copyright laws of the United States, as revised, consolidated, and amended by act of congress approved July 8th, 1870. 8 p. 8°. Washington, Government printing office, 1870.

—— Directions for securing copyrights under the revised act of congress which took effect August 1, 1874. 4 p. 8°. [Washington, Library of Congress, 1874.]
Note.—Furnished, upon application, by the Librarian of Congress, Washington, D. C.
—— The law of copyright in the United States. In force August 1, 1874. From the Revised Statutes of the United States, in force December 1, 1873, as amended by act approved June 18, 1874. 4 p. 8°. [Washington, Library of Congress, 1874.]
Note.—Supplied, upon application, by the Librarian of Congress, Washington, D. C.

—— The law of patents and copyrights, as revised, simplified, arranged, and consolidated, by the commission appointed for that purpose, from the various acts of congress now in force, in whole or in part. 24 p. 8°. Washington, Government printing office, 1868.
Contains: Chapter III, of copyrights, p. 20-24.

—— The patent, trade-mark and copyright laws of the United States of America. From the Revised Statutes of the United States, with the amendments since 1874. And a full index. 48 p. 8°. New York, Baker, Voorhis & co., 1878.
Contains: Chapter 3. Copyright, p. 38-44.

—— Revision of the United States statutes. Title lxiii. : Patents, trade-marks, and copyrights. As drafted by the commissioners appointed for that purpose. Title leaf, 34 p. 4°. Washington, Government printing office, 1872.
Contains: Copyrights, p. 27-33.

UNITED STATES DIGEST ; a digest of decisions of the various courts within the United States to the year 1870. By B: Vaughan Abbott. 14 v. 8°. Boston, Little, Brown & co., 1874-76.
Contains: Copyright, v. 3, p. 607-612.

—— *Same :* New series, v. 1-9. Annual digest. 1870-1878. By B: V. Abbott. 8°. Boston, Little, Brown & co., 1872-79.
Contains: Copyright, v. 1, 1870, p. 167-168 : v. 2, 1871, p. 166-167 : v. 3, 1872, p. 159-160 : v. 4, 1873, p. 182-183 : v. 6, 1875, p. 176 : v. 7, 1876, p. 177-178 : v. 8, 1877, p. 172-173.

—— *Same :* New series, v. 10. Annual digest. 1879. By J: E. Hudson and G: F: Williams. 8°. Boston, Little, Brown & co., 1880.
Contains : Copyright, p. 152.

—— *Same :* New series, v. 11-14. Annual digest. 1880-1883. By G: F: Williams. 8°. Boston, Little, Brown & co., 1881-84.
Contains: Copyright, v. 11, 1880, p. 162 : v. 12, 1881, p. 164 : v. 13, 1882, p. 176-177 : v. 14, 1883, p. 165-166.

UNIVERSITY of Cambridge. *England.* Further statement ordered by the syndics of the University of Cambridge to be printed and circulated. 8°. Cambridge, 1818.

—— *Same : In* "A vindication of the right of the universities of the United Kingdom to a copy of every new publication. By E: Christian." 3d ed. 8°. Cambridge, J. Smith, 1818, p. 189-193.
Note.—For a reply see Brydges (Sir S: Egerton). Answer to the Further statement by the syndics of the University of Cambridge. 1818.

—— Observations on the copy-right bill, printed by order of the vice-chancellor, heads of colleges, &c. of the University of Cambridge. 8°. Cambridge, 1818.

—— *Same : In* "A vindication of the right of the universities of the United Kingdom to a copy of every new publication. By E: Christian." 3d ed. 8°. Cambridge, J. Smith, 1818, p. 181-188.

UNIVERSITY (The) of Cambridge against H:

LITERARY PROPERTY.

49

Bryer. Judgment, 20th November 1812. [*Anon.* report.] 15 p. 8°. [London, Strahan & Preston, *n. d.*]
—— *Same : In* "A vindication of the right of the universities of the United Kingdom to a copy of every new publication. By E: Christian." 3d ed. 8°. Cambridge, J. Smith, 1818, p. 85–107.
—— *Same : In* "Reports of cases argued and determined in the court of king's bench. By E: Hyde East." v. 16. 8°. London, A. Strahan for J. Butterworth & son, 1814, p. 317–334.
—— *Same : In* "Reports of cases in the court of king's bench. By E: Hyde East." v. 16. New ed., by T: Day. 8°. Philadelphia, M. Carey & son, 1817, p. 315–333.

UNPARTHEYISCHES bedenken, worin aus allen natürlichen, göttlichen und menschlichen, civil- und criminalrechten und gesetzen klar und deutlich ausgeführet und bewiesen wird, dass der unbefugte nachdruck privilegirter und unprivilegirter bücher ein grob- und schändliches, allen göttlich- und menschlichen rechten und gesetzen zuwiderlaufendes verbrechen, und infamer diebstahl sey. 8°. Cöln, 1742.
Note.—According to Weller (Emil) Die falschen und fingirten druckorte, v. 1, Leipzig, 1864, it was printed by Püttner in Hof.

UNRECIPROCATED copyright. [*Anon.*] *In* "The New monthly magazine and humorist. Edited by W. Harrison Ainsworth." v. 93. 8°. London, no. 369, Sept. 1851, p. 122–126.

URHEBERRECHT und nachdruck. *In* "Die Grenzboten. Zeitschrift für politik und literatur." 20. Jahrgang, 1. semester, 1. band. 8°. Leipzig, 1861, p. 52–63?

VATIMESNIL (— de). Opinion de m. de Vatimesnil, sur l'effet des prorogations accordeés par le projet, quant aux priviléges dont l'auteur ou ses héritiers auraient traité avec un tiers. *In* France. *Commission de la propriété littéraire.* Collection des procès-verbaux. 4°. Paris. Pillet aîné, 1826, p. 305–307.

VEIT (Moritz). Die erweiterung des schutzes gegen nachdruck zu gunsten der erben verdienter autoren. 8°. Leipzig, Veit & co., 1855.

VELDEN (M. B. J. van den). Over het kopijregt in Nederland. 8°. 's Gravenhage, S. de Visser, 1835.

VERGÉ (Charles Henri). *See* Lacan (Adolphe Jean Baptiste) *and* Paulmier (Charles Pierre Paul).—Pataille (Henri Jules Simon) *and* Huguet (Auguste).—Rendu (Ambroise).

VERMEIRE (P.) Le libre travail, ou abolition des brevets, droits d'auteur, garantie de dessins, remplacé par un système plus efficace et plus naturel, suivi d'une critique par Ch. Le Hardy de Beaulieu et P. Paillotet. 8°. Bruxelles, A. Decq, 1864.

VERNET (Jean Émile Horace). Du droit des peintres et des sculpteurs sur leurs ouvrages. *In* "La France littéraire." Nouvelle série, v. 4. 8°. Paris, 7 mars 1841, p. 257–268.

VERPLANCK (Gulian Crommelin). The law of literary property. *In* "Discourses and addresses on subjects of American history, arts, and literature. By Gulian C. Verplanck." 12°. New York, J. & J. Harper, 1833, p. 215–227.

VERTHEIDIGUNG des eigenthums gegen den raub oder prüfung der schrift: Wider und für den büchernachdruck, aus den papieren des blauen mannes. [*Anon.*] About 70 p. 8°. Schwaben, 1790.

VESQUE VON PÜTTLINGEN (Johann, freiherr). Das musicalische autorrecht. Eine juristisch-musicalische abhandlung. Mit unterstützung durch die Kaiserliche Academie des wissenschaften. x., 205 p. 8°. Wien, W: Braumüller, 1864.
—— Oesterreichs gesetzgebung über literarisches und artistisches eigenthum. *In* "Œsterreichische zeitscrift für rechts- und staatswissenschaft." 23. Jahrgang. 8°. Wien, 1847, p. 92–*seq.*

VIETOR (J. Fresemann). Eene bijdrage tot het leerstuk van den intellectueelen eigendom. About 106 p. 8°. Utrecht, J. L. Beijers, 1868.
—— Het auteursrecht. Kantteekeningen op het ontwerp van wet tot regeling van het auteursrecht. 66 p. 8°. Utrecht, J. L. Beijers, 1877.

VIGNY (*Le comte* Alfred de). De mademoiselle Sédaine et de la propriété littéraire. Lettre à messieurs les députés. *In* "Revue des deux mondes." v. 25, 4ème série. 8°. Paris, 15 jan. 1841, p. 220–252.

VILLEFORT (Alfred). De la propriété littéraire et artistique au point de vue international. Aperçu sur les législations étrangères et sur les traités relatifs à la répression de la contrefaçon, suivi d'un appendice contenant : 1° le texte des conventions diplomatiques conclues ; par la France avec la Grande-Bretagne, la Sardaigne, le Portugal et le Hanovre ; par la Grande-Bretagne avec la Prusse et la Hanovre : 2° le texte en français de la loi portugaise sur la propriété littéraire. 2 p. l., 103 p. 8°. Paris, Cosse, 1851.

VILLEMAIN (—) Projet de loi sur les droits de propriété littéraire et artistique, présenté par m. Villemain, voté par articles et rejeté au vote final par la chambre des députés en 1841. *In* "Législation de la propriété littéraire et artistique, par Jules Delalain." 8°. Paris, 1862, p. 102–108.

VINCENT (C: E: Howard). The law of criticism and libel. A handbook for journalists, authors, and the libelled. 58 p. 16°. London, E. Wilson, 1876.

VINDICATION (A) of the exclusive right of authors to their own works : a subject now under consideration before the twelve judges of England. [*Anon.*] About 45 p. 8°. London, 1762.

VIOTTA (H. A.) Het auteursrecht van den componist. Academisch proefschrift. About

4 p. l, 83 p. 8°. Amsterdam, L. Roothaan, 1877.

VIVIEN (Alexandre François Auguste). De la répression de la contrefaçon en France des ouvrages publiés en Sardaigne.—Rapport de m. Vivien. *In* " Revue de législation et de jurisprudence." 10e année, nouv. série. v. 20. 8°. Paris, 1844, p. 512-525.

VOLKMANN (Adalbert Wilhelm). Ein wort über die lage deutscher verleger von werken nicht deutscher urheber. [Signed V. S. *anon.*] *In* " Deutsche Vierteljahrsschrift." 2tes heft, 1846. 8°. Stuttgart & Tubingen, nr. 34, p. 196-204.

—— Das getheilte eigenthum unter dem bestehenden gesetze gegen nachdruck. *In* " Zeitschrift für rechtspflege und verwaltung, zunächst für das königreich Sachsen." Neue folge, bd. 14. 8°. Leipzig, 1855, heft 2, nr. iv., p. 110-125.

—— Ist der unbefugte nachdruck des rechtmässigen verlegers, welcher in der ueberschreitung der vertragsmässigen anzahl der exemplare liegt, ein betrug? *In* " Neue jahrbücher für sachsisches strafrecht." 4. bd. 8°. Dresden & Leipzig, 1846, nr. 7, p. 117-*seq.*

—— Ueber die grenzen des den geisteswerken gebührenden rechtsschutzes. Mit besonderer rücksicht auf das gesetz vom 22. Febr. 1844. *In* " Zeitschrift für rechtspflege und verwaltung, zunächst für das königreich Sachsen." Neue folge, 6. bd. 8°. Leipzig, 1847, nr. 9, p. 262-282.

—— Ueber die strafrechtliche seite der verletzungen des urheberrechts. *In* " Neue jahrbücher für sachsisches strafrecht." 5. bd. 8°. Dresden & Leipzig, 1848, nro. 2 & 9.

—— Die werke der kunst in den deutschen gesetzgebungen zum schutze des urheberrechts. Mit besonderer bezugnahme auf das königlichsächsische recht beleuchtet. 8°. München, 1856.

—— Widerlegung der hauptsächlichsten gründe der vertheidiger des nachdrucks. *In* " Allgemeine presszeitung. Annalen der presse, der literatur und des buchhandels. Redigirt unter der leitung von dr. J. E. Hitzig." Jahrgang 1845. 8°. Leipzig, 1845.

—— Zusammenstellung der gesetzlichen bestimmungen über das urheber- und verlagsrecht. Aus den bundesbeschlüssen den deutschen territorialgesetzgebungen und den französischen und englischen gesetzen in auftrag des Börsenvereins der deutschen buchhändler bearbeitet. xviii., 174 p. 8°. Leipzig, E. Polz, 1855.

—— *Same :* Deutsche gesetze und verträge zum schutze des urheberrechts. Im auftrage des Börsenvereins der deutschen buchhändler, zusammengestellt von A. W. Volkmann. 2. abdruck. About 177 p. 8°. Leipzig, 1877. *A non. notice in* " Journal du droit international privé." 5me année, 1878. 12°. Paris, no. 11-12, p. 659.

W. The law of copyright with respect to abridgments. 1847. *See* Walker (Timothy).

WÄCHTER (Oscar), Das autorrecht nach dem gemeinen deutschen recht systematisch dargestellt. viii., 352 p. 8°. Stuttgart, F. Enke, 1875. *A non. notice in* " Journal du droit international privé." 2me année. 8°. Paris, no. 11-12, nov.-dec., 1875, p. 480.

—— Das recht der briefe und photographien. [*Anon.*] *In* "Deutsche vierteljahrs-schrift." 26ster jahrgang, 1863. 8°. Stuttgart, 2tes heft, nr. 102, 2te abtheilung, p. 173-203.

—— Das recht des künstlers. [*Anon.*] *In* "Deutsche vierteljahrs-schrift." gang, 1859. 8°. Stuttgart, 4tes heft, p. 178-223.

—— *Same :* Das recht des künstlers gegen nachbildung und nachdruck seiner werke. Nach den in Deutschland geltenden rechten und den neuesten legislativen anträgen dargestellt. Aus der Deutschen vierteljahrsschrift abgedruckt. About 48 p. 8°. Stuttgart, J. G. Cotta, 1859.

—— Schutz der autoren gegen übersetzung. [*Anon.*] *In* " Deutsche vierteljahrs-schrift." 1855. 8°. Stuttgart & Augsburg, 2tes heft, p. 278-327.

—— Das urheberrecht an werken der bildenden künste, photographien und gewerblichen mustern. Nach dem gemeinen deutschen recht systematisch dargestellt. vii., 348 p. 8°. Stuttgart, F. Enke, 1877.

—— Das verlagsrecht mit einschluss der lehren von dem verlagsvertrag und nachdruck nach den geltenden deutschen und internationalen rechten mit besonderer rücksicht auf die gesetzgebungen von Œsterreich, Preussen, Bayern und Sachsen systematisch dargestellt. 2 parts. 1 p. l. x., 484 p. 1 l. 485-920 p. 8°. Stuttgart, J. G. Cotta, 1857-58.

WALKER (Timothy). The law of copyright with respect to abridgments. [*Anon.* signed W. With appendix : Case of Story v. Holcombe, from notes by J: McLean.] *In* " The Western law journal." v. 5. 8°. Cincinnati, no. 3, Dec. 1847, p. 97-108 : no. 4, Jan. 1848, p. 145-154.

WALRAS (Léon). De la propriété intellectuelle position de la question économique. *In* " Journal des économistes." 2e série, v. 24. 8°. Paris, 1859, p. 392-407.

WARBURTON (W:, bishop of Gloucester). A letter from an author to a member of parliament, concerning literary property. [*Anon.*] About 23 p. 8°. London, Knapton, 1747.

—— *Same :* In " The Works of W: Warburton." A new ed. v. 12. 8°. London, for T. Cadell & W. Davies, 1811, p. 405-416.

WARNER (C: Dudley). *See* The Publishers' weekly.

WARNER (Susan). *See* The Publishers' weekly.

WASHBURN (P: Thacher). The law of copyright. Laws of the United States, now in force, relating to copy-rights ; with notes and references to adjudged cases. *In* Blake (Alexander V.) The American bookseller's trade list." 4°. Claremont, N. H., S. Ide, 1847, p. 225-232.

WATERMAN (T: Whitney). Of injunctions to

restrain the infringement of copyright. *In* Henley (Robert Henley, 2d baron Henley). A compendium of the law and practice of injunctions. 3d ed. 8°. New York, Banks, Gould & co., 1852, 113 p. of vol. 2.

WEBSTER (Dr. G:) Observations on the law of copyright, in reference to the bill of mr sergeant Talfourd, in which it is attempted to be proved that the provisions of the bill are opposed to the principles of English law ; that authors require no additional protection ; and that such a bill would inflict a heavy blow on literature, and prove a great discouragement to its diffusion in this country. [*Anon.*] About 48 p. 8°. London, Scott, Webster & Geary, 1838.

WEBSTER (Noah). Origin of the copy-right laws in the United States. *In* "A collection of papers on political, literary and moral subjects. By N. Webster." 8°. New York, Webster & Clark, 1843, p. 173-178.

Note.—For an account of Mr. Webster's efforts to secure a copyright law see an anonymous communication from the New York Commercial advertiser, entitled : Copyright law, in " Niles' Weekly register," v. 40, or v. 4, 4th series. 8°. Baltimore, no. 1032, July 2, 1831, p. 319-320 ; and " Noah Webster. By Horace E. Scudder." (American men of letters. Edited by C: Dudley Warner.) 12°. Boston, Houghton, Mifflin & co., 1882, p. 52-68.

WEBSTER (T:) On the protection of property in intellectual labour as embodied in inventions, books, designs, and pictures, by the amendment of the laws of patent-right and copy-right. *In* National association for the promotion of social science. Transactions. 1859. 8°. London, J. W. Parker & son, 1860, p. 237-244.

WEISKE (Dr. Julius). Rechtslexikon für juristen aller teutschen staaten, redigirt von dr. Jul. Weiske. 8°. Leipzig, O. Wigand, 1838-43.

Contains : Buchhandel, v. 2, 1840, p. 495-501. Eigenthum, literarisches, artistisches, v. 4, 1843, p. 170-196.

WEISSER (Friedrich). Ueber den büchernachdruck. 8°. Stuttgart, Macklot, 1820.

WELCKER (Carl Theodor). *See* Rotteck (Carl Wenzeslas Rodecker von) *and* Welcker.

WHARTON (G: Mifflin). *See* Lieber (Francis) On international copyright. 1840.

WHEATON (H:) *and* DONALDSON (Robert) *vs.* Peters (R:, jr.) *and* Grigg (John). Report of the copy-right case of Wheaton v. Peters. Decided in the supreme court of the United States [Jan. term, 1834]. With an appendix, containing the acts of congress relating to copy-right. 176 p., 1 slip errata. 8°. New York, J. van Norden, 1834.

—— *Same :* *In* " Reports of cases argued and adjudged in the supreme court of the United States. By R: Peters." v. 8. 8°. Philadelphia, Desilver, jun., & Thomas, 1834, p. 591-699.

Anon. review, signed S. [i. e. H: J: Shepherd ?] : Law of copyright in America. *In* " The Law magazine ; or quarterly review of jurisprudence." v. 13. 8°. London, May, 1835, p. 331-342.

Anon. review in " The Westminster review." v. 24. 8°. London, no. 47, Jan., 1836, p. 187-197.

WHELPLEY (James Davenport). Ideal property. *In* " The Atlantic monthly." v. 22. 8°. Boston, no. 130, Aug. 1868, p. 167-173.

WHIPPLE (Edwin Percy). *See* The Publishers' weekly.

WHITE (R: Grant). The American view of the copyright question. By an American author. [*Anon.*] *In* " The Broadway annual." 8°. London & New York, May 1868, p. 656-667.

—— *Same :* The American view of the copyright question. Reprinted from the " Broadway magazine " [i. e. Broadway annual] May, 1868. With a postscript. 70 p. 12°. London & New York, G: Routledge & Sons, 1880.

Contents : Prefatory, p. v.-viii. The American view of the copyright question, p. 9-29. Postscript. [An account of the efforts of the Copyright association to secure copyright legislation], p. 30-62. Appendix. The right of copyright. By S. Irenæus Prime, p. 63-68. Extract from mr. G: Haven Putnam's address on international copyright. [Delivered in New York, Jan. 29, 1879], p. 69-70.

Anon. review in " The Athenæum." 4°. London, no. 2782, Feb. 19, 1881, p. 257-258.

Anon. notice [by Eaton Sylvester Drone] in " New York Herald," March 28, 1881, p. 10.

Editorial notice in " The Publishers' weekly." v. 19. 8°. New York, no. 480, March 26, 1881, p. 333.

—— The copyright question as it stands. *In* The Copyright association for the protection and advancement of literature and art. International copyright. 8°. New York, 1868, p. 35-40.

WHITMAN (C: Sidney). Patent laws and practice in the United States and foreign countries ; including copy-right and trade-mark laws. xi. p. 1l., 708 p. 12°. Washington, W. H. & O. H. Morrison, 1871.

WHITNEY (Adeline D. Train). *See* The Publishers' weekly.

WHITTLESEY (C:) Rights of authors outside of copyright. (Hesperian, September, 1839.) *In* " Fugitive essays. By C: Whittlesey." 12°. Hudson, Ohio, Sawyer, Ingersoll & co., 1852, p. 75-90.

WIDER und für den büchernachdruck aus den papieren des blauen mannes. Bey gelegenheit der zukünftigen wahlkapitulazion ; gedruckt im reich und für das reich. [*Anon.*] About. 79 p. 8°. [*n. p.*], 1790.

WIEBE (Eduard, translator). *See* Putnam (G: Haven). Internationaler schutz gegen den nachdruck. 1880.

WILSON (Daniel). The law of copyright. Pike vs. Nicholas. *In* " The Canadian journal of science, literature, and history : conducted by the editing committee of the Canadian institute." New series, v. 12. 8°. Toronto, no. 71, or v. 12, no. 5, April 1870, p. 415-429.

WINSOR (Justin). *See* The Publishers' weekly.

WITZLEBEN (C. D. von). Das Norddeutsche Bundes-nachdruckgesetz. *In* " Deutsche vierteljahrs-schrift." 33 ter jahrgang, 1870. 8°. Stuttgart, I stes heft, nr. 129, p. 98-161.

—— Zur frage einer einheitlichen deutschen nachdrucksgesetzgebung. Mit besonderer beziehung auf die dem bundestag vorgelegten gesetzentwürfe der österreichischen regierung und des Börsenvereins der deutschen buchhändler. [*Anon.*] *In* " Deutsche vierteljahrs-schrift." 26 ster jahrgang, 1863. 8°. Stuttgart, heft 1, nr. 101, p. 219–292.

—— Zur frage über die anwendbarkeit des gesetzlichen schutzrechts gegen nachdruck auf erzeugnisse der tagespresse. *In* " Zeitschrift für rechtspflege und verwaltung, zunächst für das königreich Sachsen." Neuefolge, band 14. 8°. Leipzig, 1855, heft 1, p. 1–33.

WOLOWSKI (Louis François Michel Raymond). Projet de loi sur la propriété littéraire en Allemagne. *In* " Revue de législation et de jurisprudence." v. 2. 8°. Paris, 1835, p. 53–*seq.*

WOOLSEY (Theodore Dwight). *See* The Publishers' weekly.

WORDSWORTH (W:) *See* Southey (Robert).

WORMS (Fernand). Étude sur la propriété littéraire, décret du 1er germinal an xiii [March 22, 1805.] Avec une préface de m. E. Pouillet. Suivie du procès des œuvres posthumes d'André Chénier, de la jurisprudence, des lois et traités diplomatiques, des rapports et exposés des motifs de 1777 à 1866 par F. Worms. 2 v. 1 p. l. viii., 411 p. ; 2 p. l. 480 p. 16°. Paris, A. Lemerre. 1878.

Contents: v. 1. Préface [Signed Eugène Pouillet], p. i.–viii. Étude sur le décret de l'an xiii., p. 1–63. Tribunal civil de la Seine. Audiences des 7, 14, 21 et 28 juillet, et 11 août 1876. Comte rendu du procès relatif aux œuvres posthumes d'André Chénier. MM. Charpentier & cie, éditeurs, contre m. Gabriel de Chénier et et m. Alphonse Lemerre, éditeur, p. 64–147: Cour d'appel de Paris, audiences des 8, 15, 22 février, et 1er, 15 et 29 mars 1878, p. 149–306. Jurisprudence relative aux questions soulevées par le procès Chénier, p. 307–408. v. 2. Historique: I. Rapports et exposés des motifs des lois et projets de loi sur le droit des auteurs de 1777 à 1866, p. 1–337: II. Législation littéraire et artistique, p. 338–415: III. Analyse des conventions diplomatiques entre la France et les pays étrangers, p. 416–476. *Anon. notice in* " Journal du droit international privé." 5me année, 1878. 12°. Paris, no. 11–12, p. 658–659.

—— Questions de propriété littéraire. Les œuvres posthumes au point de vue légal et critiques du décret de l'an iii. *In* " Le Livre." 2e année, tome 2 : Bibliographie moderne. 8°. Paris, 3e livraison, 10 mar, 1881, p. 139–144.

—— *See also* Delalande (E.)—Pouillet (Eugène).

WRANGELL (Dr. baron Constantin von). Die prinzipien des literarischen eigenthums mit specieller rücksicht auf dessen juristische form, öconomische, sociale und internationale bedeutung, sowie auf die natürliche begrenzung seines inhaltes und seiner ausdehnung. 4 p. l. iii., 150 p. 1 l. 8°. Berlin, H. Peters, 1866.

WURM (Christian Friedrich). Der schutz des verlagsrechts gegen auswärtigen nachdruck. *In* "Deutsche vierteljahrs-schrift." 3 tes heft, 1841. 8°. Stuttgart & Tübingen, nr. 15, p. 237–312.

ZUR frage einer einheitlichen deutschen nachdrucksgesetzgebung. 1863. *See* Witzleben (C. D. von).

ZUR verständigung über ein allgemeines deutsches pressgesetz. Mit besonderer beziehung auf die schrift: Ideen zur einführung eines deutschen pressgesetzes, Berlin, &c. 1845. Von einem Süddeutschen. [*Anon.*] *In* "Deutsche vierteljahrsschrift." 1 stes heft 1846. 8°. Stuttgart & Tübingen, nr. 33, p. 248–286.

ABBOTT (B : Vaughan). History of copyright. *In* " The Literary world." v. 10. 4°. Boston, no. 109, March 1, 1879, p. 73-74.

—— The year book of jurisprudence for 1880. 8°. Boston, Little, Brown, & co., 1880. *Contains :* Copyright, p. 113-118.

—— *and* ABBOTT (Austin). A digest of the reports of the United States courts, to the year 1867. 4 v. 8°. New York, Diossy & Cockcroft, 1867-69. *Contains :* Copyright. Revised by G : Ticknor Curtis, v. 2, p. 1-11.

—— *Same.* Supplements. By B : Vaughan Abbott. 1868-80. 4 v. 8°. New York, Diossy & co., 1872-80. *Contains :* Copyright, v. 5, p. 144-147 : v. 6, p 170-172 : v. 7, p. 213-215; v. 8, p. 241-242.

—— *Same.* Abbott's national digest. [Revised] to 1885, by B: V. Abbott. v. 1-2. 8°. New York, G. S. Diossy, 1884. *Contains :* Copyright, v. 2, p. 1-32.

ACTES de la Conférence internationale pour la protection des droits d'auteur réunie à Berne du 8 au 19 septembre 1884. 3 p. l., 7-87 p., 1 l. fol. Berne, imprimerie K. J. Wyss, 1884.

ADAM (G. Mercer). New aspects of the copyright question. *In* " Rose-Belford's Canadian monthly and national review." v. 1. 8°. Toronto, no. 3, Sept. 1878, p. 369-376.

ALFONSO (Luis) *and* LERMINA (Jules). Rapport présenté au Congrès littéraire international ; au nom de la 3e commission. About 31 p. 8°. Paris, Chaix & ce., 1878.

ALLEZARD (Charles). Considèrations économiques et juridiques sur la propriété intellectuelle. (Article extrait de " La France judiciaire.") 8°. Paris, G. Pedone-Lauriel, 1882.

AMAR (Moise). Dei diritti degli artisti in Italia ed all' estero : studii. About 106 p. 8°. Torino, tip. Camilla, 1880.

ANCILLON DE JOUY (George). De la propriété littéraire et artistique en droit romain ; de la propriété artistique en droit français. About 319 p. 8°. Nancy, imp. Crépin-Leblond ; Paris, Larose, 1880.

ANDERS (Josef, freiherr von). Beiträge zur lehre vom literarischen und artistischen urheberrechte. Eine civilistische studie mit besonderer beziehung auf das deutsche und österreichische recht. 1 p. l. xviii p. 1 l., 298 p. 1 l. 8°. Innsbruck, Wagner, 1881.

ARCHIVES de droit et de législation. v. 1-4. 8°. Bruxelles, Société Belge de librairie, 1837-41. *Contains :* Théorie des droits des auteurs sur les productions de leur intelligence. [By Augustin Charles Renouard], v. 1, p. 27-49 (of 1st pagination.) Traité des droits d'auteur. Par. A. C. Renouard. [*Anon review*], v. 3, p. 920-224.

ARNOLD (Matthew). Copyright. *In* " Irish essays and others by Matthew Arnold." 12°. London, Smith, Elder & co., 1882, p. 244-280.

ASSOCIATION for the reform and codification of the law of nations. London. Report of the ninth annual conference, held at Cologne, August 16th-19th, 1881. x p. 1 l. 243 p. 8°. London, W : Clowes & s ns, 1882. *Contains :* International copyright, p. 145-165 : (Report of committee on international copyright,p. 146-153 : Remarks, p.153-155 : The Scandinavian copyright laws. [By Alfred Kirsebom], p. 155-162 : Industrial and artistic copyright [By C: H: E: Carmichael], p. 163-165.)

ATLANTIC monthly. v. 22. 8°. Boston, 1868. *Contains :* Ideal property. By James D. Whelpley, p. 167-173.

ATLAS (The) company of Scotland *v.* A. Fullarton and company. Report of the trial at the instance of the Atlas company of Scotland against A. Fullarton and company, publishers, Edinburgh and London. Tried before a jury at Edinburgh on the 27th, 28th, and 29th days of July 1853. By I. M. Duncan, advocate. 2 p. l. 44 p. 8°. Edinburgh and London, W: Blackwood & sons, 1853.

AUGER (Louis Simon). Observations lues en la séance du 26 décembre 1825. *In* France. *Commission de la propriété littéraire.* Collection des procès-verbaux. 4°. Paris, Pillet Aîné, 1826, p. 73-78.

AZEVEDO (Fernand d'). Étude sur la propriété littéraire, pérpétuité, droit international. About 72 p. 16°. Paris, ve Aillaud, Guillard & cie, 1873.

BAER (H. J.) Der internationale vertrag zum schutze literarischer erzeugnisse mit spezieller beziehung auf Frankfurt am Main vom theoretisch-moralischen und praktisch-materiellen standpunkt aus beleuchtet. (Als manuskript gedruckt.) 8°. [n. p., n. d., Frankfurt a. M., 1856.]

—— *Same.* II. Nachträgliche bemerkungen und erläuterungen. (Als manuskript gedruckt.) 8°. Frankfurt a. M., 1857.

BALZAC (Honoré de). Notes remises à MM. les députés composant la commission de la loi sur la propriété littéraire. About 24 p. 8°. Paris, Hetzel & Paulin, 1841.

BARTOCCINI (Nicola). I diritti ed i doveri degli autori delle opere d'ingegno in relazione all'arte della pittura. About 80 p. 4°. Roma, tip. frat. Pallotta, 1881.

BECKER (Rudolf Zacharias). Das eigenthumsrecht an geisteswerken, mit einer dreyfachen beschwerde über das bischöflich-augsburgische vikariat wegen nachdruck, verstümmelung und verfälschung des noth-und hülfsbüchleins. About 94 p. 8°. Frankfurt & Leipzig, F. C. W. Vogel, 1789. *Review* by Chr. Sigismund Krause in " Neuen teutschen museum." v. 3. 8°. Leipzig, Sept. 1790, p. 934-962.

BERGSÖE (Jörgen Vilhelm). Provinspressen og den literære ejendomsret. 8°. Kjöbenhavn, 1882.

BIEDERMANN (Karl). Das geistige eigenthum mit bezug auf zeitungen und zeitschriften. Ein referat für den dritten deutschen journalistentag. 8°. Berlin, F. Duncker, 1869.

BIELITZ (Gustaf Alexander). Versuch, die von dem verlagsrecht geltenden grundsätze aus der analogie der positiven gesetze abzuleiten. 8°. Dresden, Grimmer, 1799.

BIGNON (Louis Pierre Édouard). Lettre à M. Ambroise Firmin Didot, sur la contrefaçon étrangère. [Verclives, 5 Octobre 1837.] *In* " Histoire de France sous Napoléon. Par M. Bignon." v. 7. 8°. Paris, F. Didot frères, 1838, pp. i.-xxxvi.

BIRNBAUM (J. A.) Eines aufrichtigen patrioten unpartheiische gedanken über einige quellen und wirkungen des verfalls der jetzigen buchhandlung, worin insonderheit die betrügereien der bücherpränumerationen entdeckt, und zugleich erwiesen wird, dass der unbefugte nachdruck unprivilegirter bücher ein allen rechten zuwiderlaufender diebstahl sei. 8°. Schweinfurt, 1733.

BLAINE (Delabere Roberton). On the laws of artistic copyright, and their defects. For the use of artists, sculptors, engravers, printsellers, etc. viii., 85 p. 1 l. 8°. [London], J: Murray, 1853.

——Report to the committee on artistic copyright [of the Society of arts. With the report of the committee.] *In* " The Journal of the Society of arts." v. 6. 4°. London, no. 279, March 26 1858, p. 293-301.

BLANC (Étienne). Traité de la contrefaçon en tous genres. 4e éd. 2 p. l. xvi., 820 p. 8°. Paris, H. Plon; Cosse, 1855.

—— *and* BEAUME (Alexandre). Code général de la propriété industrielle, littéraire et artistique. 2 p. l. viii., 643 p. 8°. Paris, Cosse, 1854.

BLUNTSCHLI (Johann Caspar). Rights of authors. *In* " Cyclopædia of political science. Edited by J: J. Lalor." v. 1. 8°. Chicago, Rand, McNally & co., 1881, p. 182-183.

BOHN (H: G:). The question of unreciprocated foreign copyright in Great Britain. A report of the speeches and proceedings at a public meeting held at the Hanover square rooms, July 1, 1851, Sir E: Bulwer Lytton. bart., in the chair. With notes. viii., 68 p. 8°. London, Bohn, 1851.

BOSWELL (James). The decision of the court of session, upon the question of literary property ; in the cause J : Hinton of London, bookseller, pursuer ; against Alexander Donaldson and J: Wood, booksellers in Edinburgh, and James Meurose bookseller in Kilmarnock, defenders. 1 p. l., iv., 37 p. 4°. Edinburgh, J. Donaldson, for A. Donaldson, 1774.

BOZZO-BAGNERA (Giovanni Battista). Sulla perpetua proprietá letteraria ed artistica. Studio. 2a edizione riveduta e corretta. 48 p. 12°. Milano, C. Barbini, 1871.

BREULIER (Adolphe). Du droit de perpétuité

de la propriété intellectuelle. Théorie de la propriété des écrivains, des artistes, des inventeurs et des fabricants. About 140 p. 8°. Paris, A. Durand, 1855.

BRIEF (A) statement on the subject of assumed foreign copyright ; addressed to British authors, publishers, and others interested in British literature. About 16 p. 8°. London, 1851.

BRIGGS (C: F:). Literary piracy. [*Anon.* review of " Letters on international copy-right. By H. C. Carey." Philadelphia, A. Hart, 1853.] *In* " Putnam's monthly magazine." v. 3. 8°. New York, no. 13, Jan. 1854, p. 96-103.

BRITO (José). Legislacion Mexicana. Indice alfabetico razonado de las leyes, decretos, reglamentos, ordenes y circulares que se han expedido desde el año de 1821 hasta el de 1869. [Apendice, 1870-'71.] 3 v. 8°. México, imprenta del gobierno, á cargo de J. M. Sandoval, 1872-3.
Contains : Propiedad literaria, v. 3, p. 194-200, apendice, p. 785-789.

BRITTON (J:). The rights of literature. 77 p. 8°. London, for the author, by A. J. Valpy, 1814. *Contains :* A catalogue of tracts concerning literary property, etc. 35 titles, p. 71-77.

BROUSSE (M.—). Propriété littéraire. *In* " Répertoire de la nouvelle législation civile, commerciale et administrative ; par Favard de Langlade." v. 4. 4°. Paris, 1823, p. 618-661.

BRUZZO (Gian Carlo). Del diritto di proprietà sulle produzioni dell'ingegno. About 51 p. 8°. Genova, tip. del R. istituto sordomuti, 1881.

BUMP (Orlando Franklin). The law of patents, trade-marks, labels and copyrights. 2d ed. ccxviii., 667 p. 8°. Baltimore, Cushings & Bailey, 1884. (Copyrights, p. 492-526.)

BÜRGER (Gottfried August). Vorschlag, dem büchernachdrucke zu steuern. *In* " G. A. Bürger's Sämmtliche werke. Herausgegeben von Karl v. Reinhard." v. 6. 8°. Berlin, 1825.

BURKE (P:) The copyright law and the press : an essay to show the necessity of an immediate amendment of the copyright law upon the removal of the stamp duty from newspapers. 8°. London, S. Low & son, 1855.

—— Society for promoting the amendment of the law. 20th session. The present state of the law of copyright in literature and the fine arts, with a view to its amendment. (A paper by mr. serjeant Burke, read at a general meeting of the society, held on monday, 1st June, 1863, and ordered to be printed.) 15 p. 8°. [London, M'Corquedale & co., 1863.]

CAILLEMER (Exupère). Études sur les antiquités juridiques d'Athènes. 6e étude. La propriété littéraire à Athènes. 8°. [Caen] ; Paris, E. Thorin, 1868.

CALLENDER (E: B.) The law for playwrights. *In* Southern law review." New series,

v. 8. 8°. St. Louis, no. 1, April-May, 1882, p. 13–32.

CALMELS (Antoine Edouard). De la propriété et de la contrefaçon des œuvres de l'intelligence, comprenant : les productions littéraires, dramatiques, musicales ; les œuvres artistiques de la peinture, du dessin, de la gravure et de la sculpture ; les titres d'ouvrages, [etc.] Avec le texte des lois et décrets sur la matière. vii., 866 p. 1 l. 8°. Paris, Cosse, 1856.

—— Projet du code pénal portugais. Observations sur le chapitre viii. concernant la répression des contrefaçons et autres délits en matière de propriété littéraire et artistique, [etc.] Adressées à m. Levy Maria Jordão. 2 p. l. 51 p. 8°. Paris, au bureau des annales de la propriété industrielle, artistique et littéraire, 1862.

CAPPELLEMANS (Victor). De la propriété littéraire et artistique en Belgique et en France. Histoire, législation, jurisprudence, convention du 12 août 1852 avec commentaire. Règlements d'exécution en Belgique et en France. Notes explicatives, etc. 2 p. l. xxvii., 375 p. 12°. Bruxelles, Delevingne & Callewaert ; Paris, J. Renouard & comp., 1854.

CASES (The) of the appellants and respondents in the cause of literary property. [*Anon.*] 4 p. l. 59 p.+3 p. 4°. London, printed for J. Bew, W. Clarke, P. Brett, and C. Wilkin, 1774.

CATTREUX (Louis). Étude sur le droit de propriété des œuvres dramatiques ct musicales. About 217 p. 8°. Bruxelles, imp. A. Lefèvre ; lib. F. Larcier, 1883.

CELLIEZ (Henry). Plaidoirie de me Celliez. [Cour impériale de Paris, 12 déc., 1857. Revendication de la propriété exclusive du pseudonyme Nadar.] *In* "La Tribune judiciaire, par J. Sabbatier." v. 5. 8°. Paris, C. Borrani, 1857, p. 295–311.

CHAMPEIN (Marie François Stanislas). Réflexions de m. Champein, lues dans la séance du 27 février 1826. *In* France. *Commission de la propriété littéraire.* Collection des procès-verbaux. 4°. Paris, Pillet aîné, 1826, p. 241–249.

CHAPMAN (J:) The commerce of literature. [*Anon.*] *In* "The Westminster review." [v. 57], n. s., v. 1. 8°. London, J: Chapman, no. 112, n. s. no. 2, April 1, 1852, p. 511–554.

—— *Same :* Cheap books, and how to get them. Being a reprint of the article on "The commerce of literature," together with a brief account of the origin and progress of the recent agitation for free trade in books. To which is added, the judgment pronounced by lord Campbell. 8°. London, J: Chapman, 1852?

CHATAIN (Marcel). Faculté de droit de Paris. De l'in bonis en droit romain. De la propriété littéraire en droit français. Thèse pour le doctorat. L'acte public sur les ma-

tières ci-après sera présenté et soutenu le 23 décembre, 1880. 3 p. l. 5–86 p. 1 l. 5–190 p. 8°. Paris, F. Pichon & A. Cotillon, 1880. De la propriété littéraire, 5–190 p.

CLEVELAND (H.) Copy-right [and] Copy-right law. *In* "The American monthly magazine." New series. 8°. Philadelphia, Boston and New York, 1837: (No. 1. To the writers of America. *Anon.*), v. 3, Feb., p. 153–158 : (No. 2. To the publishers of America. *Anon.*), v. 3, March, p. 283–287 : (No. 3. To the readers of the United States. *Anon.*, signed H. C.), v. 4, Oct., p. 374–377.

CLUNET (Édouard). Extrait du compte rendu sténographique du Congrès international de la propriété artistique, tenu à Paris du 18 au 21 septembre 1878. 40 p. 8°. Paris, imprimerie Nationale, 1879.

—— *Same. In* "Congrès international de la propriété artistique. Compte rendu." 8°. Paris, imp. Nationale, 1879, p. 119–158.

COMMERCE (The) of literature. 1852. *See* Chapman (J:)

CONGRÈS de la propriété littéraire et artistique tenu à Bruxelles, les 27, 28, 29, et 30 septembre 1858. 1. Organisation du congrès et adhésions. 2. Analyse des séances du congrès. 3. Discours et rapports. 4. Résolutions du congrès. *In* "Annales de la propriété industrielle artistique et littéraire." v. 4. 8°. Paris, 1858, p. 401–454.

CONGRÈS international de la propriété artistique. *See* France.

CONSTANT (L.) De la propriété en général et de la propriété littéraire. [Séances du 30 juin au 7 juillet 1844.] *In* Société littéraire de l'université catholique de Louvain. Choix de mémoires. v. 3. 8°. Louvain, Fonteyn, 1845, p. 185–254. I. De la propriété en général, p. 187–225 : II. De la propriété littéraire, p. 225–254.

COPYRIGHT. [*Anon.*] *In* "The Leisure hour." v. 14. 4°. London, 1865, I., in no. 728, Dec. 9, p. 774–776 : II., in no. 729, Dec. 16, p. 788–791 : III., in no. 730, Dec. 23, p. 804–807.

COPYRIGHT (The) act. The law of copyright, regarding authors, dramatic writers, and musical composers ; as altered by the recent statute of the 5 & 6 Victoria [1st July 1842], analysed and simplified : with an explanatory introduction, and an appendix, containing, at full, the new copyright and the dramatic property acts. By a barrister. [*Anon.*] 40 p. 8°. London, J. Gilbert, [1842.]

COPY-RIGHT (The) law. [*Anon.*] *In* "The Monthly review." [v. 145], new series v. 1. 8°. London, E. Henderson, no. 1, Jan. 1838, p. 52–63. A review of 1. "Speech of mr. serjeant Talfourd on literary property, 18th of May 1837." London, Sherwood & co. 2. "Remarks on the speech of serjeant Talfourd. By T: Tegg." London, Tegg, 1837.

CURTIS (G: Ticknor). Copyright. *In* "A law dictionary. By John Bouvier." 14th ed. v. 1. 8°. Philadelphia, J. B. Lippincott & co., 1882, p. 363–366.

CURTIS (G: Ticknor). *See also* Abbott (B: Vaughan) *and* Abbott (Austin). A digest of reports. 1867-69.

CYCLOPÆDIA of political science. *See* Lalor (J: J., editor).

DAMBACH (Otto). Der deutsch-französische litterar-vertrag vom 19. April, 1883. Mit erläuterungen. About vi., 74 p. 8°. Berlin, T. C. F. Enslin, 1883.

—— Einige bemerkungen zur lehre von urheberrechte. *In* "Zeitschrift für die deutsche gesetzgebung und für einheitliches deutsches recht." v. 6. 8°. Berlin, 1872, p. 51-60.

—— Die strafbarkeit des vorsatzes und der fahrlässigkeit beim vergehen des nachdrucks im preussischen rechte. About 32 p. 8°. Berlin, I. Guttentag, 1864. [Aus Preussischer anwaltszeitung, 1864, besonders abgedruckt.]

DAWSON (S. E.) Copyright in books : an insight into its origin, and an account of the present state of the law in Canada : a lecture ; being one of the occasional lectures delivered before the law school of Bishop's college at Sherbrooke, Thursday, Jan. 26, '82. About 40 p. 8°. Montreal, Dawson brothers, 1882. *Anon. notice in* "The Albany law journal." v. 26. 8°. Albany, no. 11, Sept. 9, 1882, p. 201. *Anon. notice in* "The Popular science monthly." v. 21. 8°. New York, no. 5, Sept. 1882, p. 704. *Anon. notice in* "The Publishers' circular." v. 45. 8°. London, no. 1077, Aug. 1, 1882, p. 655-656.

DELALAIN (Auguste Henri Jules). Législation de la propriété littéraire et artistique suivie des conventions internationales. Nouv. éd., revue et augmentée. x., 240 p. 8°. Paris, typographie et librairie Delalain, 1858.

—— Nouvelle législation des droits de propriété littéraire et artistique accompagnée de notes explicatives et suivie d'un résumé de la législation des pays étrangers. 6ème éd., revue et augmentée. x., 84 p. 12°. Paris, J. Delalain, 1867.

DENKSCHRIFT über den büchernachdruck ; zugleich bittschrift um bewürkung eines deutschen reichsgesetzes gegen denselben. Den erlauchten, bei dem congress zu Wien versammleten gesandten deutscher staaten ehrerbietigst überreicht im namen deutscher buchhändler. 3 p. l. 38 p. 8°. Leipzig, P. G. Kummer, 1814.
Signed by Friedrich Justin Bertuch, Weimar ; Johann Georg Cotta, Stuttgart ; Johann Friedrich Hartknoch, Paul Gotthelf Kummer, Carl Friedrich Enoch Richter, Friedrich Christian Wilhelm Vogel, Leipzig.

DESCHAMPS (E.) Étude sur la propriété industrielle, littéraire et artistique au point de vue de la cession des droits de l'inventeur, du fabricant et de l'auteur. About 120 p. 8°. Paris, Larose & Forcel, 1882.

DESMAREST (Ernest). Plaidoirie de me Desmarest. [Cour impériale de Paris. 12 déc., 1857. Revendication de la propriété exclusive du pseudonyme Nadar.] *In* "La Tribune judiciaire. Par J. Sabbatier." v. 5. 8°. Paris, C. Borrani, 1857, p. 311-322.

DUBLAN (Manuel) *and* LOZANO (José María). Legislacion mexicana ó coleccion completa de las disposiciones legislativas expedidas desde la independencia de la republica. Edicion oficial. v. 1-11. [1687-1871.] fol. México, imprenta del Comercio, á cargo de Dublan y Lozano, hijos, [etc.]. 1876-79.
Contains: Decreto de 10de Junio de 1813.—Reglas para conservar á los escritores la propiedad de sus obras, v. 1, p. 412. Diciembre 3 de 1846. Decreto del gobierno. Sobre propiedad literaria, v. 5, p. 227-228.

DUNCAN (I. M.) *See* Atlas (The) company of Scotland. vs. A. Fullarton and company.

DUVAL (Alexandre). Observations de m. A. Duval, lues à la séance du 3 février 1826. *In* France. *Commission de la propriété littéraire.* Collection des procès-verbaux. 4°. Paris, Pillet aîné, 1826, p. 181-190.

EBERS (Georg). Der nachdruck deutscher bücher in Holland. Eine zuschrift an das Magazin. *In* "Das Magazin für die litteratur des in- und auslandes." 53. jahrgang. 4°. Leipzig. nr. 2, den 12. Januar 1884, p. 29-30 : nr. 6, den 9 Februar 1884, p. 93-94.

EHLERS (Martin). Ueber die unzulässigkeit des büchernachdrucks nach dem natürlichen zwangsrecht. About 194 p. 8°. Dessau und Leipzig, 1785.

ENSLIN (Adolph). Ueber internationale verlagsverträge mit besonderer beziehung auf Deutschland. About 41 p. 8°. Berlin, T. C. F. Enslin, 1855.

"ENTERED at Stationers' hall." A sketch of the history and privileges of the company of stationers. With notes on Francis Moore, John Partridge, and other distinguished personages. [*Anon.*] 2 p. l. 32 p. 12°. London, printed by M. Thomas, sold by E. Truelove, 1871.

ENTWURF eines gesetzes für Deutschland zum schutze des eigenthums an werken der wissenschaft und kunst gegen nachdruck und nachbildung, nebst motiven. Als manuskript gedruckt. About 172p. 4°. Berlin, J. Sittenfeld, 1857.

FAIDER (Charles). Note sur le congrès de la propriété littéraire et artistique, tenu à Bruxelles, en Septembre 1858. *In* "Bulletins de l'Académie royale des sciences, des lettres et des beaux-arts de Belgique." 27e année, 2me série, v. 5. 8°. Bruxelles, Hayez, 1858, p. 521-531.

—— *Same. In* "Compte rendu des travaux du congrès de la propriété littéraire et artistique, par Édouard Romberg." v. 2. 8°. Bruxelles & Leipzig, É. Flatau, 1859, p. 312-318.

FERRARI (Paolo). Introduzione storica. *See* Rosmini (Enrico). La legislazione e la giurisprudenza dei teatri e dei diritti d'autore. 1872-73.

FICHTE (Johann Gottlieb). Beweis der unrechtmässigkeit des büchernachdrucks. Ein räsonnement und eine parabel. *In* "Berliner monatsschrift." v. 21. 8°. Berlin, Mai 1793, p. 443-483.

FICHTE (Johann Gottlieb) *Same. In* "Johann Gottlieb Fichte's sämmtliche werke. Herausgegeben von J. H. Fichte." 8 ter bd. 8°. Berlin, Veit & comp., 1846, p. 223–244.

FIELD (G: W.) Field's lawyers' briefs, consisting of treatises on every important legal subject, alphabetically arranged. v. 2. 8°. Albany : New York, Banks & brothers, 1884.
Contains: Copyright, p. 136–153.

FINNAMORE (J:) Imperial copyright law, as affecting the colonies. *In* " The Victorian review." v. 4. 8°. Melbourne, no. 24, Oct. 1, 1881, p. 712–722.

FLINIAUX (Charles). Essai sur les droits des auteurs étrangers en France et des auteurs français en pays étrangers. *In* " Revue générale du droit." 8°. Paris, 1879, p. 25–50, 140–150.

FRANCE. *Ministère de l'agriculture et du commerce.* Exposition universelle internationale de 1878, à Paris. Congrès et conférences du Palais duTrocadéro. Comptes rendus sténographiques publiés sous les auspices du comité central des congrès et conférénces et la direction de m. Ch. Thirion. Congrès international de la propriété artistique tenu à Paris du 18 au 21 septembre. no. 27 de la série. 2 p.l. 213 p. 8°. Paris, imprimerie Nationale, 1879.

FRANZOS (Karl Emil). Autorrecht und leihbibliothek. *In* " Das Magazin für die litteratur des in-und auslandes." 53. jahrgang. 4°. Leipzig, nr. 1, 5. Jan. 1884, p. 4–6 : nr. 2, 12. Jan. 1884, p. 18–20.

FRORIEP (Robert). Schutz vor nachbildung der kunstwerke. Nach dem königl. preuss. gesetz vom 11. Juni 1837 für künstler und kunstverleger erläutert. 8°. Berlin, Sachse & comp., 1839.

GANZ (Johann Friedrich Ferdinand). Uebersicht der gründe wegen des strafbaren des büchernachdrucks und vorschläge, wie diesem übel durch ein allgemein verbindliches reichsgesetz vorgebeugt werden könne. About 66 p. 8°. Regensburg, 1790.

GAUTHIER (Hippolyte). De la propriété littéraire sur les livres d'éducation. Question de jurisprudence. Arrêt de la cour impériale de Paris dans le procès Jeannel et Delagrave contre Taulier et Eug. Belin. About 16 p. 8°. Paris, imp. Rouge frères, Dunon et Fresné, 1868.

GERBER (Carl Friedrich von). Ueber die natur der rechte des schriftstellers und verlegers. *In* " Gesammelte juristische abhandlungen von C. F. von Gerber." 2. Bd. 8°. Jena, Dufft, 1872, p. 261–310.

GERHARD (Friedrich). Der nachdruck deutscher schriften in den Vereinigten Staaten, und seine gegner. 50 p. 12°. New York, [Randel & Bloemeke], 1867.
**" Wird gratis ausgegeben und kann in beliebigen Parthieen vom Verfasser bezogen werden."

GERMANY. Gesetz, betreffend das urheberrecht

an schriftwerken, abbildungen, musikalischen kompositionen und dramatischen werken. Vom 11. Juni 1870. 24 p. 16°. Berlin, F. Kortkampf, 1870.

GESCHICHTE des büchernachdrucks. *In* " Journal für Deutschland, historisch politischen inhalts, herausgegeben von Fr. Buchholz." 8°. Berlin, 2. Bd., 1815, p. 581–620 : 3. Bd., 1816, p. 44–67, 198–216.

GLASER (Matthäus Christian). Ueber kauf und verkauf der gedanken, oder können gedanken marktwaare sein ? 8°. Kulmbach & Coburg, wittwenversorgungsanstalt, 1820.
——*Same.* Ueber den diebstahl der nachdrucker. Ein nachstück zu " Ueber kauf und verkauf der gedanken." 8°. Kulmbach & Coburg, 1821.

GODSON (R :) A practical treatise on the law of patents for inventions, and of copyright in literature, the drama, music, engraving and sculpture, and also in ornamental and useful designs for the purposes of sale and exhibition. 2d ed. To which is added a supplement, bringing the patent and copyright law down to the present time. 2 p. l. vii.–xxxv., 496 p. +94 p. +viii., 236 p. 8°. London, W : Benning & co., 1851.
Copyright, p. 305–496 (1st pagination); p. 57–102 (3d pagination.)

GREAT BRITAIN. The law reports. The public general statutes. 1882–1884. v. 18–20. 8°. London, 1882–84.
Contains : An act to amend the law of copyright relating to musical compositions. [45 & 46 Victoria, chapter 40, 10th Aug. 1882], v. 18, p. 144–145.

GROLMANN (Karl Ludwig Wilhelm von). Der büchernachdruck in seiner neuesten gestalt. *In* " Bibliothek für die peinliche rechtswissenschaft und gesetzkunde." 1. Bd. 8°. Herborn, 2. stück, 1798, p. 269–278.

GUTACHTEN des königlich preussischen geheimen ober-tribunals über den begriff des strafbaren nachdrucks und der demselben nach § 3 des gesetzes vom 11. Juni 1837 zum schutze des eigenthums an werken der wissenschaft und kunst gegen nachdruck und nachbildung, gleichzuachtenden vergehungen, auf veranlassung des justiz ministers Mühler abgegeben am 13. Februar 1844. 4°. Berlin, Heymann, 1844. [Aus dem Justiz-ministerial-blatt, 1844, besonders abgedruckt.]

HEYDEMANN (Ludwig Eduard). Der internationale schutz des autorrechtes. *In* " Gesammelte aufsätze und mittheilungen aus dem Börsenblatt für den deutschen buchhandel." 8°. Leipzig, 1875, p. 278–297.

INTERNATIONAL copyright. — The claims of literature. [*Anon.*] *In* " The United States democratic review." New series, v. 42. 8°. New York, Dec. 1858, p. 454–464.

ITALY. *Ministero di agricoltura, industria e commercio. (Direzione dell'industria e del commercio.)* Annali dell'industria e del commercio 1879, num. 7. Notizie statistiche intorno ai diritti d'autore sulle opere d'ingegno ed Alle privative industriali, marchii e segni distin-

tivi e disegni e modelli di fabbrica. 26 p.
12°. Roma, tipografia E. Botta, 1879.

Notizie statistiche intorno ai diritti d'autore sulle opere
d'ingegno, p. 5–13.

JENAISCHE responsum juris sammt völligem
beifall dreyer juristenfacultäten, worinnen
dargethan wird, dass denen autoribus der in
druck gegebenen bücher und deren cession-
ariis, welche von hohen obrigkeiten keine
privilegia darüber ausgewirkt, kein mono-
polium solches bücherverkaufs zustehe, noch
vor weltlichen gerichten ein recht zukomme,
andern den nachdruck solcher bücher zu
verbieten oder wider selbige desshalben um
bestrafung anzusuchen. 8°. Erfurt, 1726.

KAERGER (Karl). Die theorien über die juristische natur des urheberrechts. Eine kriti-
sche studie. Inaugural-dissertation zur erlangung der juristischen doctorwürde in der
rechts- & staatswissenschaftlichen facultät
der universität Strassburg. 47 p. 8°. Berlin,
Puttkammer & Mühlbrecht, 1882.

KAISER (Hermann). Entwurf eines gesetzes
für den norddeutschen Bund, zum schutze
der original-photographien gegen unbefugte
nachbildung. Nebst erläuterungen und einer denkschrift über die schutzberechtigung
der orig.-photographien. About 72 p. 8°.
Berlin, Schroeder, 1868.

KENT (James). Commentaries on American
law. 13th ed., edited by C: M. Barnes. 4 v.
8°. Boston, Little, Brown, & co., 1884.

Contains: Copyrights of authors, v. 2, p. 521–538.

KIRSEBOM (Alfred). The Scandinavian copyright laws. In "Association for the reform
and codification of the law of nations. Report
of the 9th annual conference, Cologne, Aug.
1881." 8°. London, W: Clowes & sons, 1882,
p. 155–162.

KNIGGE (Adolph Franz Friedrich Ludwig,
Freiherr von). Ueber schriftsteller und
schriftstellerei. 8°. Hannover, Hahn, 1793.

KRISIS (Die) des teutschen buchhandels, her-
beigeführt durch teutsche buchhändler. Oder
abgedrungene beleuchtung der denkschrift
über den büchernachdruck. About 39 p. 8°.
Reutlingen, 1815.

LACHMANN (Karl). Ausgaben classischer
werke darf jeder nachdrucken. Eine war-
nung für herausgeber. 8°. Berlin, Besser,
1841.

Concerning the reprinting of certain works by Lessing,
out of the collected edition by Lachmann.

LAHURE (Charles). Observations sur la de-
mande faite par des libraires réunis en commission, de reconnaître chez nous, et sans
condition, la propriété littéraire des étrangers ; et moyen de paralyser les contrefaçons
belges sans nuire à aucune des branches de
notre industrie. About 32 p. 8°. Paris, imp.
de Crapelet, 1840.

LALOR (J: J., editor). Cyclopædia of political
science. v. 1–3. 8°. Chicago, Rand,
McNally & co., [etc.], 1881-84.

Contains: Rights of authors (by Johann Caspar
Bluntschli), v. 1, p. 182-183. Copyright (by H: Dunning

Macleod), v. 1, p. 642-648. Literary property (by G:
Haven Putnam), v. 3, p. 392-411.

LAST (Albert). Das autorenrecht und die
leihbibliotheken. Vortrag, gehalten auf dem
schriftstellertage zu Darmstadt am 10. September 1883. 8°. Wien, E. Last, 1883.

LEA (H: C:) International copyright. An open
letter [to Hon. S: J. Randall, M.C. ; Philadelphia, February 18, 1884.] 8 p. 8°. [Phila-
delphia, 1884].

LLOYD (E:) Consolidation of the law of copyright. In "The Solicitors' journal and reporter." v. 6. 8°. London, 1862, no. I. in
June 28, p. 626–'7 ; no. II. in July 5, p. 645–
'6 ; no. III. in July 12, p. 663–'5 ; no. IV. in
July 19, p. 681–'2 ; no. V. in July 26, p. 702–
'3 ; no. VI. in Aug. 16, p. 751–'3 ; no. VII.—
The new copyright act, in Aug. 23, p. 767–'8.

LOOSE leaves by a literary lounger. About
authors and copyrights. [Anon.] In "The
United States magazine, and democratic review" New series, v. 12. 8°. New York,
no. 57, March 1843, p. 290–300.

LUTHEREAU (Jean Guillaume Antoine). Opinion d'un voleur artistique et littéraire sur
la contrefaçon ; moyens de l'abolir sans
leser les intérêts matériels du pays. 8°.
Bruxelles, 1852.

MACAULAY (T: Babington, baron Macaulay).
Speeches. In two volumes. 8°. New York,
W. J. Widdleton, 1866.

Contains: The copyright bill. February 5, 1841,
v. 1, p. 387-403. The copyright bill. April 6, 1842, v. 2,
p. 78-88.

MCCRARY (G: W.) The literary property of
authors. In "The Central law journal."
v. 17. 8°. St. Louis, no. 14, Oct. 5, 1883,
p. 268–271.

MENZEL (Wolfgang). Antrag, die Württem-
bergische regierung um ein gesetz zu bitten,
wodurch der nachdruck als ein, das eigenthum beeinträchtigendes, der öffentlichen
moral schädliches, und die ehre des Würt-
tembergischen namens vor dem auslande
verunglimpfendes institut unbedingt aufge-
hoben würde, vorgetragen in der sitzung der
kammer der abgeordneten vom 2. Juli. ·8°.
Stuttgart, Metzler, 1833.

MERTENS (G.) Ueber nachdruck, mit rücksicht auf C. M. von Weber's clavier-compo-
sitionen. Erste rechtmässige gesammttaus-
gabe revidirt und corrigirt von H. W. Stolze.
Eine skizze aus der tagesgeschichte. (Als
manuskript gedruckt.) 8°. Berlin, 1857.

MODIFICATIONS proposées au projet de loi présenté à la chambre des députés le 18 janvier
sur la propriété littéraire, et observations
soumises au gouvernement par des libraires
de Paris. 4°. Paris, imp. de F: Didot, 1841.

MUQUARDT (Charles). De la contrefaçon et de
son influence pernicieuse sur la littérature, la
librairie et les branches d'industrie qui s'y
rattachent ; suivi d'un projet de convention
entre la Belgique et la France pour l'abolition de la contrefaçon. Mémoire adressé à la

chambre des représentants belges. 8°. Bruxelles, 1844.

NOLL (Ferdinand). " Suum cuique ! " (Jedem das seine !) Das geistige eigenthum oder das urheberrecht an werken der arbeit jeder art, wie an schriften, tonwerken, erfindungen von maschinen &c. gegen nachahmung. Mit einem gesetzentwurfe und erläuterungen zu demselben. (Schutz der werke der wissenschaft und kunst, musterschutz, erfindungspatente.) About 51 p. 8°. Berlin, Reichardt & Zander, 1862. [Betrachtungen über die gesammten erwerbsverhältnisse des preussischen staates. 4. heft.]

—— "Suum cuique !" (Jedem das seine !). Die staats-verträge, das eigenthum überhaupt, das urheber-eigenthum (geistige eigenthum an schrift-, ton-, bild-werken, an sogenannten mustern und andern erfindungen) insonderheit. About 47 p. 8°. Berlin, Geelhaar, 1865. [Betrachtungen über die gesammten erwerbsverhältnisse des preussischen staates. 5. heft.]

NORWAY. Kongeriget Norges 25de ordentlige Storthings forhandlinger i aaret 1876. 4°. Kristiania, [1876].
Contains: Om udfærdigelse af en lov om beskyttelse af den saakaldte skrifteiendomsret, v. 3, oth. prp. no. 8, 29 p. Indstilling fra justitskomiteen angaaende den kongelige proposition til lov om beskyttelse af den saakaldte skrifteiendomsret, v. 6 B., p. 145-153. (The law protecting literary property, as now in force in Norway, is contained, p. 149-153).

—— 26de ordentlige storthings forhandlinger i aaret 1877. 4° Christiania, [1877].
Contains: Ang. udfærdigelse af en lov om beskyttelse af den saakaldte kunstneriske eiendomsret, v. 3, oth. prp. no. 13, 12 p. Indstilling fra justitskomiteen, v. 6 B., p. 51-53. Ang. udfærdigelse af en lov om beskyttelse af fotografiske billeder, v. 3, oth. prp. no. 14, 6 p. Indstilling fra justitskomiteen, v. 6 B., p. 54-55. (The two reports contain the texts of the laws, now in force in Norway, protecting artistic property and photographs).

ORELLI (Aloys von). Das Schweizerische Bundesgesetz betreffend das urheberrecht an werken der litteratur und kunst, unter berücksichtigen der bezüglich-staatsverträge erläutert. About viii., 174 p. 8°. Zürich, Schulthess, 1884.

PARSONS (Theophilus, jr.) The law of contracts. 6th ed. 3 v. 8°. Boston, Little, Brown, & co., 1873.
Contains: The law of copyright, v. 2, p. 338-360.
—— *Same.* 7th ed. With additions by W: V. Kellen. 3 v. 8°. Boston, Little, Brown, & co., 1883.
Contains: The law of copyright, v. 2, p. 329-349.

PENZENKUFFER (Christoph Wilhelm Friedrich). Beitrag zur endlichen festen bestimmung des rechtsverhältnisses zwischen autor und verleger. 8°. Nürnberg, Verfasser, 1823.

PIC (François Antoine). Code des imprimeurs, libraires, écrivains et artistes, ou recueil et concordance des dispositions législatives qui déterminent leurs obligations et leurs droits. 2 v. 8°. Paris, Corby, 1826.

PLEADINGS (The) of the counsel before the house of lords, in the great cause concerning literary property. iv., 39 p. 4°. London, printed

for C. Wilkin, S. Axtell, J. Axtell, and J. Browne, [n. d., 1774.]

POPULAR (The) science monthly. v. 22. 8°. New York, 1883.
Contains: Piratical publishers. By Leonard Scott, no. 5, march, p. 656-659. Law against right. [Editorial], no. 5, march, p. 699-702. " Piratical publishers," or a piratical government. [Editorial], no. 5, march, p. 702-704.

PRESSGESETZ (Das), nebst den gesetzen über das urheberrecht, dem musterschutz- markenschutz und patentgesetz. Textausgabe mit kurzen anmerkungen und sachregister. Herausgegeben von einem prakt. juristen. [*Anon.*] About 134 p. 16°. Leipzig, P. Reclam jun., 1883. [Universal - bibliothek, nr, 1704.]
—— *Same :* 2. Auflage. 134 p. 16°. Leipzig, P. Reclam jun., 1884.

PUTNAM (G : Haven). Literary property. *In* "Cyclopædia of political science. Edited by J: J. Lalor." v. 3. 8°. Chicago, M. B. Cary & co., 1884, p. 392-411.
—— *Same.* 8°. Chicago, A. H. Andrews & co., 1884.
Anon. notice in " The Nation." v. 39. 4°. New York, no. 1016, Dec. 18, 1884, p. 523-524.

RENOUARD (Augustin Charles). Théorie des droits des auteurs sur les productions de leur intelligence. *In* "Archives de droit et de législation." v. 1. 8°. Bruxelles, 1837, p. 27-49 (of 1st pagination).
" Ce mémoire a été lu à l'Académie des sciences morales et politiques dans la séance du 7 janvier 1837."

ROGERS (H: Wade). Literary property at common law, [etc.] *In* "The Federal reporter." v. 17. 8°. Saint Paul, West publishing co., 1883, no. 7, Sept. 18, p. 593-603.

ROSMINI (Enrico). La legislazione e la giurisprudenza dei teatri e dei diritti d'autore. Trattato dei diritti e delle obbligazioni degli impresari, artisti, autori delle direzioni, del pubblico, agenti teatrali, ecc., contenente le leggi, i regolamenti e decreti, nonche le note ministeriali, i pareri del consiglio di stato, le decisioni dei tribunali e delle corti, anche straniere, in materia teatrale, e sopra i diritti degli autori d'opere drammatiche, musicali e coreografiche, coi trattati internazionali, ecc. Preceduto da introduzione storica del prof. Paolo Ferrari. 2da edizione. 2 v. c., 564 p.; 782 p. 8°. Milano, F. Manini, 1872-73.

SAUNDERS (Robert) *and* BENNING (W:) *vs.* SMITH (J: W:) *and* MAXWELL (Alexander). Copyright in law reports. The case of Saunders v. Smith. Before the vice-chancellor [June 8th and 9th, 1838] ; and on appeal before the lord chancellor [June 22d and 23d, 1838]. With a preface, table of cases cited, notes, and an appendix. By G: Morland Crawford. vii p. 2 l. 60 p, 8°. London, A. Maxwell, 1839.

SETON (Sir H: Wilmot). Forms of decrees, judgments, and orders ; with practical notes. 1st American from the 4th English edition, by Franklin Fiske Heard. xvi., 862 p. 8°. Boston, Little, Brown, & co., 1884.
Contains: Injunctions; section vii. Infringement

of copyright, p. 126-135, sec. viii. Letters and documents, p. 135-139.

SHORTT (J:) The law relating to works of literature and art. 2d ed. About 840 p. 8°. London, Reeves & Turner, 1884.

SLATER (J: Herbert). The law relating to copyright and trade marks, treated more particularly with reference to infringement. Forming a digest of the more important English and American decisions, together with the practice of the English courts and forms of informations, notices, pleadings, and injunctions. xvii. p. 1 l. 466 p. 8°. London, Stevens & sons, 1884.

Contents: Copyright, p. 1-229. Trade marks, p. 230-331. Appendix A. Forms, p. 335-354; B. Statutes, p. 355-424.

Anon. notice: Sundry law books, in "The Nation." v. 39. 4°. New York, no. 1016, Dec. 18, 1884, p. 526.

SWITZERLAND. Uebereinkunft mit Deutschland vom 13. Mai 1869, 23. Mai 1881 betreffend den gegenseitigen schutz des literarischen und künstlerischen eigenthums.— Convention avec l'Allemagne du 13. Mai 1869, 23. Mai 1881 concernant la garantie réciproque de la propriété littéraire et artistique. *In* "Entscheidungen des Schweizerischen Bundesgerichtes aus dem jahre 1882. Amtliche sammlung. 8. band." 8°. Lausanne, imprimerie G. Bridel, 1882, p. 762-769.

THOMPSON (Joseph Parrish). On international copyright. (Prepared for the conference of the "Association for the reform and codification of the law of nations," held at Antwerp, August 28, 1877.) *In* "American comments on European questions, international and religious, by Joseph P. Thompson." 8°. Boston, Houghton, Mifflin & co., 1884, p. 151-167.

UEBER den rechtlichen schutz gegen plagiate an literarischem und artistischem eigenthume. Veröffentlicht durch die k. b. priv. kunstanstalt von Piloty und Löhle in München aus anlass der von der A. H. Payne'schen kunstanstalt zu Leipzig in dem werke "Der Kunstverein III. serie" publizirten stahlnachstiche der gesetzlich deponirten lithographien jenes institutes aus den k. b. gallerien zu München und Schleissheim. 8°. München, 1853.

UEBER die verhältnisse der buchhandlung F. A. Brockhaus in Leipzig zu herrn hofrath dr. J. P. Eckermann in Weimar in beziehung auf das werk "Gespräche mit Goethe in den letzten jahren seines lebens." Aus den acten zusammengestellt und als manuskript gedruckt. 8°. Leipzig, 1846.

UNFEHLBARES mittel den büchernachdruck zu verhindern; zum besten rechtmässiger verleger und der schriftsteller. [*Anon.*] 4°. Tübingen, 1790.

VERGARA (Mariano). De la propriedad literaria, discurso leido en el acto de recibir la investidura de doctor en la facultad de derecho, seccion de derecho administrativo. About 87 p. 8°. Madrid, impr. de M. Arcas y Sanchez, 1862.

ZALDÍVAR (Luis G.) Diccionario de la legislacion mexicana, que comprende las leyes publicadas desde el 1° de enero de 1870, hasta el 31 de diciembre de 1871. Fol. México, imprenta del gobierno, á cargo de J. M. Sandoval, 1872 [i. e., 1871-74.]

Contains: Propiedad literaria [Orden, Marzo 15de 1871, & Abril 22de 1871], p. 705-706.